Gadamer and the
Social Turn in Epistemology

SUNY series in Contemporary Continental Philosophy

Dennis J. Schmidt, editor

Gadamer and the
Social Turn in Epistemology

CAROLYN CULBERTSON

Published by State University of New York Press, Albany

© 2024 State University of New York

All rights reserved

Printed in the United States of America

No part of this book may be used or reproduced in any manner whatsoever without written permission. No part of this book may be stored in a retrieval system or transmitted in any form or by any means including electronic, electrostatic, magnetic tape, mechanical, photocopying, recording, or otherwise without the prior permission in writing of the publisher.

For information, contact State University of New York Press, Albany, NY
www.sunypress.edu

Library of Congress Cataloging-in-Publication Data

Name: Culbertson, Carolyn, 1982– author.
Title: Gadamer and the social turn in epistemology / Carolyn Culbertson.
Description: Albany : State University of New York Press, [2024] | Series: SUNY series in contemporary continental philosophy | Includes bibliographical references.
Identifiers: LCCN 2023048139 | ISBN 9781438498164 (hardcover : alk. paper) | ISBN 9781438498171 (ebook) | ISBN 9781438498157 (pbk. : alk. paper)
Subjects: LCSH: Gadamer, Hans-Georg, 1900–2002. | Hermeneutics—History—20th century.
Classification: LCC B3248.G34 C85 2024 | DDC 121/.686—dc23/eng/20240308
LC record available at https://lccn.loc.gov/2023048139

10 9 8 7 6 5 4 3 2 1

Contents

Acknowledgments — vii

Introduction — 1

Part 1:
Gadamer's Hermeneutic Conception of Understanding

1 The Central Question of Hermeneutics: What Does It Mean to Understand? — 15

2 The Limitation of Two Historical Models of Knowing: The Enlightenment and Romanticism — 45

3 Interpretation, Truth, and Hermeneutic Realism — 69

Part 2:
Gadamerian Hermeneutics and Social Epistemology

4 The Central Question of Social Epistemology: What Does It Mean to Recognize Epistemic Practices as Social Practices? — 97

5 Feminist Contributions to Social Epistemology — 117

6 Gadamer's Hermeneutic Conception of Understanding as
   Social Epistemology   141

Notes   165

Bibliography   185

Index   193

Acknowledgments

If this book sheds any light on the virtues of Gadamer's account of understanding, it is due in large part to the opportunities that I have had to develop and refine these ideas with other philosophers over the last five years. Above all, I am indebted to the experiences I have had at meetings of the North American Society for Philosophical Hermeneutics. Since becoming involved in the society in 2016, I have learned a good deal from presentations by and conversations with a number of scholars who have been involved in the society, including Cynthia Nielsen, David Vessey, Ted George, Jim Risser, Nancy Moules, Karen Davis, Greg Lynch, Darren Walhof, Carlo DaVia, David Liakos, Kristi Sweet, and Magnus Ferguson. I am also thankful to the society for the invitation to give a talk on and receive feedback on this project at the 2022 annual NASPH meeting, hosted that year by the University of Dallas.

I am also indebted to the Canadian Hermeneutics Institute, an organization for applied hermeneutics research, whose annual conference I attended in 2022. Having the opportunity to share a portion of this project at that event and to enter into dialogue with the nurses and other practitioners who participate in the institute was a true delight and has given me high hopes for what a productive interplay between hermeneutic theory and professional practice might entail. Opportunities to present portions of this project at the 2020 meeting of the Southeast Association for the Continental Tradition and to the philosophical communities at New College of Florida and Texas A&M University were also helpful in its formation.

The philosophical community at my home institution, Florida Gulf Coast University, has been a source of constant support and motivation for me as I have worked on this project. Kevin Aho, Landon Frim, Miles

Hentrup, Eli Portella, Glenn Whitehouse, and Larry Busk have each offered encouragement as I toiled on this project and helped to sustain my spirit when crises (first, a pandemic and then, a major hurricane) interrupted the rhythm of the research process and the flow of the work. Miles Hentrup has been especially helpful in reading and commenting on early versions of my chapters and, as usual, I am indebted to him for his thorough feedback on these first drafts. Years ago, a community reading group that I coordinated with two other colleagues, Jordan Von Cannon and Laci Mattison, helped me begin to recognize the fruitful points of intersection between feminist theory and hermeneutic theory. I am also quite thankful for several students who have joined me in my study of *Truth and Method* over the past few years—especially in my Gadamer seminar and in my Philosophy of Human Communication course. Working with them as they understand, apply, and critically reflect on the text has given me valuable perspectives on it that I surely would not have developed on my own. I am thankful also to the Office of the Provost and the Dean of the College of Arts and Sciences at Florida Gulf Coast University for awarding me a sabbatical period during the fall semester of 2022, which helped me to complete the manuscript.

I thank the editors at SUNY Press for supporting the project early on and the anonymous reviewers selected by the editors for their thorough and insightful feedback on my original manuscript.

Finally, I want to thank Rowman and Littlefield for the permission to use a version of a chapter that I published in *Gadamer's Truth and Method: A Polyphonic Commentary* edited by Cynthia Nielsen and Greg Lynch (Rowman and Littlefield, 2022). A revised version of the chapter I published in that volume appears as chapter 2 in this book.

Introduction

What, if any, role do historical traditions play in the process by which we arrive at understanding? Contemporary attitudes on the matter vary greatly. On the one hand, we believe that real understanding requires that we examine the world unhindered by historical traditions so as to achieve as objective an understanding as possible. This attitude is preserved in a certain ideal of science and technology to which appeals are still regularly made in the twenty-first century. According to this ideal, part of what makes science and technology so trustworthy as processes for arriving at understanding is their indifference to particular historical traditions. In the scientific process, one need not consult history at all but can arrive at knowledge simply by collecting data and making sound inferences. While this attitude remains pervasive, it is by no means the only one common in the twenty-first century. Alongside appeals to the idea that the scientific process will free thinking from the confines of historical tradition, we find appeals to the idea that thought must remain absolutely grounded in a given tradition. On this view, historical tradition provides a template to which posterity must continually adhere. The opposition between these two common attitudes is reflected in opposing attitudes toward historical texts. When historical tradition is assigned no proper role in the process of understanding, the study of historical texts plays no significant role in the process. On the other hand, when historical tradition is regarded as providing a template from which later thinking cannot legitimately stray, historical texts come to be seen as the sources of those templates and the "literal" meaning of these texts is anxiously sought. Alongside these two attitudes toward the role of historical tradition in the process of understanding is a third—one that is less common but increasingly familiar in our contemporary world. This orientation is one that looks out for the hidden, typically unacknowledged influence of historical traditions on thought, including their influence on those scientific processes that many imagine to proceed indifferently to history. On this view, the inertia of historical traditions is indeed the cause of many social problems, but simply proceeding with the intention of being free of them provides no guarantee that one has actually accomplished such independence of thought. Instead, one must be constantly vigilant in recognizing and neutralizing these hidden biases.

Philosophers too express this same divergence of attitudes toward the role of historical tradition in the process of knowing. Some engage very little with the history of philosophy and see the essential activity of the discipline as reasoning set free from the preconceptions of the past. For others, engaging with the history of philosophy is essential. Yet there are diverging ideas about how and why it is essential. Do we read the history of philosophy in order to be able to better recognize the historical baggage that we as a society bring with us as we deliberate about issues in the present day? Or do we turn to certain texts in the history of philosophy because they set forth the parameters within which our own thought in the present day must proceed? Research in philosophy looks incredibly different depending on a given philosopher's approach. One philosopher may produce philosophical research on the ethics of leadership, for example, by spending years examining the behavior of those generally believed to be leaders in contemporary society, carefully identifying implicit points of disagreement among their leadership styles, and using principles of sound reasoning to argue for one of these styles or for an alternative. Another philosopher may produce research on the same topic by spending years working through Aristotle's *Nicomachean Ethics* and carefully identifying ancient arguments about the ethics of leadership that would, after the influence of social contract theory, become largely forgotten in the modern context. As this example suggests, then, philosophers differ nearly as much as the rest of the general population when it comes to thinking about this issue.

This confusing assortment of attitudes suggests a deep ambiguity today in the way that we think about the relevance of historical consciousness and historical texts for the process of understanding. It suggests a difficulty reconciling two insights that, although each quite convincing on its own, stand in tension with one another. On the one hand, there is the insight that, when we go to try to understand something, we do not do so as a blank slate. Our attempt is conditioned by aspects of our historical orientation whether we recognize it or not. For the most part, when we go to investigate a topic, whether it is the ethics of leadership or the social intelligence of cats, we draw from a set of questions and interests that prefigure our present investigation and from a history that has given rise to the very concepts we are investigating (e.g., intelligence, leadership, the ethical). What we seek to understand is rarely, if ever, something completely independent of the development of human consciousness. Indeed, we might even say that attempts at understanding the world can almost always be described as attempts to elaborate on and better understand ideas that are already familiar to us by virtue of our historical orientation. Yet we struggle to reconcile this insight with our observation that, in order for us to advance in our understanding of things, we cannot allow ourselves to be unduly influenced by the beliefs, questions, and habits of those who came before us. We find ourselves wishing to understand something, after all, when we experience it as new and unfamiliar. It is its unfamiliarity that would seem to demand from us that we put aside the templates that we have ready to hand.

Against this backdrop the third attitude described emerges as one possible path of reconciliation. If one cannot ever come to know the world except through a particular historical consciousness, a historical consciousness so fundamental to our cognition that it cannot ever be completely uprooted, then perhaps the best one can do in order to answer the demand of the unfamiliar is simply to acknowledge the role that one's historical biases play in one's attempt at understanding. This approach has the virtue of not taking for granted the ideal at which our attempts at understanding aim. Indeed, it radically reconceives the goal of understanding, highlighting above all the importance of self-awareness. Yet it is hard to imagine that self-awareness of one's historical biases is equivalent to understanding itself.

This book proposes that Hans-Georg Gadamer's theory of understanding in his major work, *Truth and Method*, constitutes an alternative and, in fact, a better way of thinking about the role of historical tradition in the process of understanding. Like many, Gadamer takes seriously the way that our historical context informs how we encounter, inquire into, and make sense of things. His theory of understanding has this in common with a number of other schools of thought that have gained traction over the last century—from social constructivism to communitarianism. Yet it is distinct from other treatments of the historicity of understanding on a couple of significant points.

First, most of those who highlight the role of historical traditions in understanding retain as an ideal what Lorraine Code describes as the "disinterested and dislocated view from nowhere."[1] They argue that human understanding (e.g., of reality, of the good) is such that it can never achieve this ideal and thus that human inquirers must be content with understanding what is true and what is good *for us who share a particular historical tradition*. For the constructivist, for example, we can know things only insofar as they are organized or constructed according to the template provided by our very own historical horizon *but not as they are in themselves*. Gadamer's theory of understanding, by contrast, does not preserve as an ideal the "view from nowhere" and thus does not look at historical consciousness as a defect in understanding. What he develops in *Truth and Method* is, instead, an account where the mediation of historical consciousness is essential to the event of understanding. It is the condition for its possibility rather than an indication that one has not fully understood. As Gadamer argues, "the important thing is to recognize temporal distance as a positive and productive condition enabling understanding."[2]

Second, most who address the ways that one's historical consciousness mediates their attempts at understanding conceive of this historical consciousness as something that one can, at most, become aware of but that, crucially, one cannot revise or expand. This is, in part, due to the perception of tradition as something that is relatively fixed and unchanging. It also seems to follow naturally from the observation of how very difficult, if not impossible, it is to step outside of a historical tradition that has long informed one's mode of thought and self-understanding. On this basis, it would seem that, at best, one can learn to become aware of the influence of historical traditions upon one's life but that one cannot hope to subject them to any kind of critical revision. Gadamer's theory of understanding offers an explanation, however, of the way that, as they mediate new encounters, historical traditions can become expanded and revised. Traditions need not function as rigid, unresponsive frameworks, and the horizons that they impart need not remain unchanged over time. Even texts, which many anxiously look to for the origins of their traditions, are, for Gadamer, sources of meaning in development. Indeed, for Gadamer, while immersion in a historical tradition is a condition for any understanding whatsoever, it is often the problematization of one's historical tradition that is required for genuine understanding.

Now, to present Gadamer's *Truth and Method* as offering a theory of understanding will, for some readers, seem to misconstrue the general character of the book, presenting the project as epistemological instead of ontological. *Truth and Method*, after all, addresses not just how we understand works of art but the ontology of art, not just language as a medium of understanding but the nature of things such that they come to presentation in language. In other words, it explores the nature of being and not just what we can know about it.[3] Moreover, there are moments in *Truth and Method* where Gadamer seems to distinguish hermeneutics as he understands it from components of epistemology traditionally construed. For example, in part 2 of the book, he describes the progress made by Edmund Husserl's description of the lifeworld (*Lebenswelt*) as a step in "overcoming of the epistemological problem through phenomenological research" (TM, 244), a formulation that suggests that epistemology is a limited framework for philosophical examination best replaced by a different set of problems and questions. In addition, Gadamer makes clear on a couple of different occasions, including in the opening paragraphs of the introduction, that it is not his intention to develop a method for how understanding *should* proceed and that his exploration of the hermeneutic phenomenon is not concerned with "amassing verified knowledge, such as would satisfy the methodological ideal of science" (TM, xx).[4]

The efforts that Gadamer makes to distinguish his project of philosophical hermeneutics from certain aspects of traditional epistemology have led many commentators to read Gadamer's work as a complete departure from questions about truth and justification that have long been essential to epistemology and, indeed, to the identity of the philosophical discipline. Some commentators regard this as a significant shortcoming in Gadamer's thought and argue that any serious philosophical examination of understanding has to provide an account of the phenomenon that has methodological normative relevance. In other words, it must provide a general method for arriving at legitimate knowledge or a set of general criteria for distinguishing between more justified and less justified claims. Shortly after the publication of *Truth and Method*, both Emilio Betti and Karl-Otto Apel offered criticisms of the project along these lines.[5] More recently, Michael Forster has argued that Gadamer's account of understanding implies that the indebtedness of thought to historical traditions is "epistemically insurmountable, that it is impossible to abstract from one's own specific pre-understanding."[6] Other commentators have praised what they see as Gadamer's move away from certain metaphysical commitments that have traditionally grounded epistemological concerns. Richard Rorty, for example, praises Gadamer for offering a description of understanding that is no longer bound up with a metaphysics of truth and, on this basis, identifies Gadamer as a nominalist, one who holds that to understand something better does not mean to achieve better, more justified understanding but simply "to be able to tie together the various things previously said in a new and perspicuous way."[7] Although these readings of Gadamer's work differ from one another in significant ways, all of them have in common the belief that Gadamerian hermeneutics is not an epistemology in the proper sense. In the chapters that follow, I refer to these interpretations collectively as *the anti-epistemological reading of Gadamer*.

There are a couple of reasons to resist the anti-epistemological reading of Gadamerian hermeneutics, though. First, Gadamer states explicitly throughout the book that, while not concerned with developing a general method for knowing, he is still very much concerned with questions about truth and knowledge. Consider the fuller context of the passage from the introduction quoted in part above:

> The hermeneutic phenomenon is basically not a problem of method at all. It is not concerned with a method of understanding by means of which texts are subjected to scientific investigation like all other objects of experience. It is not concerned primarily with amassing verified knowledge, such as would satisfy the methodological ideal of science—*yet it too is concerned with knowledge [Erkenntnis] and with truth [Wahrheit]*. . . . But what kind of knowledge and what kind of truth? (TM, xx; emphasis added)

Gadamer goes on to argue that it is shortsighted to take the concepts of truth and knowledge implicit in the natural sciences as the only viable ways of thinking about these things. What he aims to do in *Truth and Method*, he explains, is to consider the nature of truth and knowing when examined through those forms of understanding that are formally articulated in the human sciences. What is the nature of understanding at play in those situations where one is trying to *understand* a historical event? What is the nature of the truth at issue when one claims that a given interpretation of a literary work is *true* or when one experiences an actor's performance as a *true* portrayal of a particular character? While it may be tempting to think that what is sought in such situations is simply the objective historical event, the objective meaning of the literary work, and so on, and while there have certainly been attempts to develop such methodologies in the humanities disciplines,[8] Gadamer argues that such experiences actually provide us with a model of truth and understanding that is strikingly different from that model from the natural sciences to which we are most accustomed. For example, while we are accustomed to thinking about the objects we want to understand as independent of and indifferent to the situations from which we inquire, Gadamer notes that what historical, textual, and aesthetic kinds of understanding seek is something different. What makes one curious about a historical event or a historical text is what it means for one's own present situation. The essence of what one wants to know is not simply some immediate being lodged in the past. Likewise, that which demands to be understood in a work of art is not simply the artist's original intention but something for which the spectator's historical consciousness is essential. Such experiences put us in touch with senses of truth and knowing that differ from the ideals associated with the natural sciences.

Some will object, however, that what engagements of this kind strive for is *understanding*, not *knowledge*. The former term typically refers to the way that one integrates a new experience, information, or skill into one's own already-existing set of beliefs and practical abilities. The latter refers, instead, to the possession of a belief that lines up with some objective reality, that is, how something is in itself. While it is true that we have begun to develop two distinct sets of vocabulary along these lines, one cannot conclude from this fact that interest in understanding is not interest in knowledge. We still sometimes use the term *know* to refer to an individual's integration of new information, as when in conversation one asks another: "Do you *know* what I am saying?" More importantly, even if this were not the case, it would still be valid to ask whether a frequent differentiation in usage is actually indicative of an unbridgeable rift between two domains. While it is true that Gadamer speaks more frequently of understanding (*Verstehen*) than knowledge (*Erkenntnis*) in the book, he consistently problematizes the basis upon which this distinction is typically made. He does this through two closely related arguments that problematize the distinction independently and in combination. First, drawing directly from Heidegger's discussion of "the fore-structure of the understanding," he argues that, whenever we set out to gain knowledge about something, we inevitably bring with us anticipatory projections with which we must integrate the object we are attempting to know. Going through this process of understanding (i.e., integrating the object with one's own horizon of anticipatory projections) is the condition for the possibility of gaining any knowledge. What's more, he argues that, in many cases, the very things that we seek to know are not ontologically separate from the historical horizons that we bring with us and with which they must be integrated to understand them.[9] In such cases, the understanding one achieves through the application of one's historical horizon does not simply mediate the meaning of the object for the subject but is also part of that object's meaning. It is this second argument that Gadamer presents when he writes: "Understanding must be conceived as a part of the event in which meaning occurs, the event in which the meaning of all statements—those of art and all other kinds of tradition—is formed and actualized" (TM, 164). It is not, then, that Gadamer is interested in the process by which new information is integrated through personal understanding but not in the way in which the real meaning or truth of something is made clear. What interests him in *Truth and Method* is the essential role that the former (understanding) plays in the latter.

This helps shed light on a second reason to question the anti-epistemological readings of Gadamer, namely, the fact that such readings tend to assume a rather narrow conception of epistemology. To say, for example, that Gadamerian hermeneutics does not provide a way of thinking about truth because it tracks how understanding proceeds for subjects situated in particular historical traditions is to accept that no theory that considers the historical situation of knowing subjects can qualify as a theory of knowledge. Yet this idea is increasingly contested by contemporary epistemologists. Since "the social epistemological turn" that transformed the field of epistemology toward the end of the twentieth century, more and more epistemologists accept the axiom that we cannot figure out what we ought to believe (i.e., what is true) independently of an examination of how people come to arrive at their beliefs (i.e., how understanding arises) and that the latter requires us to consider the role of social and historical factors in this process.[10] Feminist epistemology, which has been at the forefront of this development, has had an especially strong impact in encouraging not only awareness of the way particular historical traditions (like androcentrism) can tacitly condition inquiry and research in the present day but also in probing how, in light of such conditioning, to distinguish justified from unjustified beliefs. In addition to the strength of Gadamer's own arguments, which he frames on several occasions as contributing to a clarification of knowledge and truth, then, these recent developments in epistemology suggest that we should think twice before excluding Gadamerian hermeneutics from the field of epistemology. If he is problematizing some of the background assumptions of the field and attempting to reconceive what truth, justification, objectivity, and so on might mean when considered independently of these assumptions, this in no way distinguishes him from what a number of epistemologists today are doing. In fact, it suggests that mainstream epistemology has good reason to revisit Gadamer's major work and to see what light it might shed on questions still unresolved in the field.

When we consider the ways that contemporary epistemologists have been engaged in a renegotiation of the aims, scope, and basic questions of the field, we come to see Gadamer's remarks in *Truth and Method* where he seems to distance himself from epistemology in a new light. When he praises early phenomenologists for finding a way to "overcome the epistemological problem," we need not take this as evidence that Gadamer is not interested in contributing to theories of knowledge, justification, or truth. We can instead understand him to be problematizing some of the assumptions often made by epistemologists in the twentieth century and still influential in how we tend to think about the process of knowing today. We can read him, in other words, as problematizing aspects of the field in a way that is similar to the interventions made by social epistemologists and feminist epistemologists.[11]

Finally, a third and especially important reason to highlight the contributions that Gadamerian hermeneutics makes to theories of truth, justification, and knowledge is the positive difference that they can make to the broader public discourse on these topics today. This is a public discourse in which, on the one hand, people continually fall prey to what Sandra Harding calls "objectivism," that idea that beliefs and theories are justified only if they arise out of a process that is neutral with regard to historical or cultural biases.[12] As we put more and more trust in the collection and analysis of data and, increasingly, in the technological instruments that perform these operations for us, it becomes harder for us to take their results as anything other than "the god's eye view." When we become less capable of recognizing the questions, interests, and historical orientations that condition a body of research, we become, in turn, less capable of reflecting on and critically evaluating these conditioning factors. The popular alternative to this objectivism leaves us in a situation that is in no way better. What emerges in response to the dominance of technological rationality is an insistence that truth is entirely an effect of the historical and social traditions considered inessential to knowledge according to objectivism.[13] Neither of these ways of thinking about truth and knowledge encourages us to engage in any kind of serious reflection on the historical horizons that are at play when we go to inquire into things. Gadamer's account in *Truth and Method*, however, encourages such reflection and, indeed, regards it as essential to understanding and to what it means to be an epistemically responsible subject.

In the chapters that follow, I offer a reading of Gadamer's *Truth and Method* that highlights the contributions it makes to the field of epistemology. Part 1 of the book, entitled "Gadamer's Hermeneutic Conception of Understanding," introduces readers to key elements of the theory of understanding that Gadamer develops, including his argument for the positive role that historical fore-conceptions play in inquiry (chapter 1), his description of how fore-conceptions come to be revised (chapter 2), his critique of the Enlightenment's "prejudice against prejudice" (chapter 2), and his hermeneutic conception of truth (chapter 3). While part 1 serves, in some sense, as an overview of these core parts of his theory, my treatment of the text focuses especially on how Gadamer's theory of understanding is helpful both for recognizing the way that understanding proceeds from particular historical and social situations and for thinking through the implications of this insight for normative epistemological questions. Readers who are new to Gadamer's philosophy will find part 1 of the book especially helpful in explaining some of the core questions, arguments, and contexts of *Truth and Method*. Readers already familiar with Gadamer's work are likely to be more interested in how I distinguish my reading from versions of the anti-epistemological reading of Gadamerian hermeneutics and the connections that I make toward the end of part 1 between my reading and "hermeneutic realism," a new current in Gadamerian hermeneutics.

In part 2, I look to other developments in recent epistemology to contextualize Gadamer's contributions to the field, exploring important points of agreement between Gadamer and arguments central to the emergence of social epistemology (chapter 4) and feminist epistemology (chapter 5). Like Gadamer, epistemologists following these currents in the field reject the idea that real knowing entails transcending one's immersion in a historical tradition or shared lifeworld. Indeed, feminist epistemology becomes nearly synonymous with what within its tradition is known as the "situated knowledge doctrine." Moreover, there is, I argue, a growing consensus among social and feminist epistemologists that situating epistemology in this way need not and should not entail a relativistic retreat from making normative claims and distinctions. There is less consensus, however, on how to avoid such a position. In chapter 6, I spell out how I think aspects of Gadamer's hermeneutic epistemology, particularly the hermeneutic theory of truth, could offer helpful guidance on this point. While chapters 4 and 5 are intended primarily to introduce readers of Gadamer's work who might be unfamiliar with social and feminist epistemology to relevant developments in these fields, chapter 6 describes how these developments shed light on and may be further enriched by the theory of understanding that Gadamer develops in *Truth and Method*.

Part 1
Gadamer's Hermeneutic Conception of Understanding

Chapter 1

The Central Question of Hermeneutics
What Does It Mean to Understand?

> For the text must be understood as an answer to a real question.
> —Gadamer, *Truth and Method*, 383

Gadamer's *Truth and Method* leads us into one of the most important and profound questions that philosophy can explore: What is understanding? This question is important because, as human beings, we are constantly oriented toward understanding. This is apparent even in situations where achieving it in any perfect and final way seems difficult. On a given day, one may, for example, drive by a statue in one's neighborhood and wonder what its standing there means today, have a conversation with a friend where one tries to understand with her the significance of the current health crisis, listen to a colleague and try to understand their concerns about a recent meeting, read an article that attempts to make sense of changing attitudes toward sexual relationships, and watch a television show that deepens one's understanding of the characters one has been following since the beginning of the series and the tragedy in which the characters are embroiled. These are just some of the ways that we find ourselves oriented toward understanding.

The question of what it means to understand emerges, though, as soon as we realize that, in each of these cases, understanding is something that we do not appear simply to be striving for but that we are already in some sense within. Wanting to understand in each of these cases would seem to mean wanting to understand better, more completely, or more deeply. It does not entail grasping something for the first time but, rather, grasping something—the parts or content of which one has already encountered—as a meaningful whole. Thus, for example, one starts to understand that character in the television drama when one starts to see how their actions and reactions form a meaningful unity. Moreover, understanding in these cases also seems to require that one recognizes what this meaningful whole implies about the beliefs or practices circulating in one's lifeworld. Thus, for example, one feels one has understood the character in the television drama when one recognizes the character as an archetype of modern alienation. Similarly, one feels that one has understood the concerns expressed by one's colleague when one sees how the concerns point to a change that is needed in the way the department's meetings are run. Seen in this light, the need to understand something (e.g., a character, the articulation of a set of concerns, a changing set of social patterns) would appear to be renewed every time doing so would shed new light on some commonly accepted belief or practice. In this way, it seems that the task of understanding something might be satisfied once and then reopened at some later time.

These initial descriptions are not meant to answer the question "What is understanding?" or to regard classic epistemological questions as settled. Instead, the point of these preliminary descriptions is to draw out the question posed to us by aspects of what we experience and refer to in ordinary language as "understanding." To follow Gadamer in his exploration of understanding, we have to begin by attuning ourselves to the question that prompts Gadamer in this exploration. Questions, after all, have a hermeneutic priority for Gadamer. We cannot engage in an inquiry without first allowing ourselves to be addressed by a claim that requires the suspension of some of our commonly held beliefs. This suspension of commonly held beliefs, Gadamer says, "has the logical structure of a question" (TM, 310). In part 1 of this book, we are tracing out Gadamer's question: What is understanding? This question comes into relief as we explore the phenomenon that we experience and refer to as understanding and track the aspects of this phenomenon that call for reconsideration of some of our commonly held beliefs and practices related to understanding, knowledge, and truth.

This suspension, however, cannot be absolute. It is all too common today for us to imagine that inquiry is only genuinely undertaken when one embarks on it free of all preconceptions and prejudices. We may be tempted to take Gadamer's doctrine of the hermeneutic priority of the question to be putting forward a similar ideal for the method of inquiry. This is neither the meaning of Gadamer's doctrine of the hermeneutic priority of the question nor the sense of the question that guides us in this chapter, however. Understanding becomes a proper object of philosophical questioning not when we believe that we have no familiarity with and can say nothing at all about it but when certain determinate features of our commonly held beliefs and practices related to understanding are problematized. Inquiring into a subject matter presupposes some familiarity—that it belongs already to one's lifeworld. This is what Gadamer means when he says: "Posing a question implies openness but also limitation. It implies the explicit establishing of presuppositions, in terms of which can be seen what still remains open" (TM, 372).

My goal in this chapter is to develop an appreciation for the sense in which Gadamer took understanding as a question and the way in which this question still addresses us today. As I will attempt to demonstrate, Gadamer's line of inquiry in *Truth and Method* introduces important challenges to what I will call the *transcendence model* of knowing according to which knowledge of something requires the neutralization of the conditions in which we first encounter it. It does this by exploring two important aspects of the lifeworld within which much human inquiry takes place, namely, history and language. It demonstrates that, in both cases, the situatedness of the inquiry in history and language plays a positive, enabling role in the process of understanding. While this claim has been widely criticized for giving free rein to subjectivity and for abandoning the epistemological ideal of objectivity, I argue that many of the critics fail to grasp the way that Gadamer is attempting to rethink not just the process of understanding and not just the mediating factors in this process but *the nature of understanding itself*. Throughout the chapter, I attempt to demonstrate the necessity of Gadamer's challenge to the transcendence model of knowing by showing how it fails to adequately account for what transpires in historical understanding, textual interpretation, and educational experience.

The Challenge Posed by Existential Phenomenology to the Traditional Epistemological Model

There is a long legacy of thinking about knowledge as something that the inquirer does not yet possess. One seeks knowledge. One attempts to acquire knowledge. Philosophers throughout history have developed different methods for doing just this. The ancient skeptics sought legitimate knowledge by suspending judgment, for example, and early modern rationalists did so by articulating what is self-evident and beyond doubt. In fact, it is hard to even conceive of knowledge in any way other than something that the inquirer initially lacks and seeks to possess. After all, as Meno reminds us, if one already has knowledge of something, it seems quite unnecessary to inquire into it. Moreover, knowledge is a normative or evaluative concept. In a society that holds that our practical decisions should be grounded in knowledge, claiming to know that something is the case implies that it ought to be given due consideration in our practical deliberations. The normativity of knowledge claims implies that we must necessarily posit that there are some claims that count as knowledge and others that do not—some people who possess knowledge of a subject and others who lack it. This normative dimension seems to preclude the possibility that knowledge is something that we all already possess from the start when we begin to inquire. Knowledge must therefore be in some sense independent and transcendent of what is already understood by the inquirer.

This model of knowledge is so deeply embedded in our way of thinking that it is hard for us to take seriously the question of whether it is adequate or the possibility of any alternative account. We imagine that a serious inquirer, for example, is a person who is fixated on the object and the object alone—one who has put aside their own personal and cultural biases and thus is better able to attend to the matter at hand—be it the historical event, the text, or the molecule. We praise the natural scientist for their objectivity and their lack of personal and cultural bias and expect other forms of inquiry (i.e., social sciences and humanities) to emulate these virtues as well. That this model of knowledge is one possible model among others becomes especially difficult to recognize as institutions structured around this model become fixtures in human society. We come increasingly to rely, for example, on algorithms to make judgments for us, putting trust in these technologies largely because they are thought to be objective and without bias. With this, the transcendence model of knowing becomes not only more deeply entrenched in our society but also significantly modified. With the technological rationalization of thought, we begin to lose patience for cultivating the questions, wonders, and values that once motivated scientific inquiry. We start to pursue not only "data-driven" answers but data-driven questions.

Over the last century, however, several influential figures and schools in the history of philosophy have questioned the adequacy of this model. Especially influential for Gadamer was the treatment of understanding in Heidegger's existential phenomenology. Heidegger challenged the transcendence model of knowing that, following Husserl, he saw becoming operationalized throughout the lifeworld in the age of technological rationality. One of the ways that he did this was by demonstrating the way that any particular inquirer, like any particular inquiry, inevitably belongs to a "world" (*Welt*). He presented understanding not as a means by which one transcends the social and historical forms of life into which one is thrown but as a means by which these forms of life are always already "there" for us prior to conscious acts of inquiry and reflection. For Heidegger, then, it would be erroneous to imagine inquiry as taking place free of presuppositions. Inquiry emerges always from within a given factical situation, that is, from within a "there" that is given to us through the elements of the "fore-structure of the understanding" (*die Vorstruktur des Verstehens*)—foresight, fore-having, and fore-conception.[1] While it leads one to new insights and realizations, it remains immersed in facticity. The factical situation into which understanding is immersed is, moreover, a historical one for Heidegger. What calls upon our understanding are matters that are bound to a history and that require interpretation grounded in historical consciousness. Heidegger develops this point already in his 1922 "Aristotle Introduction," where he argues that the situation of interpretation, "of the understanding appropriation of the past, is always the situation of a living present."[2] As such, philosophical inquiry remains always bound to factical life.[3] The task of understanding, then, is not to break away from this factical situation but to return to it in a new way—defining and bringing clarity to the new situation. Inquiry cannot simply transcend the historical and social situation of the inquirer; it necessarily involves adherence to some pretheoretical content derived from this social and historical situation. This idea is fundamental to existential phenomenology. Existential phenomenology, like transcendental phenomenology, insists that what comes to be understood cannot be separated from conditions in which understanding occurs. While, for transcendental phenomenology, these conditions are structures of consciousness, for existential phenomenology, they are the social and historical forms of the "there" that comprise the lifeworld.[4] At stake in the emphasis on the historical situation in which understanding occurs here is the question of whether understanding is best described as the accomplishment of an individual mind acting apart from its social and historical milieu.

This existential and historical turn in phenomenology had a clear influence upon Gadamer, who studied with Heidegger during this early period of Heidegger's career and who was especially influenced by Heidegger's early treatment of Aristotle and, in particular, Aristotle's practical philosophy.[5] Gadamer takes up, for example, Heidegger's articulation of the fore-structure of the understanding in *Being and Time*.[6] Indeed, as we will examine in more depth in the next chapter, Gadamer's interpretation of Heidegger's idea of the fore-structure of the understanding constitutes a central part of *Truth and Method*. According to this doctrine, all acts of understanding involve the application of some combination of foresight, fore-having, and fore-conceptions. One does not enter into the process of inquiry without taking certain things for granted. One has some things in advance by virtue of which new discoveries can be made.

Gadamer inherits from existential phenomenology a concern about decreasing recognition and acknowledgment of the role the shared historical lifeworld plays in inquiry. He inherits the idea that, while we may become more aware of the role played by fore-conceptions rooted in the lifeworld in the process of understanding, it is inappropriate to strive to extricate our understanding from this condition. "The self-awareness of the individual," Gadamer says, "is only a flickering in the closed circuit of historical life. That is why the prejudices of the individual, far more than his judgments, constitute the historical reality of his being" (TM, 276–77).

Gadamer takes from Heidegger's existential phenomenology at least four things. First, he takes from Heidegger a commitment to recognizing the factical situations within which understanding is fundamentally immersed and, on this basis, the fundamentally interpretive character of understanding. Second, he takes from Heidegger the idea that the hermeneutic situation, in which understanding calls for such interpretation, is universal. Whereas earlier hermeneutic theorists saw the need for interpretation only in special circumstances, for Gadamer, interpretation is part of the process of understanding that we are continually thrown into as social and historical beings. Third, from the early Heidegger he takes the idea that it is helpful to go back to Aristotle in order to think about the way that understanding is bound up with facticity and, fourth, that, in so doing, we will have the opportunity to grasp some fundamental philosophical concepts, such as truth and language, in a more primordial way.[7]

Yet while Heidegger dedicates much of his philosophical effort to recovering the truth of the hermeneutics of facticity through a painstaking deconstruction (*Destruktion*) of the European tradition, Gadamer's primary way of demonstrating this truth is through reflecting on interpretive activities with which we are engaged in our everyday lives. Gadamer draws our attention to exactly the sort of experiences that I referred to earlier: the experience of trying to understand a colleague's concerns as she speaks with you, trying to understand the meaning of a health-care crisis, or trying to understand the shifts in one's feelings and desires that are called for when one witnesses a tragedy either as performed in a work of art or in real life. In none of these cases would it be appropriate to bracket the social-historical lifeworld in which we are immersed in order to understand the subject matter. Yet all of us are familiar with what it is to desire and to cultivate understanding of this sort. Thus, Gadamer attempts to demonstrate the role of facticity in understanding by exploring what it is like to strive for and to cultivate understanding as it unfolds in a number of domains (e.g., the understanding of works of art, of historical events, of texts, of law, of symptoms). In the next two sections of this chapter, we will consider two contexts of understanding that Gadamer turns to in *Truth and Method* and elsewhere that demonstrate the inexorable role of the factical lifeworld in the process of understanding.

Thinking Through Our Fundamental Immersion in History

One of the clearest ways to bring to light how one's factical situation plays a role in the process of understanding is by considering what happens when we become interested in better understanding some event or historical development in the past. Even in modernity, people regularly find themselves struck by stories, sites, and artifacts from eras in the past. Gadamer observes that, in such encounters, what interests us in the past is not some immediate *factum brutum* but something that is also contemporary in some sense. One wants to know what the text or the artifact tells us about our present—about who we are, how we might live, and so on. Indeed, such objects appear as worthy of attention at all only in light of some present question or concern. In this, we recognize the hermeneutic priority of the question, for, as Gadamer asks, "What is historical research without historical questions?" (TM, xxix) This mediated condition becomes especially clear when we examine histories written even several decades before our time and easily recognize the different questions, prejudices, and interests behind them. For Gadamer, this is not a condition that we can just transcend or escape. Even those historical accounts that manage to twist free of the most obvious and dominant prejudices of the day will appear to later readers in one way or another as representative of conditions of the lifeworld at the time of their creation. In this way, our understanding of historical events is always *situated*.[8]

What's more, Gadamer argues that the object of historical understanding is not just some given object that is mediated by the present. What one is trying to better understand is what he calls an "effective history" (*Wirkungsgeschichte*)—the event as it would come to matter to history thereafter (TM, 312). Effective histories are not simply lodged in the past, because they are a significant part of what sets forth the meaning of the present. In turn, historical investigation involves reflective engagement with the present, and the object of these investigations is inextricably linked to the present. To illustrate this point, Georgia Warnke considers what exactly it is that we want to understand when we ponder the World Wars of the twentieth century.

> The meaning of events will change with changes in historical perspective. The meaning of World War I, for example, changes depending on the historical "horizon" from which it is viewed: it can be described as the Great War or the war to end all wars at a certain point in history, but only until the start of World War II. Similarly the events that comprise the start of World War II must have a different meaning before World War II becomes a recognizable entity than they do after it has achieved this identity in the consciousness of historical interpreters. The meaning of historical actions and events is contingent upon the vantage point from which they are perceived and encompasses only that meaning events have from the position in history that the historian possesses.[9]

Now, the notion that our access to the past is generally conditioned by the concerns and interests of our present is neither rare nor very difficult to understand. We have all heard the common adage, for example, that "history is written by the victors." Yet one misunderstands Gadamer's point if one takes him simply to be saying that it is present concerns and interests that are given rather than the past. This is a point that is easy to overlook. For Gadamer, though, "there is no more an isolated horizon of the present in itself than there are historical horizons which have to be acquired" (TM, 317). Our sense of the present, just like our sense of the past, emerges and becomes modified through our development of historical consciousness. Our understanding of the past is always situated in that it is always colored by what we know of history thereafter, including the present, but this immersion is itself ecstatic. We are continually reorienting ourselves in the present through our thinking about the past.

Let us consider another example to illustrate Gadamer's point. Consider this time the case of studying some historical social movement, say, the early nineteenth-century abolition movement in the United States. In studying this historical development from the twenty-first century, we cannot help but see it in light of the historical events that would later transpire (e.g., the American Civil War, the passing of the Fourteenth Amendment, the continuing subordination of Black people in America during Jim Crow) and in light of questions, concerns, and interests of the present (e.g., questions about the persistence of social inequality in the United States, concerns about systems of racial and economic subordination in the twenty-first century, and the great difficulty that people today face in challenging these systems). These are the contexts in which we generally encounter stories and artifacts of the abolition movement and thus are fore-conceptions that constrain what can come to light about the movement. Yet these are highly productive constraints. They are what make the abolition movement and artifacts of that movement relevant and thought-worthy for us today. Moreover, rather than confining our discovery to the questions and narratives already familiar to us, these fore-conceptions allow us to make new historical discoveries. For example, if I start to recognize the extent to which some of the abolitionists' original demands were left unsatisfied after the conclusion of the American Civil War, it might make me see the conclusion of the war differently. If I start to recognize the use of biblical motifs in the rhetoric of the abolitionists, it might make me see the use of such motifs in contemporary liberatory rhetoric differently.

It is not uncommon, then, at least in our orientations toward history, to experience our factical situations as inquirers as productive constraints. In a world where inquiry is generally thought of as requiring the transcendence and neutralization of an inquirer's factical situation, even deference to an impartial algorithm, though, this sort of experience leaves us with a question: What does the experience of historical understanding tell us about understanding in general? Does understanding really require absolute transcendence of one's factical situation, or is immersion within and reflection upon one's factical situation a necessary condition for understanding? These are the questions about understanding that struck Gadamer. They are questions that, while grounded in experiences of understanding, point to something rarely formulated when we think about understanding. They are also, I think, living questions for us today. The advancement of technological rationality has clearly only intensified in the decades that have passed since the publication of *Truth and Method*. This means that the question "What is understanding?" has become only more difficult to recover from the answer readily provided to us today by technological rationality.

One might object here that the way Gadamer conceives of historical understanding makes every attempt to understand the past viciously circular. How can one, after all, assume that the contemporary horizon within which one first comes to think about the past is at all appropriate? Is it not circular to say that one's attempt to understand a historical topic on the basis of present concerns and interests is legitimate because such attempts can make a difference to one's present concerns and interests? Does it not make more sense to say that understanding the end of the nineteenth-century abolition movement in light of continuing concerns about racial inequality today is not to understand the event itself but only to be able to practically apply it to our present interests? Several commentators have raised this objection to Gadamer's approach. One of the earliest and most famous versions of this objection came from Emilio Betti, an Italian jurist, theologian, and philosopher. Betti insisted that such practical applications of history were external to the basic task of historical interpretation and, contra Gadamer, the responsibility of historical interpretation should not be conflated with the task of applying historical interpretation to the interests and concerns of living communities. As he argues: "Procedures of this kind are obviously not suited to lead us to historical truth; on the contrary, they open the door to subjective arbitrariness and threaten to cover up or misrepresent historical truth and to distort it, even if only unconsciously."[10] According to Betti, Gadamer's claim that textual interpretation is necessarily immersed in the anticipatory projections of the reader leads to the same problem: enabling "a substantive agreement between text and reader—i.e., between the apparently easily accessible meaning of a text and the subjective conception of the reader—to be formed without, however, guaranteeing the correctness of understanding."[11] This is the basis for Betti's concerns about Gadamer's approach to historical understanding and about the degree to which Gadamer's account of understanding, more generally, is epistemically responsible. Betti's criticism, in fact, plays an important role in the interpretation of Gadamer's work that I will refer to as the "anti-epistemological reading."

For Gadamer, though, Betti's objection begs the question of how inquiry in general ought to proceed and how the object of inquiry ought to be conceived. It assumes that beginning inquiry with preconceptions that help shape the inquiry introduces subjective arbitrariness, adulterates the process, and renders the result of the inquiry invalid. This only follows, however, if one accepts the transcendence model of knowing and conceives of the object of knowing as something ontologically separate from that which allows it to appear. It is this model of inquiry and of knowledge that Gadamer is questioning, though, when he considers the productive role that fore-conceptions play in everyday processes of understanding such as historical interpretation. Rather than seeing the participation of fore-conceptions in inquiry as the source of a vicious circularity, Gadamer follows Heidegger in finding the inevitable circularity of thought to have an ontologically positive significance. A person trying to understand something inevitably finds themselves in "the anticipatory movement of fore-understanding" (TM, 304). The task, for both Heidegger and Gadamer, is not to exit this circle but to engage in it in the right way. This is the way that Gadamer understands Heidegger's doctrine of the "hermeneutic circle." Gadamer illustrates his understanding of this concept through his description of what is involved in reading a text. "A person who is trying to understand a text is always projecting. He projects a meaning for the text as a whole as soon as some initial meaning emerges in the text. Again, the initial meaning emerges only because he is reading the text with particular expectations in regard to certain meaning. Working out this fore-projection, which is constantly revised in terms of what emerges as he penetrates into the meaning, is understanding what is there" (TM, 279). In the case of historical understanding, this means that one ought not to regard the present horizon in relation to which the past is meaningful as an impediment to understanding the past. The task of historical interpretation is not simply to transcend and set aside the implicit bias of one's present horizon. This is, once again, though, not to say that one is simply locked into this horizon as a fixed, immovable worldview. Rather, affirming one's present horizon as the basis for historical interpretation is the condition for finding one's own present horizon altered by the encounter with the past. In this way, Gadamer is rethinking what it means to understand a historical development. At the same time, he is also rethinking what it is that we understand when we understand the historical development. Again, for Gadamer, what we understand is not some brute fact of the past but its effective history (*Wirkungsgeschichte*). The effective history of the nineteenth-century abolition movement, for example, includes those situations that first connect us to and make us interested in it as a historical event. Contrary to what Betti argues, the content of this *Wirkungsgeschichte* originates no more from any pure subject than it does from any pure object. The interests and concerns that I experience as bringing me to the past belong no more to an isolated horizon of the present than they do to an isolated horizon of the past. What we want to understand is, rather, what appears as an interplay of these two horizons but that, in truth, dissolves the fixity of both.

Betti's criticism relies on a second conceptual distinction that Gadamer questions in *Truth and Method* and elsewhere. This is the distinction between theoretical understanding and practical application. For Betti, proper historical interpretation is limited to the former. It may be fruitful to consider the lessons that people today can derive from history, but such efforts should in no way replace the work of finding out what happened during a particular historical development and what it meant for people living and involved at that time. For Betti, understanding something through practical application means not understanding it objectively, as it is in itself, but only subjectively, in the meaning it has for a particular living community. Thus, what is at stake in conflating historical interpretation and the practical application of history, for Betti, is, once again, the loss of objectivity, a loss that "cannot be offset by the subject becoming self-aware of his own historicality."[12] Gadamer questions the conceptual distinction between theoretical understanding and practical application, however. He considers the essential role of application in not only historical but also legal and theological interpretation. When interpreting a code of law, Gadamer argues, what is essential is that one understands it precisely in terms of what it says about our present concrete situation. Similarly, he argues, adequately interpreting a divine oracle or a sacred text requires that one translate the message so that it is conveyed and can be applied in the concrete lives of those the language addresses. "This implies that the text, whether law or gospel, if it is to be understood properly—i.e., according to the claim it makes—must be understood at every moment, in every concrete situation, in a new and different way. Understanding here is always application" (TM, 319–20). Here again, Gadamer's point is not that the present horizon dictates unilaterally what the text says. Rather, in considering the present horizon through which the message of the text must be concretized, one is able to attend better to both the concrete present and the text itself. The principles of legal and theological hermeneutics are not special cases, though. For Gadamer, they are exemplary of what understanding in general requires. Understanding a historical event by thinking through its practical applications within our present lifeworld, then, is not, for Gadamer, some subjective or arbitrary appropriation of the past. It is the most genuine way of grappling with the meaning of the past and present.

Thinking Through Our Fundamental Immersion in Language

Having clarified Gadamer's idea that understanding is always immersed in a historical consciousness that mediates the object of inquiry for us, let us now consider another important way that the social and historical lifeworld into which we are immersed plays a positive role in the process of understanding, namely, as language. For Gadamer, language plays a role in acts of understanding analogous to that of history. To understand an expression, one must put it into "one's own" language.

We have already seen how Gadamer makes this point about the principles governing textual interpretation. To read, one must rely on a number of anticipatory projections, including various forms of linguistic understanding. As one begins to read an essay, for instance, one's sense for the meaning of the words used and one's familiarity with the literary genre enable the reading to get underway. Like the question, these linguistic fore-conceptions constrain, to some degree, what the reader can discover in the essay. Yet, without such preconceptions, no new discoveries could be made at all. One cannot read and learn from an essay without relying on the meaning of the words already operative in the lifeworld and on stylistic conventions that provide one with rough templates for understanding the organization of the argument as a whole. Yet what can we say of the understanding that arises from such reading? Is the understanding that arises merely a subjective interpretation of the text that carries no validity for any other readers? As Gadamer sees it, what emerges from the interplay of the text and the fore-conceptions of the reader is not simply subjective. It is proper understanding, as the meaning of the text is only ever disclosed through such points of interaction. A text, Gadamer says, "does not simply speak its word, always the same, in lifeless rigidity, but gives ever new answers to the person who questions it and poses ever new questions to him who answers it." Thus, he continues, "to understand a text is to come to understand oneself in a kind of dialogue."[13]

We are accustomed, however, to thinking about textual interpretation, like historical interpretation, as originating in something purely subjective and, more often than not, as a source of error. Indeed, one of the defining qualities of the technological rationality of modern culture is its pervasive suspicion that no person on their own can achieve understanding that goes beyond subjective interpretation. The only way to achieve real, reliable understanding, it is thought, is to try to neutralize biases stemming from one's particular subject position as much as possible. And even then, many suspect, the understanding that results will be arbitrary beyond a certain point due to sources of bias that are impossible to remove. In part 2 of this book, we will see why some recent epistemologists take issue with the tendency to conceive of knowledge as inherently free of bias (or "value neutral"). For the moment, let us just recognize the tendency we have to think about language as one such bias. In modern societies organized by technological rationality, we tend to think about natural human language as having a subjective, arbitrary relationship to the world and to consider human thought's reliance on natural language primarily, therefore, as a source of error. Generally speaking, we distrust thought to the extent that it relies on language for its expression. Gadamer was well aware of this modern distrust of language. In his essay "To What Extent Does Language Preform Thought?," Gadamer describes "the fundamental doubt" that we harbor today "about the possibility of our escaping from the sphere of influence of our education which is linguistic, of our socialization which is linguistic, and of our thought which is transmitted through language" (TM, 568). Alongside this doubt comes a related suspicion about interpretation. If language is an untrustworthy medium for understanding, then so too is the whole enterprise of linguistic interpretation that we rely on to understand speeches and texts.

This attitude toward language, however, is relatively new within the history of philosophy. Throughout most of this history, by contrast, philosophers have regarded the principles that we use to understand a speech or a text as fundamental to the development of understanding in general. This is the premise of Aristotle's *On Interpretation*—one of Aristotle's logical treatises that was most studied during the Middle Ages. It is also the basis for the close association between philosophy, disputation, jurisprudence, and rhetoric that is present in the organization of major works in philosophy and of university faculties up until the seventeenth century. During this period, philosophical thought is deeply interwoven with and in some ways indistinguishable from the activity of interpretation and disputation. Moreover, many of the treatises on interpretation during this period aim not at a general theory of interpretation but at a theory of interpretation as bound to a given text or set of texts—for example, a particular body of sacred scripture or a particular code of law. This is the case, for instance, for studies on the principles of biblical interpretation such as Rabbi David Adani's fourteenth-century *Midrash HaGadol* and Matthias Flacius Illyricus's *Clavais Scripturae Sacrae* (1567) and for studies on the interpretation of particular codes of law like Constantius Rogerius's study of the Roman Code of Justinian in *De Iuris Interpretatione* (1463). In each of these cases, valuable understanding is thought to emerge through the careful interpretation of texts of historical significance and through the articulation of the principles that guide such interpretation.

With the advent of writing, texts come increasingly to play an important role in the organization of human society and human thought. When texts begin to play this role, and especially when divergent interpretations of these texts start to arise, people naturally start to wonder what exactly might indicate whether a text is being properly understood. They start to consider, in other words, the principles of understanding these texts—what is indicative of and necessary for understanding them and what might thwart this understanding. Such questioning arises especially of texts where there is a general consensus regarding their importance and the centrality of their role in the organization of social life, for example, in the case of written codes of law—whether secular or religious. This is the context in which systematic inquiry into understanding and interpretation—what eventually comes to be identified as the field of "hermeneutics"—begins. Over time, hermeneutic treatises of a more general scope start to emerge. By the late seventeenth century, one finds the emergence of, not only texts that address the principles of legal and theological hermeneutics in general, but those that address the interpretation of texts more broadly. Early examples of the latter include Johannes von Felde's *Treatise on the Science of Interpretation* (1689), Johann Heinrich Ernesti's *On the Nature and Constitution of Secular Hermeneutics* (1699), and Johann Martin Chladenius's *Introduction to the Correct Interpretation of Reasonable Discourses and Books* (1742), all of which attempt to generate principles of interpretation that apply to a broad set of texts. Thus, even many Enlightenment thinkers found it necessary, when thinking about human understanding, to consider the way that understanding can arise through the proper interpretation of texts.

By the late seventeenth century, hermeneutics had begun to broaden into an exploration of understanding texts in general—or, at least, into an exploration of understanding any and all historical texts where, for proper comprehension, the original intention of the work needed to be deciphered. In this way, general hermeneutics began to emerge as a field on its own—independent of explorations of jurisprudence or theology bound to a particular tradition and to a particular set of texts. Yet this period also saw a narrowing of the field of hermeneutics as well. Enlightenment thinkers, who generally aspired to think free of the guardrails of any tradition, no longer saw the interpretation of texts as central to the task of understanding. Nor did they see the principles of textual interpretation as a blueprint for understanding in general. They recognized a need to secure proper understanding of historical and legal texts, but they did not believe that there was anything to gain through such interpretation other than information about the past and an understanding of the intentions behind the writing. This is the context in which Christian Wolff addresses hermeneutic theory, for example, in his discussion of understanding historical texts in his *Rational Thoughts on the Powers of the Human Understanding and Its Proper Use in the Cognition of Truth* (1713). Thus, the epistemic value of hermeneutics would be secured at this time only by restricting it to a particular domain. Hermeneutics would be a valuable tool for understanding but only for understanding the limited set of things that we can only make sense of through texts.

For the most part, this narrowing of the field of hermeneutics persists during the period of Romantic hermeneutics at the turn of the nineteenth century. For Romantic thinkers like Friedrich Schlegel and Friedrich Schleiermacher, hermeneutics is still very much bound to the interpretation of speech acts—of texts and, secondarily, of living speech. Yet thinkers during this period also began to return to the earlier notion that understanding a text involves recognizing the dialectical movement of which the text is a part. For Schleiermacher, "every act of understanding is the reverse side of an act of speaking, and one must grasp the thinking that underlies a given statement."[14] For the Romantics, the task of hermeneutics is still limited to understanding the intentional thought of the author, but, consistent with the Romantic doctrine of the genius, the intentional thought of the author is understood in terms of how the whole comes to appear at this particular moment. For Schleiermacher, every act of interpretation requires that we understand what is said by considering both the context of the possibilities that exist within the speaker's language and the event of thought taking place in the thought of the speaker. This means, for Schleiermacher, that one must regard the person and their speaking "exclusively as occasions for the language to reveal itself."[15] This is a significant development in the enterprise of hermeneutics, because it reconceives the nature of that which is understood by interpretation. For the Romantics, interpretation of a historical text can reveal the author's intended meaning but only insofar as this meaning is understood as a moment in the development of a broader system of discourse. On this view, interpretation of a given text, then, can increase the interpreter's understanding of more than just the meaning intended by the text's author.

Gadamer furthers this line of thought by considering the kind of understanding that is called for in response to the address of a text. Understanding a text requires, first of all, interpretation. Interpretation is not a subjective imposition onto a text but the path one must follow in order to bring forth the work itself. As one contemporary hermeneutic thinker, Günter Figal, puts it, "The work does not arrive without the activity of interpreters; to experience it in its presence is always only possible through interpretation."[16] Furthermore, Gadamer argues that understanding a text means primarily engaging with the truth at stake in the discussion rather than simply registering the author's intended meaning or reconstructing the original historical horizon of the text. It means preparing oneself to encounter claims about what is or is not, what should be or should not be and to have some portion of one's current beliefs and habits challenged. This entails reading specifically with an eye to the way what is said coheres with and is thus intelligible within one's current horizon but also with an eye to how it expands or revises this horizon in some way.

Thus, Gadamer describes the task of understanding a text as follows:

> What is stated in the text must be detached from all contingent factors and grasped in its full ideality, in which alone it has validity [*Geltung*]. Thus, precisely because it entirely detaches the sense of what is said from the person saying it, the written word makes the understanding reader the arbiter of its claim to truth. The reader experiences what is addressed to him and what he understands in all its validity [*Geltung*]. What he understands is always more than an unfamiliar opinion: it is always possible truth. (TM, 412)

For Gadamer, then, the primary point of reading the work of an author—be it Plato, Dōgen, or Virginia Woolf—is not to learn about who these authors were as people or about the character of people living in this particular place and time. Nor is the point to encounter unfamiliar opinions that leave us struck with how different these authors' own historical horizons are from ours in the present day. If we say that what the interpretation yields is only an illumination of the author's unique genius or of strange ancient belief systems, we underestimate what transpires in the process of interpretation. We miss the epistemic relevance when we imagine that what emerges from reading is only a reflection of the interpreter's own horizon prior to the encounter or the horizon of the original text. In fact, both of these horizons are abstractions from the subject matter to be understood. As Gadamer says, "There is no more an isolated horizon of the present in itself than there are historical horizons which have to be acquired. Rather, understanding is always the fusion of these horizons supposedly existing by themselves" (TM, 317). When one grapples with the truth claims of a text, one is not simply learning about some closed horizon of the past and leaving unbothered one's present understanding of their hermeneutical situation. The point of reading these works is to receive, think through, and respond to the claim that they make on us. It is to grapple with works created by humans past in order to hear what they have to say to us today—to mine them for their "possible truth."

Although texts, with their relative autonomy from authorial intentions, are paradigmatic objects of hermeneutic understanding for Gadamer (TM, 417), the same dynamics also characterize the understanding called for in the case of conversation. We will explore what Gadamer sees as emerging from conversation in chapter 3. For now, let us just consider the nature of the understanding that is sought when people enter into conversation. The point of a conversation is not to extract information from the other person in a disinterested way—information, say, about the beliefs they hold, their present mental state, or their past experiences. Nor is the point to get inside the other person's head and figure out just what they mean to say about a topic. Because this is the case, conversation, just like textual interpretation, requires that we take what the other says as meaningful and intelligible and as disclosive in some way of the truths at stake in the discussion. As Gadamer puts it:

> Conversation is a process of coming to an understanding. Thus it belongs to every true conversation that each person opens himself to the other, truly accepts his point of view as valid [*seine Gesichtspunkte wirklich gelten läßt*] and transposes himself into the other to such an extent that he understands not the particular individual but what he says. What is to be grasped is the substantive rightness of his opinion, so that we can be at one with each other on the subject. Thus we do not relate the other's opinion to him but to our own opinions and views. (TM, 403)

Of course, not all forms of verbal interaction can be described as genuine conversations. When your physician or your psychiatrist asks you questions in order to make a diagnosis or a detective interrogates you as a suspect for a crime, they do not do this in order to think along with you about the subject matter. They are simply trying to get information from you. Such interactions are the exception, however. When we are speaking to one another in conditions of relative trust and cooperation, listening to one another means being attuned to what is disclosed about the matter at hand. Consider, after all, how inappropriate it would be in most contexts to respond to a person who speaks to you by simply describing their intention. Imagine that your partner says to you: "The storm's intensity is increasing. We had better get inside." It would clearly be absurd in this case to limit your response entirely to "You mean to say that the weather is worsening and that we should relocate." It certainly might help to make sure that you have understood them, but such a response, by itself, is clearly inadequate. The proper response is, in Gadamer's words, to grasp "the substantive rightness" of what your partner is saying. This does not necessarily mean agreeing with their conclusion. By listening carefully to and following along with their *logos*, you may find yourself drawn to a conclusion other than theirs. Your partner's vivid description of the strengthening storm may, for instance, persuade you not to run inside but to secure loose items you have in the yard. Likewise, although there is no evidence that Plato intended to argue for such a point in the *Republic*, one may come away from the *Republic* struck above all by the conviction that real justice is not possible in a society where one's role in society is determined at birth. In both cases, it is clear that the understanding that unfolds is not a matter of simply getting the intention behind the speaker's words right.

Gadamer helps us to see, then, how in interpreting a text, I must look for, articulate, and grapple with the truth of what is at issue. What I take away from interpretation, then, is not isolated to the meaning of the text as an object that was already present at the beginning of the encounter. A text refers us to and attempts to enlighten us about some subject matter beyond the text itself. This point is pivotal in understanding how Gadamer's thought relates to other phases in the history of hermeneutics. By claiming that the interpretation of works can aid, not only in the understanding of those works, but in the development of understanding as such, Gadamer departs from the narrowing of hermeneutics that had first occurred through the Enlightenment and had then become reinforced through Romanticism. He returns instead to an earlier relationship between philosophy and interpretation, where interpreting works is a fundamental source of knowledge about the world.

Not surprisingly, Gadamer's account of textual interpretation has been subjected to the same criticisms as his account of historical interpretation. Thus, for people like Emilio Betti and E. D. Hirsch, responsible interpretation requires that one try one's best to understand the author's original intention, the meaning the text had for its original audience, and to guard against the unwarranted imposition of one's own subjective interests in the process. For these critics, we ought not to give the title of "knowledge" or even of "understanding" to what emerges from a process of reading that is conditioned by one's own linguistic and historical preconceptions. If a reading is mediated in this way, it simply cannot, for these anti-epistemological readers of Gadamer, give us the truth of the object.[17]

The idea that what is at stake in the process of textual interpretation is the apprehension of truth is also rejected, albeit for very different reasons, by Richard Rorty and John Caputo. For both, hermeneutics is essentially a move away from classical epistemological concerns about truth, and it is this radical shift enacted by hermeneutics that, for Rorty and Caputo, makes it so compelling. Wary of philosophy's traditionally foundationalist aspirations, both find in Gadamer's thought at least the promise of another sort of philosophical project that can illuminate the way to a meaningful life that is not underwritten by a metaphysics of truth. For Rorty, hermeneutics is "an expression of hope that the cultural space left by the demise of epistemology will not be filled."[18] Gadamer's work is an important part of the development of hermeneutics, for Rorty, then, insofar as it presents the course of human thought as aimed at "continuing a conversation rather than at discovering truth."[19] For Rorty, the aim of hermeneutic engagement is not the acquisition of knowledge; it is ongoing self-edification (*Bildung*).

While Caputo finds the seed of what he calls "radical hermeneutics" in Gadamer's thought, he criticizes Gadamer's hermeneutics for remaining oriented toward the pursuit of knowledge and the truth in several ways. In suggesting that it is truth that is at stake in textual interpretation, Caputo argues that Gadamer took hermeneutics in a "conservative" rather than "radical" direction.[20] Caputo's concerns here take their lead from the late twentieth-century tradition of deconstruction and, in particular, from the work of Jacques Derrida. Following Derrida, Caputo finds any talk of truth in the process of interpretation to be a reactionary attempt to eliminate "the uncontrollable play of dissemination"[21] and to direct hermeneutics back toward a metaphysical tradition to which Caputo believes radical hermeneutics seeks to provide an alternative. Insofar as it presents the process of interpretation as a way of grappling with truth claims, *Truth and Method*, Caputo argues, "remains within the metaphysics of truth"[22] and lacks the courage (Caputo frequently presents the error as a defect of character) to affirm the play of dissemination.[23]

These criticisms, all of which I take to belong to the anti-epistemological tradition of reading Gadamer's work, are at odds with each other in a couple of significant ways. Rorty praises Gadamer's thought for parting ways with the field of epistemology, which he takes to be inevitably bound up with the aspirations of foundationalist philosophy, while Caputo criticizes Gadamer for ultimately remaining bound to the discourse of truth and the metaphysics that it implies. More significantly, Caputo criticizes Gadamer's account of textual interpretation in *Truth and Method* for remaining bound to exactly what a number of other commentators (e.g., Betti, Hirsch, and Apel) claimed he did not take seriously enough, namely, epistemological concerns about truth and knowledge.

I do not wish to defend Gadamer's project in *Truth and Method* from Caputo's charge, as I think that the concern underlying the charge is misguided. I disagree with Caputo that the pursuit of truth and understanding is a way of avoiding the play of dissemination. More emphatically, I do not consider the play of dissemination that is detached from the pursuit of truth and understanding to be a worthy aim.[24] What must be emphasized in response to all of these critics, though (e.g., Betti, Rorty, and Caputo), is that it is inappropriate to assess Gadamer's project with a theoretical model that he is questioning. As we have seen, *Truth and Method* raises the question of how we ought to think about the processes by which we arrive at knowledge. It raises questions about aspects of the transcendence model, the theoretical framework that we typically rely on to conceive of knowledge. Both Betti and Rorty, however, take recourse in this framework when they claim that *Truth and Method* is not interested in the pursuit of truth and knowledge. For them, any critique of the transcendence model of knowing or the objectivity model of truth must be an abandonment of epistemology. What they and Caputo fail to see, however, is how Gadamer is opening up a space in which to rethink the meaning of these traditional epistemological models.

Gadamer opens up this space for questioning by considering how, in the case of historical and textual interpretation, one's factical situatedness in the social-historical lifeworld is not something that one must simply transcend. Almost without exception, the text or the historical event that I find myself striving to understand is not some object indifferent to my own interpretive horizon. It is the text or the historical event as it has something to say to us today. In the last section of this chapter, I want to clarify this insight into understanding further by thinking about what it means for the practice of education.

Understanding as a Process of (Self-)Education

We are accustomed to thinking about the object of knowing as something separate and distinct from the self of the knower. We feel we must set aside our backgrounds and our interests in order to encounter what is really there and that the reality that we will encounter, if successful, is indifferent to our existence. This assumption belongs to the transcendence model of knowing. Despite the dominance of this theoretical model, though, our everyday experiences of understanding often have a highly personal quality. One picks up the book because one anticipates that what it has to say will be timely and enlightening for one's own life. Questions in the present day make one curious to study some past culture, and one comes away from the study with new insight into modern culture and the possibilities that are laden within it. This quality of understanding is not limited to historical or textual interpretation, though. Part of the fascination that one has with the story and the characters in a television drama is curiosity about what these characters might reveal about those people around us today and how the story might shed light on our own historical moment.

On this view, one's present situation does more than simply mediate access to the object; it is actually part of what is revealed to one in the process of understanding. Consider again the experience of an audience. Watching a performance of Shakespeare's *Hamlet*, the audience identifies the character of Hamlet in terms of something that is familiar to them. They may identify him early on as, for example, a depressive type—a kind of personality type that is familiar and meaningful to them in their own historical situation. Of course, the story and the level of drama that ensues is novel. If it were completely continuous with the spectator's ordinary life, there would be little reason to attend the performance. At the same time, the story and the performance afford them new discoveries, say, about the depressive personality type that was familiar to them. They see how this personality type transitions easily into rage. As the performance dramatizes this connection, they begin to consider the ways that the connection is evident in their own twenty-first-century American society and even perhaps in themselves. In this way, the performance allows some aspect of their present situation, what is already familiar to them, to come to light in a new way. As Gadamer puts it, "To see that 'this is how it is' is a kind of self-knowledge for the spectator, who emerges with new insight from the illusions in which he, like everyone else, lives" (TM, 133).

Is this personal dimension really essential for understanding, though? Is the self-knowledge that emerges from such encounters not incidental to what it means to actually understand the meaning of the play? Recall once again Gadamer's rejection of the distinction between theoretical understanding and practical application. While Betti and others insist that knowing how to apply what one has learned to one's life is incidental to actual learning, Gadamer argues that one cannot be said to have understood properly if one is not able to find the relevant practical application. Just as one has not properly understood the nineteenth-century abolition movement if one fails to consider it in light of, say, continuing concerns about racial and economic justice, one has not properly understood the performance of Hamlet if one takes it as a story of mere historical interest with nothing to say about our lives today. For Gadamer, then, the relevance of a play to one's present situation is not of merely subjective interest. To understand the play is to be in dialogue with it.

We tend to think about the self today as distinct from many other sorts of things that we might seek to understand. To learn about history or the natural world, we think, is not to learn about the self. If one wants to learn about the self, it is thought, one needs to focus on a domain that is separate from the others, namely, the domain of psychology. Gadamer's claim that all understanding is self-understanding, though, problematizes this view. It suggests that a number of domains that we think of as domains for objective inquiry cannot be undertaken without self-examination. Conversely, it implies that self-examination cannot be undertaken independently of inquiry into history, literature, and so on. This is an important point to bear in mind lest one take Gadamer to be saying that the understanding yields insights of merely subjective relevance. For Gadamer, though, it is not that one learns about one's present situation *as opposed to* the story, historical event, characters, and so on. It's just that the truth of the latter comes to light through events of self-realization.

Gadamer uses the term *Bildung* to describe this process by which one immerses oneself in something new, foreign, unfamiliar in a way that deepens one's self-understanding. In this, Gadamer makes it clear that the process of understanding that he is offering is something familiar to most of us as an important aspect of the education and cultivation of the self. Following Hegel, Gadamer sees *Bildung* as the practice of "keeping oneself open to what is other—to other, more universal points of view" (TM, 16) for the sake of educating the self beyond its own initial and particular point of view. When one goes to the theater to immerse oneself in an unfamiliar story or performance that will compel one to see one's own time and place differently, one is engaging in *Bildung* in this sense.

Those who are consistently engaged in *Bildung* are not content to remain comfortably within their initial point of view when other points of view that present warranted challenges to their own are within reach. They relate to others and to other expressions of human activity as sources from which they might learn and grow. In this way, *Bildung* would seem to have a sort of ethical value that is relatively easy to recognize in societies with liberal egalitarian ideals like our own. It characterizes a human way of life that, rather than persisting in points of view that are indifferent to relevant insights from new experiences, takes new experiences and new people as opportunities for self-edification.

Does *Bildung* also have epistemological value? Recall that, on Rorty's reading, Gadamer's interest in the self-edification that is possible in hermeneutic encounters betrays his lack of interest in any epistemic value that they might be said to have. Attending a theatrical performance, on this view, affords an opportunity for valuable self-edification but not for deepening one's understanding of the world. Must one see these two as mutually exclusive, though? Must one choose between saying that an experience was personally edifying and that it was genuinely educational? And does Gadamer accept this opposition?

We have already considered some of the arguments that Gadamer presents for why the understanding sought by the study of a particular text or historical development is often inseparable from the particular point of access that one first had into it. It is not just that historical, social, and linguistic forms of mediation play a role in shaping how one comes to think about the object. More importantly, what calls for our understanding is what Gadamer calls the *Wirkungsgeschichte*, the effective history of the text or the event. In conceiving of the object of understanding in this way, Gadamer makes it clear that there are many cases where understanding a text or a historical event in its truth is identical to understanding what it means for one's own historical situation. Thus, Rorty is wrong to say that interest in *Wirkungsgeschichte*, for Gadamer, means interest in self-edification rather than in knowledge, since Gadamer himself sought to challenge this very opposition.

Is Rorty nevertheless right to insist on the opposition, though? Is he perhaps just clarifying the natural conclusion that should be derived from Gadamer's hermeneutics? Is it not one thing to find oneself personally transformed by an encounter and another thing for it to have taught you something about the world? To evaluate the merit of this distinction, let us consider a practice and an institution that has for centuries played a significant role in *Bildung*: education.

What is the goal of education? In a famous article that lays out the rationale and a program for "critical pedagogy," Paolo Freire observes that, when many people think about education, what they imagine is a fairly unidirectional process. Students come in bereft of knowledge and receive new knowledge through their teacher and the books that they are assigned. They are passive absorbers of information. Freire calls this the "banking concept of education."[25] For Freire, this model of education, as popular as it is, misconstrues the role students play in the educational process. While students inevitably encounter new ideas and make new discoveries in the process, what makes this experience an *educational* one is the act of taking these experiences as opportunities to critically examine existing beliefs—the student's own and those with traction in their society. To have an educational experience is to take what one learns as posing a question—for example, for our historical self-understanding, for our sense of purpose and what matters moving forward, for our understanding of our place in this world, and so on. This requires that students help to discover and articulate these questions and, thus, to draw upon the preliminary, anticipatory understanding in which they are already immersed (e.g., their present historical understanding, their present sense of purpose, their preliminary understanding of their place in the world, etc.).

To some extent, Freire's criticism of the banking concept of education is now accepted as mainstream educational theory. Most educators today strive for a "student-centered" approach and readily acknowledge that it is necessary to begin and ground inquiry where students are. For some, this means engaging the preconceptions that particular students in the classroom have. For others, it means exploring a topic by engaging those preconceptions that are most pervasive in a given generation and that naturally play a large role in how a particular group of students will approach the topic. When understood as a point about the process of learning, the theory is quite uncontroversial—even trivial. Nobody would deny that, in order to learn something new, one needs to access it through something that is familiar. For Freire and for humanistic educators, though, "student-centered" education is more than a means to get students engaged. It is intrinsic to the exploration of the topic itself.

Hermeneutic theorists offer a similar account of education. In *Hermeneutics and Education*, for example, Shaun Gallagher argues that educational experience has a hermeneutic structure. It requires that the student not just passively soak up but *interpret* what they encounter, finding in it a question for them and their time and thus an opportunity for greater self-understanding. As Gallagher says, "Education does not occur if one stands back and acts as an external observer. Nor is education simply a gathering of information that does not affect the student. To be educational, experience requires self-transcendence, an involvement that gives education its moral dimension."[26] Such a concept of educational experience follows naturally from the Gadamerian exploration of the process of understanding.[27] Indeed, Gallagher is persuasive when he argues that it is educational experience in particular that provides the very best paradigm for this process.

Now, this does not mean that the experience of some insight as self-edifying is, in and of itself, an indication of understanding. To put the criterion this way would be too formal and subjective. Self-understanding is always involved when understanding occurs, but its occurrence is not a sufficient condition for the occurrence of understanding. Equally important is the revelation of the subject matter. When understanding occurs, the subject matter is revealed in a new way. This is the objective dimension of understanding, which is a necessary counterpart to what takes place within the self-understanding of the learner. We will return in chapter 3 to explore this dimension more fully. For now, I want simply to point out that the highlighting of self-understanding as a key ingredient in educational experience should not be mistaken to imply that education amounts to an experience of mere *self*-discovery void of any content understood. Learning is neither a matter of world-disclosure without self-discovery nor self-discovery without world-disclosure. Both of these possibilities fall short of the real goal of education.

We can now articulate what is wrong with Rorty's claim that the self-edifying quality of an educational experience is in every instance irrelevant to its epistemic value. While there may be times when one's attempt to understand something is self-edifying in a merely idiosyncratic way, for the most part, what makes a particular experience of interpretation self-edifying is also what gives it epistemic value. The opposition that Rorty draws between an interest in knowledge and an interest in self-edification is thus a false one. That human thought is oriented toward self-edification (*Bildung*) does not mean that it is not oriented toward the expansion of knowledge, for, as Gadamer demonstrates, understanding is an event that requires the personal interest and involvement of inquirers. That it is personally engaging in no way disqualifies an experience from being educational.

As I have suggested here, this insight emerges not simply from Gadamer's own reflections on understanding, though. It also emerges from reflection upon the concrete experiences of teaching and learning. That Gadamer's insights into the nature of understanding should be helpful in analyzing what happens in educational experience is a point worth emphasizing today, though, since it helps us recognize the relevance of Gadamer's account of understanding for practical questions about education today. After all, it is common in many places like the United

States today for education to be seen primarily as technical training and, thus, as a way of transmitting technical knowledge and know-how. This approach to education puts little emphasis on the personal character of an educational experience except perhaps as an expedient to transmitting the objective content. Gadamer, however, helps us to see why education cannot be reduced to such a unidirectional process of transmission and why humanistic disciplines like philosophy play such a vital role in not only education but the production of knowledge. The humanistic forms of inquiry that have long made up an important part of the educational process have an essential purpose, namely, to think more carefully through the historical and social situations in which we find ourselves immersed. To neglect this task is, as a society, to be diminished in our capacities as knowers.

The questions Gadamer raises, then, have profound implications, not only for how we approach formal education but for how we conceive of the process of understanding in general. While Gadamer certainly recognized the growing monopoly of technological rationality during his time, he could not have fully grasped the extent to which its power would soon be amplified by rapid advancements in information technology at the beginning of the twenty-first century. In the twenty-first century, we conceive of the process of understanding as requiring one to leave oneself and one's situation behind so as to properly represent what exists independently of one and one's situation or assume that such neutralization of bias is automatically achieved through the rigorous application of scientific method. What's more, we assume that it is achieved very simply through the use of analytic instruments and especially "smart" technologies. Indeed, there is little epistemic value recognized in any cognitive activity beyond those that are anchored or replaced by such instruments today. For Gadamer, though, the process of understanding involves a much vaster portion of our activity as human beings. It requires that we find ourselves belonging to situations—historical, social, and linguistic—that, while familiar, require some reflective engagement to understand.

Such a concept of understanding will appear unsatisfactory to those who take it as the duty of philosophy to renounce the initial way in which we make sense of things as people, just as it will appear peculiar to those who conceive of education as the passive reception of information. From these vantage points, it will appear to not only confuse knowledge with subjective meaning but to offer little in its defense against the skeptical questions that have long motivated epistemological inquiry. As we shall see in part 2 of this book, however, Gadamer is not alone in his argument that the particular situations in which inquirers first find themselves play a productive role in the process of understanding, nor is he alone in rejecting the idea that real understanding is that which meets the challenge of the skeptic. Before exploring other developments in epistemology that share these features with Gadamer's thought, however, let us look more closely at two important aspects of his account of understanding: first, how, if at all, it accounts for the way that we come to critically reflect on and revise our fore-conceptions (the subject of the next chapter), and second, the theory of truth that Gadamer's account of understanding implies (the subject of the third chapter).

Chapter 2

The Limitation of Two Historical Models of Knowing
The Enlightenment and Romanticism

> Hence we would do well not to regard historical consciousness as something radically new—as it seems at first—but as a new element in what has always constituted the human relation to the past.
>
> —Gadamer, *Truth and Method*, 294

In the previous chapter, we explored how Gadamer's thought challenges a common attitude about the historical situation of understanding. In reality, there are two attitudes regarding the historicity of understanding commonly held today. On the one hand, we believe that we only achieve a real, worthwhile understanding of a topic when our thinking manages to break free from the dogmas of the past. We believe that this transcendence of the historical situation of thought is both possible and desirable. We applaud those whose thought appears to us to proceed unhinged by traditional dogmas, whether those dogmas be old habits of scientific thought or traditional ideas about social life. We celebrate as epistemic heroes those who discover their own way of thinking. This attitude toward the historicity of thought stems from the popular transcendence model of knowing introduced in the last chapter. On the other hand, many accept as a general rule that our understanding is inevitably bound to the particular historical and cultural situations in which we are embedded. Accordingly, they insist that there is no transcending the historicity of the understanding and thus no epistemic heroes to applaud. Despite the tension between these two positions, most people find each compelling enough to invoke with some frequency today.

Gadamer's *Truth and Method* makes the case that both these common positions on the historicity of understanding—that based on the transcendence model of knowing and the alternative based on what we may call the *immanence model of knowing*, are mistaken. According to Gadamer's account, understanding does not require that one simply abandon the prejudices of tradition at the start. Inquiry always begins in a situation where prejudices are operative. This is inevitable. However, contrary to what the immanence model of understanding suggests, inquiry is not locked into these prejudices in a way that would exhaustively determine what can emerge from it. In the previous chapter, we examined how Gadamer's exploration of the nature of understanding in *Truth and Method* raises questions about the transcendence model of epistemology and encourages us to consider the inevitable and positive role played by the mediating factors of history and language. In this chapter, I want to look more closely at the way that Gadamer's thought also problematizes the alternative model. Given the rise of neotraditionalist attitudes toward the historicity of human thought in the twenty-first century, I am particularly interested in how Gadamer's problematization of the immanence model helps us to account for not just the inevitability of fore-conceptions that come with the historical situation of thought but also the necessity of critically examining them.

The core of this argument is presented in the section of *Truth and Method* entitled "The Elevation of the Historicity of Understanding to the Status of a Hermeneutic Principle" (hereafter referred to as "The Elevation of the Historicity of Understanding"). As such, this chapter will focus on Gadamer's account in this important section of his major work. In particular, we will examine Gadamer's argument that the task of understanding requires critical self-reflection on the fore-conceptions operative at the beginning of an inquiry and, in light of this account, his attempt to articulate a model of understanding that differs both from that model inherited through the legacy of the Enlightenment and from that model that emerged with Romanticism in reaction to this one. Along the way, I will highlight some issues related to historical consciousness in the contemporary world that put into relief the continuing relevance of Gadamer's account in "The Elevation of the Historicity of Understanding."

The Necessity of Fore-Conceptions

Gadamer begins "The Elevation of the Historicity of Understanding" by reflecting on Heidegger's concept of the "fore-structure of the understanding." As indicated in the previous chapter, Heidegger introduces this concept as a way of explaining why understanding is not a matter of simply passively absorbing new information. When one goes to understand something, one inevitably brings with one anticipatory projections ("fore-conceptions") of what one is going to understand. As we saw in the last chapter, Gadamer follows Heidegger in arguing that the fore-structure of the understanding is operative all of the time—that is, whenever understanding is at work. Even further, he attempts to demonstrate the inexorable role that fore-conceptions play in human inquiry by asking us to imagine what this inquiry would be like if we could not rely on fore-conceptions and know-how from the lifeworld.

For example, to read a text, one must anticipate each step of the way. We anticipate what comes next—whether it is the next step in the plot of a story or in a theoretical argument. As Gadamer puts it, "One projects meaning for the text as a whole as soon as some initial meaning emerges in the text" (TM, 279). When we read a historical text, we inevitably bring with us a preliminary sense of the historical context and historical significance of the work. Finally, we inevitably read by anticipating the meaning of the terms used in the text. This entails taking for granted a preliminary, operative understanding of the terms based on their conventional meaning in the genre of the text. The contextual meaning of some of these terms may indeed change under the pressure of the meaning of the text as a whole; however, we must inevitably grasp some meaning of the terms in advance of the whole in order for our reading to get underway. Hence, anticipatory projections of various kinds are inevitably at work in the process of reading.

Now, it is our instinct today to understand this process as one that unfolds when an individual subject encounters some immediate object, ontologically separate from them, and relies upon their own particular experiences and associations to guide them. If we conceive of the activity as purely subjective in this way, however, we make an important assumption that will then shape what we think we can legitimately expect to happen in reading. When we assume that what the reader seeks to understand is independent of the reader's preconceptions, then the understanding developed through reading will appear to have no bearing on the self-knowledge of the reader. Moreover, the understanding developed will appear at best to approximate the object of inquiry, disclosing very little about the subject matter itself. This assumption, then, opens the door to skepticism about what can really be accomplished through reading and, by extension, by any inquiry that engages its object through our historical preconceptions.

The fore-conceptions operative in reading a text, however, are not as a whole simply the product of a reader's individual proclivities or personal experiences. Most are effects of being situated in a social-historical lifeworld and are thus anticipatory projections that we have in common with others with whom we share this world. They stem from our being situated in what Gadamer refers to as "a web of historical effects [*wirkungsgeschichtliche Verflechtung*]" (TM, 311). So, for example, it is by virtue of being situated within the effects of history that a text would first appear to the one who picks it up within a particular context as having this or that potential significance, and so on. Educators have an intimate knowledge of this point, as they must anticipate the fore-conceptions that their students as a whole will bring with them in reading a particular text and parts of the students' lifeworld with which the ideas will most clearly connect. Students may, for example, bring with them the expectation that a text assigned from antiquity is either an artifact of an outdated worldview or a source of secret wisdom that conveys possibilities of authenticity lost to modern society. On the other hand, what they find in the ancient text may be much more familiar than they imagined. It may, from the beginning, powerfully engage and expand upon some of their most intuitive ethical ideas. Such fore-conceptions are the effects of history possessed by subjects who are historically situated in a similar way.

When the object of our inquiry is mediated by the effects of history in such ways, Gadamer argues that it is imperative to reflect on the web of historical effects that condition it and, in fact, to treat these effects as inseparable from the object itself. If the mediating web of historical effects is set aside without comment, Gadamer argues, one can only attain partial knowledge of the object.[1] This is why, for Gadamer, it is wrong to imagine the process of understanding such an object as the encounter between two completely independent horizons.

As Gadamer explains:

The Limitation of Two Historical Models of Knowing | 49

> If we are trying to understand a historical phenomenon from the historical distance that is characteristic of our hermeneutical situation, we are always already affected by history. It determines in advance both what seems to us worth inquiring about and what will appear as an object of investigation, and we more or less forget half of what is really there—in fact, we miss the whole truth of the phenomenon—when we take its immediate appearance as the whole truth. (TM, 311)

We can now grasp how Gadamer challenges one of the attitudes toward the historical situation of the understanding with which we began. According to the transcendence model, one achieves real understanding by setting aside any effect of history that would mediate between the knower and the object. For Gadamer, though, this commits the error of taking the immediate appearance of the object as its truth and ignoring what mediates this appearance. When this happens, Gadamer argues, there is an actual "deformation of knowledge [*Deformation der Erkenntnis*]" (TM, 312). This deformation takes place, for example, when one presents knowledge of some historical subject without recognizing or analyzing the mediating, pretheoretical effects of history that have imbued the subject with a particular significance and positioned it within a particular context. Something similar happens, Gadamer explains, when one professes to "let the 'facts' (or the 'data') speak for themselves." Whether it is some historical fact or some data point, Gadamer continues, the danger lies in "simulat[ing] an objectivity that in reality depends on the legitimacy of the questions asked" (TM, 312). For Gadamer, genuine understanding (and, indeed, truthful speaking) requires not that one set aside one's "consciousness of being affected by history [*wirkungsgeschichtliches Bewusstsein*]" (TM, 312) but that one, in fact, recognizes this as consciousness of one's hermeneutical situation.

We can now understand part of what Gadamer means when he says that fore-conceptions have a productive role in the process of understanding. Contrary to the view that genuine inquiry requires that one set aside all prejudices and approach the object as a blank slate, Gadamer argues that these fore-conceptions are a necessary part of inquiry—and, indeed, are constitutive of the hermeneutic object itself. Neither the inquiry nor the object can be adequately approached without some consciousness of this fore-structure and, in particular, without a consciousness of being affected by history. This is an inevitable part of inquiry and a *necessary* aspect of the appearance of the hermeneutic object. Does this mean, however, that it is *sufficient* for understanding the matter at hand? And if it is not sufficient, what else is involved in understanding?

The Problematization and Testing of Fore-Conceptions

Gadamer emphasizes the necessary role that fore-conceptions play in the process of understanding. He does not, however, argue that the process of understanding is complete when these fore-conceptions are operative or when one becomes aware of their operation. The next and crucial step in the process is, as Gadamer puts it, "working out" these fore-conceptions "in terms of the things themselves [*in deren Ausarbeitung aus den Sachen selbst*]" (TM, 279).[2] Gadamer returns to the example of reading to clarify this point. While, as we have seen, one needs to be immersed in a shared lifeworld for any meaning to emerge as one reads, actually developing a *justified understanding* of what one is reading requires another step. It requires that these fore-conceptions be critically evaluated (or "worked out") in light of what emerges as one reads. Only by engaging in this additional step can one determine if one's operative fore-conceptions are legitimate or illegitimate—justified or unjustified. Gadamer describes this process and the understanding that arises from it as an achievement of "objectivity" in a particular sense: "A person who is trying to understand is exposed to distraction from fore-meanings that are not borne out by the things themselves. Working out appropriate projections, anticipatory in nature, to be confirmed 'by the things' themselves, is the constant task of understanding. The only 'objectivity' [*Objektivität*] here is the confirmation of a fore-meaning in its being worked out. Indeed, what characterizes the arbitrariness of inappropriate fore-meanings if not that they come to nothing in being worked out?" (TM, 280). Our fore-conceptions, then, while not as a whole arbitrary, are nevertheless not in themselves sufficient for arriving at justified understanding. For this, Gadamer says, one must check to see whether they are confirmed by the things themselves. When reading a text, for example, one may begin by taking for granted the meaning of a certain term, and this projection will allow an initial meaning to emerge. For any reading to begin, there must be an initial, preliminary assumption of coherence between the object and one's fore-conceptions. Yet, as the reading continues, some of these fore-conceptions become problematized as one tries, one by one, to make sense of the details of the text in a way that recognizes the text as having a unified and coherent meaning. One may discover, for example, that the term's meaning in the context of this text is quite different than one first assumed. Similarly, one must be willing to revisit the meaning of a particular section of a text as further sections are examined. Thus, we can say that there are two conditions in which one may find oneself pulled up short and needing to adjust one's understanding of a text. First, when one comes to a part of the text that one cannot understand, one must project some meaning that allows for coherence with one's background understanding. Second, when one's operative understanding of some element in the text cannot account for new details uncovered in it and thus risks making one's reading of the text incoherent, understanding requires that one revises one's current operative conception. While, for Gadamer, this process is ongoing (as he puts it, it is "the constant task of understanding"), it does not fail to award us with a sense of progress. Engaging diligently in this process is the way one arrives at more justified, less arbitrary beliefs.

Lest such diligence seem too high a demand for capturing what is achieved in ordinary acts of understanding, it is helpful here to consider how the same diligence is required for understanding even the simplest forms of speech. Whenever we go to understand the speech of someone with whom we are not well acquainted, we must rely on anticipatory projections. We take what they say as it coheres with these projections and insofar as these projections enable us to apprehend the different parts of what is said as a coherent whole. If, however, in applying these projections, we find them inadequate on either front, we must revise them. Linda Martín Alcoff argues that such readiness for revision is even a requirement for understanding simple ostensive forms of communication. If I see a Martian standing in my garden, pointing at a tomato, and uttering a sound, I may very well project that the sound means "tomato." But if the Martian then points to another plant and utters the same sound, I will need to revise my understanding. Alcoff suggests that we think about the principle that guides us in this process as the desire to "maximize comprehensive coherence." She explains:

> This revising is guided by the desire to establish the maximum internal coherence of the text and the maximum coherence between the text and our interpretation. If the continued acceptance of a given prejudgment creates incoherence or

reduces coherence, it must be discarded. For example, if the Martian in my garden goes on to point to a caterpillar and repeats the word "dervit," I must develop a new interpretation of her behavior. Perhaps she is pointing out things that are alive, or things that are in a garden, or things that she eats. The particular hypotheses I consider will be determined by their ability to preserve the coherence of her behavior.[3]

With Alcoff's example in mind, we can see why Gadamer insists that the process of understanding does not begin in one sense until "something addresses us" (TM, 310). We find ourselves addressed when we find ourselves pulled up short—aware that we do not yet have a reliable understanding of what we are encountering or what is being said to us. We are clearly addressed in those situations where we find ourselves trying to understand another attempting to communicate directly to us. However, in Gadamer's sense of the term here, it is not only when someone is directly attempting to communicate to us that we may find ourselves "addressed." This happens whenever we encounter expressions of meaning—intended for us or not—that require us to tread carefully as we interpret them.[4] In such cases, we are aware of the fact that understanding is not a given and that we must work toward a more justified understanding.

As Alcoff's example illustrates, though, in many cases, this process of revising our fore-conceptions can and often does take place without any conscious effort on our part. One does not need to stop and explicitly articulate the lack of coherence in one's interpretation in order to pique one's interest in a more coherent interpretation, nor does one need to explicitly articulate one's operative fore-conception in order for it to be replaced. Indeed, at a certain level, it is misleading to envision this process as a formal procedure that one executes in a sequence of steps. For Gadamer, there is an important sense in which *understanding is not something that we execute at will*. For the most part, it is simply an event that we find ourselves caught up in. In this sense, the title *Truth and Method* can be misleading, as Gadamer's book does not present a formal method for arriving at truth.[5] As Gadamer makes clear in the introduction, he intends *Truth and Method* to be descriptive rather than prescriptive (TM, xxii), to describe the process of understanding as it takes place.

That being said, there are situations where it is helpful, even necessary, to analyze this process in terms of the discrete procedures it involves and the specific conditions that allow understanding to occur.

Above all, it may be helpful to describe the means by which one is able to determine the need for abandoning a particular fore-conception. This is what Alcoff offers in describing what she calls Gadamer's "procedural argument for coherence."[6] Recall Alcoff's argument that, for Gadamer, our acts of understanding seek to maximize comprehensive coherence. While Gadamer intends *Truth and Method* as simply a description of the event of understanding, Alcoff argues that the analysis brings to light a rule that we could use in a formal procedure to determine when an operative understanding should be replaced by a specific alternative that has come to light. Out of the two textual interpretations, for example, Alcoff explains, the better one is the one that probes more into the details of the text, bringing to light elements previously unrecognized and their relevance for the text's meaning as a whole. The better interpretation is also one that recognizes important points of coherence between the interpreter's present horizon and the meaning of the text and lets this interplay produce important questions and insights about the present. One indication that one's reading has achieved this and is striving toward comprehensive coherence is the reading's development of a genuine question. There are, on the other hand, several ways that a reading can fail to achieve this standard. It can overlook substantial portions or patterns in a text, fail to grapple with the meaning or import of what is said in the text, or also lack internal coherence. Bad readings of religious scripture, of written law, of theoretical corpuses, and of works of fiction exhibit one or more of these qualities. They may, for example, be coherent readings unto themselves but ignore significant portions of the text or corpus due, perhaps, to their unwillingness to grapple with the import of what is said in these parts of the work. According to the procedural argument for coherence, then, "the goal of maximum comprehensive coherence is the epistemic criterion for an adequate understanding" and "the test of validity, or criterion of justification, that will be used to evaluate an interpretation is its achievement of coherence."[7]

What is most striking about Gadamer's conception of this way of arriving at justified beliefs is the alternative that it provides to the common view that honest inquiry requires that we put aside all preconceptions. For Gadamer, one does not need to set aside preconceptions at the beginning. This is, after all, not possible. Instead, understanding requires that we put our preconceptions to the test. Conceiving of the process of arriving at justified beliefs in this way has a notable advantage over the alternative view. Since it is not possible to set aside all fore-conceptions when one goes to understand an object, there is a clear problem with that conception of inquiry that makes this a requirement. It not only misdescribes what takes place in the process of understanding but perpetuates a myth of epistemic heroism that discourages people from reflecting on the constitutive role that their fore-conceptions play in shaping how and what they understand. We will return to consider the dangers of this myth in chapter 5. For now, let us consider how Gadamer connects this epistemic model to the development of historicism, that is, to that approach to history that attempts to know historical events and objects by setting aside from the start any meaning that comes from the interpreter's present situation. The mistake in this, for Gadamer, is a lack of self-awareness. Without self-awareness, without "consciousness of being affected by history," one fails to recognize how historical events are laden with meaning that they do not simply possess themselves but that comes from our present-day interactions with these events. This is what Gadamer means when he says that the historical object is the counterpart of historical thinking. "The naivete of so-called historicism consists in the fact that it does not undertake this reflection, and in trusting to the fact that its procedure is methodical, it forgets its own historicity. Real historical thinking must take account of its own historicity. Only then will it cease to chase the phantom of a historical object that is the object of progressive research, and learn to view the object as the counterpart of itself and hence understand both" (TM, 310). This suggests that the fore-conceptions that come from historical consciousness cannot be regarded from the start as arbitrary. At the same time, they should not be regarded as equally harmonious with the object from the start. The only way to determine if specific fore-conceptions are arbitrary is to put them at risk and to see whether they are or are not confirmed by the object as it unfolds in the interpretive interaction. This is, for Gadamer, what it means for a historical interpretation to be justified: that it is confirmed by the object in this way.[8]

Now, this part of the process of understanding as Gadamer describes it will sound familiar and unproblematic to those accustomed to thinking about truth as the correspondence between a belief or a proposition and an independent object. As Gadamer conceives of it, though, what is involved in this process of testing is not a matter of seeing whether some fore-conception corresponds with the independent, *immediate* object that one comes upon at the beginning of the inquiry. This is because the things themselves [*die Sache*] by which one tests one's fore-conceptions are not independent objects that can be known immediately but, on Gadamer's view, come into relief only through an interpretive, self-interrogative interaction. Hence, when it comes to humanistic inquiry, Gadamer explains, "such an 'object in itself' [*Gegenstand an sich*] clearly does not exist at all" (TM, 296).[9]

Hermeneutic Virtues and Their Role in Understanding

With Gadamer's theory of the process of understanding and the role of historical fore-conceptions in this process now in view, let us turn our attention to those habits of mind that facilitate or hinder this process from taking place. For as much as Gadamer himself claims to be only describing rather than prescribing the process of understanding in *Truth and Method*, one of the things that is likely to stand out most to readers of "The Elevation of the Historicity of Understanding" is the creative redescription that it offers according to which habits of mind like openness, courage, and self-awareness are necessary for epistemic responsibility. As we will see in chapter 4, the argument that certain habits of mind positively correlate with the development of knowledge has received significant traction in recent epistemology and comprises a central focus of what is now known as "virtue epistemology." Miranda Fricker, for example, has recently argued that the state of epistemic responsibility today suffers in various ways from the idea, reinforced by the transcendence argument, that success in knowing has nothing to do with such virtues or even virtue at all.[10] In response to this tendency, Fricker and others have argued that virtues like self-awareness and open-mindedness are essential to epistemic responsibility, while opposite conditions like meta-blindness and epistemic arrogance are hindrances to it.[11] In this way, epistemic justice theorists help put into relief the historical-cultural horizon with which Gadamer's argument in *Truth and Method* addresses us today. We will return in chapter 4 to the analysis of epistemic virtues offered by contemporary virtue epistemology. For now, let us consider the specific hermeneutic virtues that can be inferred from Gadamer's description of the process of understanding in "The Elevation of the Historicity of Understanding."

One crucial hermeneutic virtue is that habit of mind that makes one aware one is being addressed by a truth claim in the way described above. Gadamer describes the role such a habit of mind plays in reading, explaining that "a person trying to understand a text is prepared for it to tell him something" and that "that is why a hermeneutically trained consciousness must be, from the start, sensitive to the text's alterity" (TM, 282). The description is helpful in clarifying why, despite Gadamer's claim to be offering only a descriptive and not prescriptive account of understanding, there is need for some account of hermeneutic virtues. The ready availability of historical phenomena that challenge one's fore-conceptions is no guarantee that one will seek out such opportunities for self-interrogation. Only those with a certain habit of mind will be receptive to such opportunities—being open to them when they arise and even actively seeking them out. Some are highly defensive of and largely unwilling to suspend their preconceptions. One may be defensive in this way, for example, if one perceives at some level that one's sense of identity or self-worth may be jeopardized if one or more of one's fore-conceptions are rationally undermined. This happens when people with certain forms of social and economic privilege, for example, are resistant to opportunities to learn about the forms of exploitation that have historically contributed to their privilege.[12] In other cases, the issue may be less that one is actively defensive against self-interrogation and more that one lacks any education in the art of questioning that opens up a hermeneutic object. Being able to ask a good question is itself, after all, a valuable metacognitive skill that many people are not taught (including many who pass through the current education system). Finally, as Whitney Mannies argues, hermeneutic encounters are often encounters with particular affective dispositions. So, for example, "for readers to feel the force of Montesquieu's argument, they must be willing to trade in nostalgia for benevolent absolutism for dignity and self-respect, they must forgo dependence and flattery for moral courage and genuine love. . . . The emotions to be cultivated in *The Persian Letters* are part and parcel of the political logic to be grasped."[13] There is some virtue, then, in allowing oneself not only to consider and allow a fair hearing to truth claims but even, in some contexts, in allowing oneself to be *moved* by them in an affective sense. In such ways, one is on guard against the "tyranny of prejudices"—willing to subject one's fore-conceptions to critical interrogation for the sake of self-edification.

While we may want to conceive of the virtue just described as the virtue of "openness," this description only works if we add an important caveat. To be open in a way that is hermeneutically virtuous is not the same as possessing no beliefs, habits of character, or affective attunements. The goal is not to be so open that one never comes to settle on any belief or quality of character at all and so that one is without any anticipatory affective attunement. After all, one must hold beliefs and qualities to some degree in order for them to be called into question. Otherwise, one cannot possibly be putting oneself at risk in the way Gadamer describes. Similarly, to be seriously open to the truth claim of another in the way that Gadamer describes requires that one be willing to adopt new beliefs in light of what emerges in the hermeneutic encounter. This, in turn, requires that one become, not more open to, but, in fact, *more closed off* to other contradictory beliefs. For example, having a conversation that convinces you to take the continuing history of racism more seriously should make you more closed off to arguments that underplay this history. To wager one's fore-conception in this situation (e.g., to wager one's understanding of the role of racism in American history up to the present) means nothing if the end result is that one is in a state of indecision regarding different claims about this history. To engage fully and honestly in the hermeneutic process of understanding, one needs to stand firmly by the beliefs and qualities of character that come from these hermeneutic encounters until there is compelling reason to put them into question.

Although it can be helpful to talk about hermeneutic virtues in the abstract, this last point helps us to see clearly why Gadamer resists presenting these virtues as part of a formal method for understanding that, if followed, would be sufficient for arriving at legitimate knowledge. While we should certainly be cautious to avoid the "tyranny of prejudices," it is not the case that every attunement, meaning, and belief should—by virtue of operating as a prejudice—be cast into doubt. Rather, they should be cast into doubt only when a legitimate challenge arises in the course of a hermeneutic encounter—when, in relying upon them, we are pulled up short by the *Sache* itself. The doctrine of hermeneutic virtue clarifies what it means to respond appropriately to this challenge. It does not, however, constitute a formal method for determining what constitutes a legitimate or illegitimate challenge. As familiar as the search for such a method would be to us moderns today, Gadamer's account is not intended to provide such a method, as this would mean that understanding is no longer grounded in historical consciousness. This point is made clear in Gadamer's critique of the Enlightenment model of understanding. It is to this part of "The Elevation of the Historicity of Understanding" that we turn next.

Gadamer's Twofold Critique of the Enlightenment and Romanticism

Recall the two common ways of thinking about the historical situation of our understanding described at the beginning of this chapter: the transcendence model and the immanence model. The claim each makes about the historical situation of thought seems obvious to us today. They seem so obvious today, in fact, that it is hard to believe that philosophers once had to argue for them and that they initially struck most of their original audience as untenable. Yet these two conclusions are the offspring of the approach to knowing once rigorously argued and advocated for by the thinkers of the Enlightenment. To think clearly about the historicity of the understanding, then, it would be helpful to bring to light the fundamental maxims of the age of the Enlightenment so as to put the beliefs inherited from this age at risk in the sense described above. This is indeed what Gadamer does in "The Elevation of the Historicity of Understanding"—particularly in two sections entitled "The Discrediting of Prejudice by the Enlightenment" and "The Rehabilitation of Authority and Tradition."

It is hard to overstate the influence of the Enlightenment on our conceptions of thinking today. Indeed, we celebrate the accomplishment of the Enlightenment today on grounds that we have inherited from the Enlightenment itself. We applaud the figures of the Enlightenment for being courageous in their thought and, specifically, for breaking away from the stronghold of the prejudices to which they would inevitably be bound if their thought remained rooted in tradition. We find perfectly understandable Francis Bacon's desire to recognize and cast away the various "idols" that tend to beset human thinking, and immediately agree with him when he writes in 1620 that "it is pointless to expect any great advancements in science from grafting new things onto old" and that, for this reason, "we must make a fresh start with deep foundations."[14] We find quite natural René Descartes's desire for a method of arriving at beliefs that he can be absolutely certain of and find intuitive his argument—again, once considered wildly counterintuitive—that, for this reason, we cannot rely entirely upon either the senses or common custom. We thus easily appreciate the praise expressed by Jean le Rond d'Alembert in the *Encyclopédie* (1760) where he attributes to Descartes "a strong imagination, a most logical mind, knowledge drawn from himself more than from books, great courage in battling the most generally accepted prejudices,

The Limitation of Two Historical Models of Knowing | 59

and no form of dependence which forced him to spare them."[15] Indeed, the Enlightenment ideal of thinking in a way that breaks free from the prejudices of tradition is so intuitive that we are taken aback when we come across indications that these Enlightenment figures were invariably observant of religious and cultural norms and working within a particular historical consciousness.

What we have inherited, Gadamer says, is a presupposition handed down to us from the Enlightenment: a "prejudice against prejudice itself" (TM, 283). Essential to Enlightenment thought was the belief that real progress in knowledge requires freeing thought from the guardrails of tradition. In the eyes of Bacon, what we inherit from tradition and custom can be summed up as the "idols of the tribe"[16]—beliefs and practices that we adhere to out of tenacity alone and thus have no real justification. Enlightenment thought, by contrast, proceeds under the banner of the motto articulated in 1784 by Kant: "*Sapere aude!* Have the courage to use your own intelligence!"[17] It is with this opposition between reason and tradition in mind that D'Alembert praises Descartes for courageously combating widely held prejudices and for not deriving his knowledge from books. Texts in particular were seen as carrying the dead weight of tradition—of passing ideas down from generation to generation in a way that did not require one to think for oneself. As such, written tradition was often presented by Enlightenment figures as a source of error. If they were not subjected to a rationalizing interpretation, such texts were nothing more than "idols of the tribe." Such a conception is still present today when people operate under the assumption that they can either think for themselves or they can spend their time reading old books.[18] This assumption—that tradition is opposed to reason and to thinking for oneself—is, ironically, an assumption born out of the historical tradition of the Enlightenment.

The Enlightenment understood itself as freeing thought and human society specifically from tradition and, by extension, viewed tradition as a powerful force from which thought and human society must be freed. According to the Enlightenment, thinking that proceeds from tradition or from any other preconception is, as a whole, illegitimate. As Gadamer puts it:

> In general, the Enlightenment tends to accept no authority and to decide everything before the judgment seat of reason. Thus the written tradition of Scripture, like any other historical

> document, can claim no absolute validity; the possible truth of the tradition depends on the credibility that reason accords it. It is not tradition but reason that constitutes the ultimate source of all authority. What is written down is not necessarily true. We can know better: this is the maxim with which the modern Enlightenment approaches tradition and which ultimately leads it to undertake historical research. It takes tradition as an object of critique, just as the natural sciences do with the evidence of the senses. (TM, 285)

This aspect of the Enlightenment is the historical basis for the transcendence model of knowing and for the first of the attitudes toward the historicity of thought described above. It is quite common today for people to believe that honest inquiry into a subject matter requires that one bracket any beliefs one has about it by virtue of the transmission of tradition, which is to say, by virtue of one's particular historical horizon. What differentiates most people today from the Enlightenment thinkers, however, is the degree of difficulty each perceives in this task. While thinkers like Descartes, Bacon, and Kant devised elaborate formal methods for determining when and to what extent a belief was rationally justified, the mass popularization of the ideal has made it so that we strain today to imagine how anyone at all could fall short of the benchmark. With the popularization of the Enlightenment, we begin to simply take for granted that, with few exceptions aside, we are all thinking for ourselves. Ironically, then, in the wake of the Enlightenment, there is comparatively little commitment to searching out, critically assessing, and revising the beliefs one has inherited from one's historical-cultural situation.

For Gadamer, though, this problem plagued the Enlightenment from the beginning. While it is true that the reception of ideas transmitted through tradition is not sufficient for knowledge, the Enlightenment, on Gadamer's view, went too far in categorizing all thought situated within a tradition as epistemically illegitimate and insisting that tradition function only as an object of critique. To understand Gadamer's assessment of this problem, let us consider, first, the argument presented above regarding the productive role of preconceptions in the process of understanding. Recall that, for Gadamer, genuine inquiry into a subject matter puts those preconceptions relevant to that subject matter into play. It requires both that one actively rely upon them and that one puts them at risk when they become problematized. In this way, Gadamer argues, contrary to the Enlightenment model, that preconceptions are not only inevitable but that they play a productive role in the process of understanding—by either bearing themselves out in terms of the subject matter or by becoming problematized in a way that changes how the subject matter comes to appear.

Gadamer has no dispute, then, with the Enlightenment thinkers' concern about our tendency to take traditional beliefs for granted and to assume that these beliefs are, without any criticism or reflection, sufficient for understanding any subject matter. As we know, Gadamer himself is concerned with the "tyranny of prejudices," that is, with what transpires when one lacks the virtue required to put traditional beliefs and meanings that have become problematized to the test. Gadamer differs from the Enlightenment thinkers, however, in insisting that it is possible to relate to prejudices in a different way. A subject with a "hermeneutically trained consciousness" will not treat the traditions to which they belong as having a validity and a significance that are beyond any question or revision. Tradition will appear to them to be equally something relied upon and something thought through and put to the test. Indeed, for them, beliefs and meanings inherited from tradition are only really epistemically relevant when they are put genuinely into play—facilitating a hermeneutic encounter that may very well fundamentally transform them. In this way, Gadamer argues that Enlightenment thinkers are wrong to treat tradition as the opposite of reason. One can certainly relate to tradition in a way that hinders critical reflection and self-interrogation, but this is not the only possible way of relating to it.

Gadamer's critique of the Enlightenment, though, is not simply a methodological correction. It is not only about how we ought to seek knowledge but also about how to properly conceive of the object of inquiry. According to the Enlightenment model, the process of understanding renders irrelevant any particular features of the inquiring subject's situation, including their historical-cultural situation. It is this model that is operative today when members of a society feel no need to inquire into the historical-cultural situation of their collective thinking on certain topics. This lack of recognition of a need for self-awareness is manifest, for example, in the way that many Americans think about race. On the Enlightenment model, no such self-reflection is required for understanding the subject matter, and the inquiry will have no bearing on the self-understanding of the inquirer. The object is, after all, taken as ontologically separate from the historical horizon in which it comes to appear. As we have seen, though, Gadamer challenges the assumption of this ontological separation on the grounds that knowledge of objects in the human sciences requires knowledge of the historical horizon within which a given object appears. As he puts it, "What appears to be a limiting prejudice from the viewpoint of the absolute self-construction of reason in fact belongs to historical reality itself" (TM, 289).[19] This is why an attempt to inquire that does not make conspicuous and put at risk relevant aspects of one's historical-cultural horizon can achieve only partial success.

In the face of this criticism of the Enlightenment ideal, it may be tempting to set up an alternative model of understanding that embraces tradition and the guardrails it offers to the understanding. Rather than conceiving of understanding as something that takes place sporadically through feats of individual epistemic heroism, we might insist that understanding is always bound to definite forms of social life. This option aligns with the second position on the historicity of understanding described above and with the immanence model of knowing on which it is premised. Here too we can see that this attitude has historical roots that are generally unacknowledged by those who take it today to be common sense. On Gadamer's account, it emerged as a critical reaction to the Enlightenment ideal. Embraced in different ways by a number of writers in modernity, the reaction is articulated, for example, by the Romantic, Novalis (Friedrich von Hardenberg), in his infamous "Christianity or Europe" (1799), where he laments the social transformations brought about by the Enlightenment and, in particular, the transfer of authority from Christian traditions and institutions to the ideas and institutions associated with the Enlightenment. Novalis describes the waning relevance of Christianity in the age of the Enlightenment as such:

> One saw in faith the source of universal stagnation; and through a more penetrating knowledge one hoped to destroy it. Everywhere the sense for the sacred suffered from various persecutions of its past nature, its temporal personality. The result of the modern manner of thinking one called "philosophy," and regarded it as anything opposed to the old order, especially therefore as any whim contrary to religion. . . . Every trace of the sacred was to be destroyed, all memory of noble events and people was to be spoiled by satire, and the world stripped of colorful ornament. Their favorite theme, on account of its mathematical obedience and impudence, was light. They

were pleased that it refracted rather than played with its colors and so they called their great enterprise "Enlightenment."[20]

Now, both Novalis and Gadamer are critical of the Enlightenment ideal insofar as both take issue with the claim that all beliefs and meanings that emerge from a particular cultural-historical worldview are epistemically irrelevant. Gadamer finds value in the insights of Romanticism up to this point. His treatment of Romanticism in "The Elevation of the Historicity of Understanding," however, is primarily critical. How does he find Romanticism's model of understanding misguided, then? According to Gadamer, Romanticism, no less than the Enlightenment, achieves only partial knowledge of its object, because it accepts the Enlightenment's basic premise that tradition is "the abstract opposite of free self-determination" (TM, 293). Gadamer holds this to be a faulty premise and its acceptance by both Enlightenment thinkers and those reacting in defense of tradition against the Enlightenment to be problematic. As Gadamer explains it: "What determines the romantic understanding of tradition is its abstract opposition [*abstrakte Gegensatz*] to the principle of enlightenment. Romanticism conceives of tradition as an antithesis to the freedom of reason and regards it as something historically given, like nature. And whether one wants to be revolutionary and oppose it or preserve it, tradition is still viewed as the abstract opposite of free self-determination, since its validity does not require any reasons but conditions us without our questioning it" (TM, 293). Romanticism, for Gadamer, longs for tradition understood in a distorted way. What it longs for is not the possession of tentative beliefs and meanings that must be renegotiated in hermeneutic encounters—a process that involves ongoing self-interrogation. Instead, it professes its devotion to "the idols of the tribe," in other words, to tradition as construed by Enlightenment thinkers. Here again we find Gadamer's account illuminating for understanding the present. After all, Gadamer's description of the Romantic misconception of tradition applies to sizable portions of the human population today who embrace as "tradition" doctrines and practices that arose only as a reaction to developments in modernity. One can find such neotraditionalists within all major religions and forms of modern nationalism today. They see themselves—as Novalis did—in conflict with, not only the tenets of modern liberal society, but with those in their own tradition for whom inhabiting that tradition means contributing to its ongoing critical and rational transformation.[21] Of course, even the neotraditionalists are innovators. This is why their conception of their own self-activity (e.g., as "fundamentalists") is false. As much as they want to view their tradition (e.g., their religious doctrine, their national identity and history) as something that never changes, their interpretations of the tradition are inevitably the result of a historical consciousness that is very much ongoing.[22] This is why such neotraditionalists, in Gadamer's words, "lag behind their true historical being" (TM, 293).

> In tradition there is always an element of freedom and of history itself. Even the most genuine and pure tradition does not persist because of the inertia of what once existed. It needs to be affirmed, embraced, cultivated. It is, essentially, preservation, and it is active in all historical change. But preservation is an act of reason, though an inconspicuous one. For this reason, only innovation and planning appear to be the result of reason. But this is an illusion. . . . Preservation is as much a freely chosen action as are revolution and renewal. This is why both the Enlightenment's critique of tradition and the romantic rehabilitation of it lag behind their true historical being. (TM, 293)

What both the Enlightenment and Romanticism have in common, then, is a denial of historical consciousness and its relevance for the process of understanding. Understanding is no more able to simply break free from the past than it is absolutely bound within the past. Both of these misconstrue not just the nature of understanding but the nature of our historicity. Yet it is common to imagine the meaning of past cultures as frozen in time. Indeed, for this form of historicism, which develops out of the same opposition between reason and tradition introduced by the Enlightenment, traditions of the past should not be interpreted through a reasoning that is informed by present historical consciousness. They should be understood as curiosities of a time no longer present. For Gadamer, though, this denies the intrinsic unity between our past and present. It misconstrues the past as something that we happen upon without any anticipatory projection. Gadamer disputes this sort of historicism on this point. For him, "the closed horizon that is supposed to enclose a culture is an abstraction. The historical movement of human life consists in the fact that it is never absolutely bound to any one standpoint, and hence can never have a truly closed horizon. The horizon is, rather, something into which we move and that moves with us" (TM, 315).²³ Thus, just as the abstract opposition between reason and tradition can prevent us from embracing the hermeneutic process of understanding described above, so too can the abstract opposition, taken for granted for the most part today, between present historical consciousness and the past.

Now, to be clear, the claim that there is an intrinsic unity between present historical consciousness and the past should not be taken to imply that every aspect of a past culture that we might possibly encounter is equally significant for present consciousness. Likewise, the claim that there is a similar unity between tradition and reason should not be taken to imply that every aspect of a tradition will turn out to be rational. If this were Gadamer's argument, after all, one would never experience the problematization of aspects of one's character or beliefs in a hermeneutic encounter and the historical phenomena that we come upon would in no sense be unfamiliar. One would not have to grapple, when reading about American history, for example, with what elements of it are attempting to speak to us today and what they are attempting to disclose about the present. There would be no problematization of beliefs and no need for interpretation in this sense. These are vital to Gadamer's conception of the process of understanding, though.²⁴ Hence, when he proposes that reason and tradition, present and past are unities, Gadamer is simply arguing that, for a self-aware historical consciousness, these cannot be regarded as abstract oppositions. A person who has self-aware historical consciousness is one who has the requisite hermeneutic virtues to engage critically and reflectively with tradition—for example, by allowing themselves to be addressed by truth claims issuing from traditions, to put to the test those beliefs that are legitimately problematized by these claims, and to critically revise traditional beliefs and practices in light of the commitments that emerge through this ongoing process of understanding. Such a person would not, like the Enlightenment thinkers, disregard tradition as a whole as epistemically relevant. Nor would they operate under the Romantic thinker's assumption that tradition contains truths that are inaccessible to reason. Finally, to operate in this way would be to inhabit historical consciousness as dynamic in the way that Gadamer describes it above—"as something which we move and that moves with us."

We can now see how Gadamer's argument in "The Elevation of the Historicity of Understanding" challenges the two common positions on the historical situation of understanding described earlier. The transcendence position, which claims that real understanding requires that we step outside of our historical situations and the particular traditions by which we find ourselves addressed, is familiar to us today in the wake of the Enlightenment. It is so familiar, in fact, that it is very difficult for us to understand these arguments as innovative proposals. The suggestion that real understanding takes the form of a thinking that has achieved independence from traditional ideas appears obvious and unquestionable to us today. Yet, as Gadamer argues, this claim rests upon a problematic premise, namely, that thinking that is historically conscious in any way is irrational. This claim is betrayed, for one, by any acknowledgment of the historical-cultural situation of Enlightenment thought. It is problematized as well by any consideration of the productive role that historical fore-conceptions play in the process of understanding. As we have seen, it is by virtue of our immersion in a social and historical lifeworld that the object we come upon and strive to understand better is already laden with meaning. In some cases, our fore-conceptions are confirmed by the object, and we are justified in holding to them—even using them as a basis for critiquing other beliefs—until they undergo a legitimate challenge. In other cases, when we go to apply a fore-conception to an object, it is problematized by it and must be revised accordingly. In either case, fore-conceptions play a productive role in the process of understanding. Indeed, when they are grounded in our historical consciousness, even those that are problematized cannot be regarded as arbitrary, since they belong to the dynamic development of historical consciousness itself.

The immanence position often emerges today in reaction to and in opposition to the transcendence position. Here too Gadamer's account in "The Elevation of the Historicity of Understanding" sheds light by allowing us to recognize the roots of the immanence position in a particular aspect of Romanticism. The ground of Romanticism's opposition to the Enlightenment is recognizable to us today as the rationale of neotraditionalism. Although these developments emerge in response to the Enlightenment, Gadamer argues, they accept from the Enlightenment its problematic opposition between tradition and reason. Tradition, for Romantics and neotraditionalists, is that which the light of reason cannot penetrate and that point at which human freedom reaches its limits. Romantics and neotraditionalists attempt to reduce historical consciousness to this moment of finding oneself bound to a particular historical-cultural situation. Historicists, in turn, inherit this conception of tradition from Romanticism by conceiving of the past not as something that we actively preserve in the present, and thus not as something grounded in human freedom, but as something that can be understood without reason and reflection on the contemporary age.²⁵

In sum, both the Enlightenment and Romanticism make the mistake of attempting to arrest the dynamic movement of historical consciousness and to ground understanding in one moment of this movement taken in abstraction from the rest of it. The Enlightenment thinker denies the historical-cultural situation of their thought. They reduce the ground of their understanding to the moment of transcendence. The Romantic and the neotraditionalist deny the reason and freedom at work in the way that their historical-cultural situation appears to them. They reduce the ground of their understanding to the moment of immanence. In place of these two dominant models of understanding, Gadamer offers instead a description of understanding this is historically dynamic and irreducible to any formal method. In this, he offers a relevant alternative to ways of thinking about understanding that, while epistemologically, ontologically, and socially problematic, are widely accepted today.

Chapter 3

Interpretation, Truth, and Hermeneutic Realism

> The world that appears in the play of presentation does not stand like a copy next to the real world, but is that world in the heightened truth of its being.
>
> —Gadamer, *Truth and Method*, 138

For Gadamer, one of the most important dimensions of our existence as human beings is our ongoing interest in self-edification. In its practical form, this involves distancing ourselves to some degree from our immediate desires and instincts so that we can habituate ourselves toward other worthy ends. In its theoretical form, it involves being attentive to where our present ways of thinking fall short as a response to the matters that confront us and integrating new ways of thinking as needed. Both require the hermeneutic virtues described in the previous chapter: an openness and willingness to be convinced by and even, at times, moved by truth claims and the ability to hold firmly to what emerges through these encounters until one has reason to be moved again. Such is not only the structure of educational experience described in chapter 1 but the ongoing pursuit of self-edification (*Bildung*) that characterizes human existence from the earliest stages to the end of a human's life.

The human interest in self-edification is clear, for Gadamer, when we consider what happens in aesthetic experience. Gadamer follows Aristotle in regarding the human interest in art as rooted in our desire for knowledge. In the *Poetics*, Aristotle argues that what pleases us about watching a theatrical performance is the joy we find in recognizing something in a new way. On stage, a familiar character, place, or event becomes manifest in a new way such that the audience is compelled to revise their understanding of it. The same goes for other fine arts. Whether it is painting, film, or poetry, art provides us with a valuable form of mediation, that is, with the opportunity to encounter something—be it a person, place, concept, or event—in a new but still recognizable way.

We have already seen how, for Gadamer, such mediation belongs to the structure of human understanding. To understand requires that one put one's relevant fore-conceptions at risk such that some are confirmed and others are revealed to fall short. To this extent, Gadamer's argument that the work of art facilitates understanding should come as no surprise. Yet to focus on the concept of "understanding" will still suggest, to some, that this mediation is only a formal, subjective necessity, that is, that it describes only how things must appear to a subject conditioned to make sense of things through interpretation. It is therefore important to consider Gadamer's argument that what comes to light in aesthetic experience is *truth*.

The suggestion that we find truth in aesthetic experience seems quite improbable today. To some extent, this is because there is still a tendency to think about art as a deceptive copy of something real that has, as Plato at times feared, the power to confuse people and lead them toward false beliefs. Much more common today, though, is the idea that art is to be valued purely on the basis of novelty—say, as a window into some particular "genius"—a subjectivity novel in comparison to that of its admirers. Gadamer is quite aware of the way both of these legacies shape our attitudes toward art today. He traces the genesis of these legacies in the opening chapters of *Truth and Method*. Yet he insists that a closer look at aesthetic experience will prompt us to reconsider the assumptions about truth implicit in these common attitudes toward art today and will lead us to reconceive the meaning of truth in a way that has rather far-reaching consequences.

In what follows, then, I want to examine Gadamer's account of truth in aesthetic experience and his reasons for rejecting those accounts of art that deny it any possible claim to truth. We will consider the reasons Gadamer offers for his claim that what is brought forth in aesthetic experience is "genuine truth" (TM, 76), what it means to conceive of truth in this way, and how this conception of truth can be extended beyond the aesthetic realm. We will also consider how to make sense of Gadamer's claim that the occurrence of truth, while entailing definite knowledge in those subjects who undergo this occurrence, nevertheless leaves room for further disclosures and thus the further determination of truth.

The Logic of the Work of Art as a Starting Point for Reconceiving Truth

It is common for us in modern, techno-rational societies today to consider art a decadence having no important function in the process of knowledge. Indeed, were a work clearly to possess such a function, many would deny it on this basis the status of art. This conception of art and its relegation to the nonfunctional is a relatively recent phenomenon. For most of human history, art has played a vital role in understanding both at the individual and social level. Gadamer frequently illustrates this point by describing the centrality of symbolic art and ritual to the history of Christianity. Throughout this history, symbolic objects and rituals have served a vital function of allowing the divine to come to presence on earth with and alongside human beings. The practice of Christianity is imbued through and through with symbolic objects, rituals, and festivals that create a bridge, according to Gadamer, between human understanding and the divinity that it seeks to understand and with which it seeks a palpable sense of unity. For such practitioners, Gadamer suggests, symbols are anything but arbitrary impositions onto this divinity. As Gadamer says, "It is possible to be led beyond the sensible to the divine. For the world of the sense is not mere nothingness and darkness but the outflowing and reflection of truth" (TM, 67). This relationship to art is not unique to the history of Christianity. Such a use of symbol pervaded the ancient world. In ancient Greece, for example, when people heard poetry or attended a theatrical performance, they experienced the very being of, say, the legendary figure or event become present.

As Aristotle himself observed, such ancient practices are premised on the audience being familiar to some extent with the subject matter. Writing *Oedipus Rex*, for example, Sophocles knows that his audience in ancient Greece is familiar with the tragic tale of Oedipus through the mythic tradition in which they were immersed. Likewise, Aristophanes composes *Lysistrata*, knowing that the setting of the comedy, the Peloponnesian War, is thoroughly familiar to his audience. Such works of art are referential in this way. They refer to things that are already to some extent familiar in the world in which the audience dwells. This is not an incidental feature. For Gadamer, like Aristotle, the work of art lies in the interaction between the presentation and the audience. More precisely, it lies in the *recognition* that occurs between the presentation and the relevant fore-meanings that the audience brings with them. As Gadamer says:

> Recognition as cognition of the true occurs through an act of identification in which we do not differentiate between the representation and the represented. For what is recognition? It does not mean simply seeing something that we have already seen before. . . . Recognizing something means rather that I now cognize something as something that I have already seen. The enigma here lies entirely in the "as." I am not thinking of the miracle of memory, but of the miracle of knowledge it implies.[1]

For Gadamer, even modern, nonrepresentational works of art that do not clearly refer to subject matters familiar to the audience by virtue of a shared history (e.g., the story of Achilles) still solicit this sort of recognition. While that to which they refer us may not be as easy to pinpoint, for Gadamer, to experience modern works of art is still to be called back to something already familiar so that it is recognized in a more comprehensive way. In the modern era, Gadamer argues, this is often a matter of art revealing to its modern audience that there is more to the subject matter with which the audience is familiar than the way it is articulated in modern techno-rational, capitalist society. In particular, Gadamer argues, nonrepresentational art can remind us that, despite the way that modern technology and capitalist forces attempt to mold everything to an arbitrary will guided by the pursuit of technological power and profit, there is still an intelligible order in the universe and one of which human judgment constitutes an integral part.[2]

Given the hermeneutic theory of understanding that we have examined so far, what Gadamer says about the integral role of the audience should come as no surprise. Gadamer consistently emphasizes that understanding requires that one put to work the fore-conceptions that one has as a social and historical being so that they can anticipate what will be revealed and potentially be transformed in the process. We have seen, for example, how Gadamer applies this theory to his account of historical understanding. Recall also Gadamer's theory of textual understanding. When a text speaks to us, Gadamer says, "it does not simply speak its word, always the same, in lifeless rigidity, but gives ever new answers to the person who questions it and poses ever new questions to him who answers it." Thus, he continues, "to understand a text is to come to understand oneself in a kind of dialogue" (PH, 57). To understand a work of art requires the same.

Gadamer's treatment of aesthetic experience, however, makes especially clear that, despite the mediation that occurs, what comes to appear through this mediation is marked by a character of *nondifferentiation*.[3] What appears is not a mere copy but the original subject matter itself. If an artwork is successful, it is not a particular "take" on the subject that appears but the subject itself. It is the hero's tale that appears as we take it in through the singing of the ballad, the performance on stage, or the composition of the painting. The temptation here today is to say that what appears is ontologically separate from the subject itself—that it is, for example, the expression of the artist's mind. In this sense, the Kantian approach to aesthetics that Gadamer discusses at length is alive and well in popular attitudes toward art in the twenty-first century. This attitude is premised on the idea that what appears through the work of art must be a subjective representation and thus not afford us real theoretical cognition of the subject matter.[4] For Gadamer, though, only by positing an ontological unity or nondifferentiation between representation and what is represented can we account for what has long interested us as a human species in art. Art interests us because it is a way for us to come to better understanding. It allows us to experience something that transcends our expectations and preconceptions about the subject matter. Something similar happens in the process of producing art. Those involved in this process know the work is not a matter of just realizing a subjective preconception. In theater, for example, both actors and playwright must put aside those parts of themselves that do not help set forth the tale that they want to tell. Those parts that can aid in this process must be oriented entirely toward that end. In this way, those involved in the production of the artwork participate in practical *Bildung* in a way similar to those taking in the performance. They too must "find universal viewpoints from which [they] can grasp the thing, 'the objective thing in its freedom,' without selfish interest" (TM, 13).

In orienting themselves toward the work of art in this way, Gadamer points out, participants behave similarly to participants in a game. A game is a playful activity. Yet for it to bring anything to light at all (e.g., if it is to determine a winner in a competitive game), participants—players and audience—must engage in it with some seriousness. This means that one must respect the boundaries and definitions that belong to the game without which the game would not exist at all. One must accept in general the rules of engagement as determining the possibilities of the game and not discard them on ad hoc bases. This means recognizing that the rules and definitions beyond the world of the game often do not apply within it and agreeing to set those that do not aside. They must also recognize that, within the field of the game, the meaning of many elements has been transformed from its ordinary meaning. For example, both the players and the audience must accept the participants first and foremost as players and their actions first and foremost as laden with intentions relevant to the game. They must accept, too, certain spatial and temporal boundaries as the definitive boundaries in which the game is played, the boundaries that establish what Johan Huizinga describes as a "temporary world within the ordinary world."[5] Only in such conditions can what transpires in a game be meaningful. Thus we experience in games the same sort of nondifferentiation described above as the achievement of art. Indeed, what is loved about the game quickly starts to dissolve when we attempt to break apart this nondifferentiation and to look behind the world of meaning particular to the game. Thus the frustration caused by the spoilsport—be it one who refuses to recognize the child in costume as the character they aim to present or whose concerns about corruption among team management or player eligibility prevent them from becoming immersed in the match. Art too requires serious engagement of this kind. For instance, only when one resolves that one has entered clearly into the world of the artwork will one allow the work the space it requires to make a true disclosure. This helps to explain the importance of the various boundary lines that have over the ages served to mark the transition between spaces designated for art and ordinary spaces. Often regarded as sacred, such boundaries include, for example, the parameters that set apart the theater, the festival, the museum, the ritual dance, and the song.

The participants' serious engagement with the artwork makes it possible for the works of art that occur in these spaces to bring something forth, to make it present, in a new and unpredictable way.

Gadamer describes this occurrence as a "transformation into structure" (*Verwandlung ins Gebilde*). As an audience takes in a performance of a play, for instance, elements in the play—characters, concepts, places—are set forth as if they are being perceived for the first time. We know that it is hard to call to mind a character whom we have seen performed by a great actor without imagining that particular actor's rendition. Similarly, if we have turned to a particular musical album frequently during a very difficult time in life, it may be hard to recall our affective attunement at that time independently of the music that accompanied it and helped one to articulate it. Hearing that album again tends to call forth what it was like to dwell in that particular emotional state. Elements of the reception and of the performance conspire to bring forth the thing—for example, the character or the emotional state—as a unified whole. As Gadamer points out, when we encounter works of art, we search for the unity to which all of the elements build up. Where does this song take me? What does this film tell us? What does this painting mean? It is the concretization of this sort of determinate meaning that is the *telos* of aesthetic experience. Thus, Gadamer explains, when one watches a play,

> the players (or playwright) no longer exist, only what they are playing. But, above all, what no longer exists is the world in which we live as our own. Transformation into structure is not simply transposition into another world. Certainly the play takes place in another, closed world. But inasmuch as it is structure, it is, so to speak, its own measure and measures itself by nothing outside of it. Thus the action of a drama—in this respect it still entirely resembles the religious act—exists as something that rests absolutely within itself. It no longer permits of any comparison with reality as the secret measure of all verisimilitude. It is raised above all such comparisons—and hence also above the question of whether it is real—because a superior truth speaks from it. (TM, 116)

If we examine things from the vantage point of aesthetic experience, then, it is wrong to say that what happens in art simply changes one's subjective view. Aesthetic experience tells a different tale; namely, the encounter with great art is a way of coming to discover the truth about something. We come to recognize something already familiar to us in a clearer, not just a different light. It tells us that what we understood before about the reality of the subject matter was not sufficient, that our previous understanding was missing something. As Richard Palmer puts it, "When we see a great work of art and enter its world, we do not leave home so much as 'come home.' We say at once: truly it is so! The artist has said what *is*. . . . The legitimation of art is not that it gives aesthetic pleasure but that it reveals being."[6] For those who seriously engage in the encounter with art, art provides "the raising up [*Aufhebung*] of this reality into its truth" (TM, 117). This is why, for Gadamer, it is a mistake to think that what one takes away from aesthetic experience is of no epistemic relevance. Works of art have an epistemic function.

In arguing that truth is at work in aesthetic experience, Gadamer imagines truth in a way that differs from many of the ways that we have become accustomed to talk about it today. While technological rationality has, in many ways, replaced most older ways of thinking about truth, one component of the Platonist conception of truth remains dominant in the twenty-first century, namely, the idea that what *is* has its being completely in itself and not through any other and that it rests frozen in time awaiting discovery rather taking place diachronically. Gadamer recognizes, however, that what emerges through artistic presentation has a different kind of temporality. This is especially clear when we think about how the being of certain works such as musical works is inseparable from their performances and presentations. The most essential way in which Chopin's *Nocturnes* exists is as a beautiful performance—a performance that allows us to hear the score as if for the first time. The composition appears more fully in the performance than in either the original copy of the written score or the sequence of symbols transcribed in it. Its temporality has the structure of play. It exists through being played. Gadamer notes that festivals have a similar temporality. A festival, Gadamer says, is not "determined by its origin so that there was once the 'real' festival—as distinct from the way in which it later came to be celebrated. From its inception—whether instituted in a single act or instituted gradually—the nature of a festival is to be celebrated regularly. Thus its own original essence is always to be something different." (TM, 126). Neither the being of the musical composition nor of the festival, then, can be properly understood as something that rests wholly in itself untouched by time or history. While works requiring performance are paradigmatic of this type of being, the same structure can be observed elsewhere. In the logic of Protestant Christianity, for example, a passage from Scripture is grasped most essentially in the sermons that attempt to elucidate it for new audiences over time. Likewise, the character of a person or historical event can be made forcefully present for us by a great portrait or even a photograph. In each of these cases, the disclosure of the being in question would appear to be bound up with interpretive and situated presentations.

Given our tendency today to separate aesthetics from epistemology and ontology, it may be tempting at this point to believe that all of what we have covered in this chapter so far makes for an interesting contribution to aesthetics but not to the more serious business of the latter investigations. For Gadamer, though, the turn to aesthetic experience at the beginning of *Truth and Method* (and elsewhere in his writing) is precisely in the interest of examining the nature of truth, knowledge, and being and, more precisely, in legitimating the knowledge and truth disclosed in hermeneutic experience (TM, 89). We have already explored the ways that situated interpretation plays a productive role in the understanding of history. If Gadamer is right that the structure of aesthetic experience belongs to hermeneutic experiences in general, though, we should be able to recognize some of the same components described above in other situations where we attempt to interpret and to understand. In the next section, we will consider the extent to which the theory of truth that Gadamer arrives at through his treatment of aesthetic experience can also help us to make sense of the disclosive capacity of human speech and conversation.

From the Truth of Art to the Truth of Conversation

Not all human speech would seem to solicit interpretive understanding. Much of the speech acts that we exchange with one another simply reflect and do not offer any critical reflection upon immersive modes of understanding acquired in the lifeworld. In such cases, one is not using the opportunity of a verbal exchange to discover a new way of understanding something. The intention is only to convey or to receive a message—a message whose meaning is equivalent to what is intended by the speech act according to conventions implicitly agreed upon in the society. So, for example, if I ask a friend who calls to tell me she is in town, "Shall we meet up for dinner tonight?," I expect her to accept, to explain why she cannot meet up, or to suggest postponing dinner or doing something else. Speech acts of this kind play an instrumental role in conveying predictable meanings and soliciting predictable responses. One may also enter into a verbal exchange in order to receive information from someone. To illustrate this point, Gadamer provides the examples of interrogation (as in the examination of a witness in a court of law) and of the administration of examinations (PH 67; TM, 403). The interrogator and the exam administrator follow a predetermined plan of questioning and have envisaged in advance what the potential outcomes are and perhaps even, as in the case of the cross-examination of a witness in court, what exactly they would like the other to say. In such cases, one is not treating the other as a source of new insight, nor is the conversation functioning as a hermeneutic event.

Such uses of language, however, do not exhaust the disclosive possibilities of human speech. Consider, for example, when one finds one's understanding provoked by a poetic description one comes across while reading or finds oneself thinking along with a lecture and, in so doing, gaining a better understanding of the subject matter. In such experiences, speech is clearly not just serving to convey a meaning already wholly familiar. Rather, one experiences speech as a hermeneutic event similar to the work of art. This is easy to see in the case of poetic description—the way that language can bring something forth through metaphor, metonymy, allegory, and so on. When a poetic description is successful, it heightens our understanding of a subject. It makes us recognize the essence of a person, an event, or a subject matter. This is why Gadamer insists that Homer's Achilles is "more than the original," "more than the being of the thing represented" (TM, 119). The same can be said of a very effective academic lecture. The lecture takes what is already somewhat familiar to the students (e.g., a text that they have read for class, a topic or a historical event that they are familiar with, etc.) and, by soliciting from them serious and personal engagement, helps them to see it in a clearer light, revealing aspects previously neglected or misunderstood.[7] Moreover, just as the reader walks away from the beautiful poem with a sense that they now know the subject matter better, students walk away from an engaging lecture with a sense that they now have a better understanding of the subject matter. In these ways, both the poetic description and the academic lecture are hermeneutic events that are disclosive in the way that artworks are disclosive.[8]

Gadamer's account of truth in aesthetic experience is especially illuminating when we consider the way it can be applied to make sense of what can transpire in conversation. For Gadamer, it is above all in face-to-face conversation where we are likely to find ourselves open to the event of language and, thus, to the power of language to bring something into presentation. Indeed, this is what leads Gadamer more than once to make the claim that language only fully realizes itself in conversation.[9] Gadamer begins the fifth chapter of *Truth and Method* on "Language and Hermeneutics" by describing what happens in conversation. Conversation, he explains, is something we fall into and that yields unexpected discoveries that we could not have predicted with any certainty in advance—understandings that emerge immanently within the conversation itself. This gives conversation the character of an unpredictable, disclosive, and transformative event. As Gadamer puts it:

> We say that we "conduct" a conversation, but the more genuine a conversation is, the less its conduct lies within the will of either partner. Thus a genuine conversation is never the one that we wanted to conduct. Rather, it is generally more correct to say that we fall into conversation, or even that we become involved in it. The way one word follows another, with the conversation taking its own twists and reaching its own conclusion, may well be conducted in some way, but the partners conversing are far less the leaders of it than the led. No one knows in advance what will "come out" of a conversation. . . . All this shows that a conversation has a spirit of its own, and that the language in which it is conducted bears its own truth within it—i.e., that it allows something to "emerge" which henceforth exists. (TM, 401)

Gadamer's claim that conversation "bears its own truth within it" recalls the above description of how works of art allow something to come to presentation, to be *there* more authentically than before. A great portrait or a great film brings a subject forth in this way, providing a new and better understanding of it. Conversation is similar in that it allows a subject matter to come to presentation and for participants to thus gain new understanding of it. What transpires in a good conversation with friends is not this or that person's "take" on the topic. What transpires is not differentiated in this way. It is, rather, the recognition of some truth about the topic itself. It is this possibility, after all, that attracts us to conversation. Should conversations not present us with some claim to truth, they would not be opportunities to reflect on our own beliefs or to refine our understanding of things. It is this possibility that leads us, however, to seek out conversations with others—especially when we know that we are confused or unclear about something.

Yet, whatever our intentions going into it, a conversation has a spirit of its own. We gain understanding only by following along with the inner necessity of the movement that takes place in the conversation. That inner necessity is dictated by neither participant themselves but by the subject matter (*die Sache*) and is, for Gadamer, what unifies the participants in their inquiry. This is what Gadamer means when he claims in the above passage that in conversation, "the partners conversing are far less the leaders of it than the led." Just as the work of art can disclose things beyond the practical intentions and expectations of those who tarry with it, so too can a conversation.[10] Indeed, the relative autonomy of what is disclosed vis-à-vis these intentions and expectations mirrors what we described above as the "transformation into structure" that characterizes aesthetic experience. Genuine conversation aims to bring to light something that was not already clear and, indeed, requires that participants follow the *logos* of the conversation wherever it goes.

To follow the *logos* of conversation is not a passive affair, however. Just as aesthetic experience requires serious engagement on the part of the audience to unfold, so too does good conversation hinge on putting into practice certain hermeneutic virtues that enable a conversation to function as a hermeneutic event. Importantly, for a genuine conversation to occur, participants must take each other's contributions to the conversation as truth claims, that is, as potentially disclosive of new understanding.[11] As previously noted, we do not always take the words of others this way. There are, for example, certain kinds of linguistic exchanges where participants are not there to collaborate in an inquiry oriented toward arriving at mutual understanding. One thinks here not only of what happens out of necessity in medical diagnosis and the administration of academic exams but also of the sort of distortions of public discourse that occur when debate on political issues degenerates into bullying, gaslighting, and political grandstanding.

Genuine conversation also requires that the participants use the conversation as an opportunity to critically reflect on their own ideas. This is what it means, for Gadamer, to exhibit openness in conversation. Here it is important to emphasize what Gadamer does not mean by openness. In keeping with his account of understanding as a hermeneutic circle, Gadamer does not believe it is necessary for one to abandon one's beliefs and habits of character in order to engage genuinely in conversation. One must, instead, be willing to put these at risk (TM, 278–80). One cannot simply put aside a belief or a feeling that one has that is relevant to the conversation at hand. However, one fails to genuinely engage in conversation as a process of understanding if one is not willing to put these fore-conceptions to the test when they come under question. Similarly, one will necessarily rely on ready-to-hand concepts to engage in conversation, just as one must rely on them in any interpretation; however, one must also be willing to question and rethink these concepts if the line of thought that emerges in the conversation demands it. After all, as we have seen, for Gadamer, the process of "working out appropriate projections, anticipatory in nature, to be confirmed 'by the things' themselves," is "the constant task of understanding" (TM, 280).

Thus, Gadamer's argument that a conversation "has a spirit of its own" that determines what occurs in it should not be taken to mean that there is no art of conversation or that every conversation yields new, valuable understanding. These days especially we are rightly concerned with the conditions that enable mutually enriching conversation and those that inhibit it. While Gadamer could not have anticipated the degree to which communication habits would change with the rapidly growing use of virtual communication technologies in the twenty-first century,[12] he was already keenly aware of some of the habits that can sidetrack us from the process of questioning and discovery made possible by conversation. In describing what is required for genuine conversation, however, Gadamer explains: "But this activity and this effort consist in not interfering arbitrarily—latching onto this or that ready-made notion as it strikes one—with the immanent necessity of thought. Certainly, the thing does not go its own course without our thinking being involved, but thinking means unfolding what consistently follows from the subject matter itself. It is part of this process to suppress ideas 'that tend to insinuate themselves' and to insist on the logic of the thought" (TM, 480).

For Gadamer, the two most instructive models in the history of philosophy of this "true method, which is the activity of the thing itself" are the writings of Plato and Hegel (TM, 479–80). For Plato's dialogues and Hegel's *Logic*, the method and content of philosophical investigation are ultimately one and the same.[13] This is what it means to say that both proceed dialectically. In their dramatic form, Plato's dialogues are especially helpful here, as the dialogues present us with characters who embody the virtues necessary for conversation to function as a medium of truth as well as those who sorely lack such virtues. Socrates exemplifies the commitment to questioning and to the path of inquiry needed for genuine conversation. He is a lover of *logos*—not in the sense of loving to win at arguments, as others so often accused him, but in his affection for conversations that function as sites of new understanding, new discovery. As Darren Walhof explains, "The goal in Socrates' exchanges is not to win every argument but to persist in questioning ever further, as a means of pursuing the truth about something, a subject common to the participants in the dialogue."[14] This comportment, so similar to the patient, interpretive comportment required to read and learn from Plato's dialogues themselves, is what allows Socrates to experience the contributions others make to the conversation as meaningful, insightful hermeneutic events.

To be clear, following the inner necessity of a conversation does not mean sticking to a predetermined topic for discussion. Indeed, just as the discoveries made in the course of a conversation cannot be determined in advance, so too must the subject matter of the conversation unfold through the dialectical movement of conversation itself. This is a tricky point, though. Those who engage in a conversation must have some notion of what the conversation is about such that they feel able to contribute and to follow along with the inquiry. Yet the subject matter must, on the other hand, come to light through the discussion. As Günter Figal puts it, it must be "grasped as yet undetermined and nonetheless as this determinant thing."[15] Here again, we find a helpful allegory in Plato's *Meno*. In the dialogue, the title character, Meno, despairs about his ability to engage in philosophical conversation with Socrates about a subject matter that he does not know (*Meno* 80d). In response, Socrates offers him an account of knowledge as recollection (*anamnesis*) meant to encourage him by making clear that, even in his present condition of unknowing, he is able to proceed productively in the inquiry (*Meno* 81a–d). In fact, Meno's condition is the necessary condition of all participants upon entering a conversation. In order for there to be a genuine conversation, participants must be familiar enough with the topic under discussion to engage and to entertain questions about it, but they cannot have full knowledge of the subject matter yet, or the conversation would not function as a process of understanding at all. Contrary to Meno's fears, then, the fact that the subject matter is not fully determined at the beginning of an inquiry does not mean that understanding is impossible. It means only that understanding emerges through a dialectical, dialogical process: the process of "working out appropriate projections, anticipatory in nature, to be confirmed 'by the things' themselves" (TM, 280), which Gadamer takes to be the ongoing task of understanding.

Notice too that, just as in aesthetic experience, in all of these cases where a linguistic exchange brings forth some truth, truth involves recognition, a clarification of something already familiar. Homer's poetic description of Achilles clarifies the figure of Achilles with whom the original audience was already familiar. The academic lecture on poverty in Europe in the Middle Ages allows its modern audience to understand poverty and Christian attitudes toward economic inequality in the contemporary world in a new way. The conversation one has with a friend about different approaches that local governments might take to improving housing affordability gets one thinking in new ways about the housing crisis that one observes in one's own community. In each case, one comes to recognize some previously undisclosed truth about a reality with which one was already familiar. Moreover, such interpretive activities, like modern works of art, reveal not just something about the topic at hand but, along with this, a sort of harmonious interplay between the matter of concern and the inquirers that becomes obscured when the topic is approached purely through technological rationality. They encourage an approach to the topic that highlights self-reflection and self-examination. The truth that emerges in conversation is also, then, like art, recognitive in its nature. It ensues as a participant comes to recognize reality—including the reality of themselves—in a more refined, more complete way.

With this account of recognition in mind, we can identify and distinguish three moments that belong to the process of disclosure that takes place in such speech situations: the linguistic presentation (e.g., the conversation, the lecture), the reality that comes to be better understood through the presentation, and the truth of that reality that is revealed through the presentation. Yet, for Gadamer, the distinction among these moments is not absolute. Rather, they belong to what he conceives of, following Hegel, as a dialectical or speculative unity.[16] This is to say that they are logically but not ontologically or metaphysically distinct. As Gadamer puts it: "To come into language does not mean that a second being is acquired. Rather, what something presents itself as belongs to its own being. Thus everything that is language has a speculative unity: it contains a distinction, that between its being and its presentations of itself, but this is a distinction that is really not a distinction at all" (TM, 491).

Thus, the theory of truth that Gadamer introduces through his consideration of aesthetic experience applies to hermeneutic situations beyond the aesthetic. In this section, we have seen how the theory helps us to make sense of what happens in genuine conversation. It helps us to understand why genuine conversations yield discoveries that the participants have not anticipated and yet in which they have a personal interest. Moreover, both this analysis of aesthetic experience and of conversation help bring to light the nature of the truth at issue in each. What interests us in both art and conversation is the truth that they might yield. The pursuit of this truth, though, is also the pursuit of *Bildung*, self-edification. This truth lies not in the correspondence between one's belief and an independent, ahistorical reality but in the discovery of something missing from our current horizon of understanding. It has a self-reflexive and corrective character—both features of which were absent from both the transcendence and the immanence models of knowing introduced in the last chapter.

Yet we are not accustomed to thinking about aesthetic experience or conversation as places where truth occurs. In an age where truth is seen as the exclusive property of the disinterested application of scientific method and increasingly of technology, these experiences are regarded as having only limited epistemic relevance. In such circumstances, it is, in fact, hard to initiate any genuine conversation about the nature of truth. This is less so because we all feel very confident about the answer to this question and more so because it hardly even seems to us today like a legitimate question. We all know what the nature of truth is, the assumption goes, we just disagree on what is true and maybe, at most, on what we need to show to justify claims to truth. If we are to make any headway, then, in taking seriously the question of the nature of truth and thinking along with Gadamer on this question, we need to draw out more explicitly our deeply held convictions about truth that are challenged by Gadamer's theory so that they can be properly examined.

Two Ways of Conceiving of Truth in Interpretation

One idea about truth that we tend to take for granted, subjecting it to little or no scrutiny, is the idea that truth in itself lies beyond the reach of any mediation such as interpretation. The basis for this idea about truth is understandable enough. We know that beliefs widely held in a society can reflect deeply entrenched interpretive habits in that society and that this can be a source of shortsightedness, encouraging people to get stuck in the ruts formed by these habits and corresponding modes of social organization. In light of this fact, it is tempting to think about the mediation that occurs in interpretation as leading us away from truth. On this view, it makes little sense to think about art and conversation, highly interpretive activities, as anything other than obstacles to truth.

How does Gadamer call into question this idea about the nature of truth, that is, that truth lies in itself unmediated by interpretation? One possibility that we must consider is the extent to which Gadamer's challenge coincides with a certain postmodern argument about truth according to which truth is *constructed* by the very interpretive actions that would seem to aim at discovering it. At times, it would seem that Gadamer's argument, after all, is that art and conversation simply *create* truth. Recall, for example, that for Gadamer, an artwork has the power to reveal the nature of something absolutely such that no external comparison could be relevant. With the "transformation into structure," Gadamer argues, what is opened up by the work of art "no longer permits of any comparison with reality as the secret measure of all verisimilitude" (TM, 83). This is, Gadamer says, the basis for the idea that art has a kind of autonomy. From this, it could be concluded that the artwork, in fact, wholly constructs its subject matter for its audience, such that the audience is not familiar at all with the subject matter as a reference in the world prior to its enactment by the work of art. According to this postmodern, constructivist reading of Gadamer, neither artwork nor conversation has any referentiality. They refer to nothing that exists outside of what they themselves create.

Some commentators offer interpretations of Gadamer along these lines. Richard Rorty, for example, reads *Truth and Method* as an antifoundationalist project, meaning, for Rorty, one that directs readers away from the search for foundational, universal rules for arriving at truth by exposing the fact that the success of explanations is due neither strictly to their adherence to such rules nor to their successful reflection of nature (the achievement of which is often thought to be the essential function of proper reasoning). Rorty compares Gadamer's contribution on this point to Thomas Kuhn's theory of incommensurability among scientific theories. Just as Kuhn argues that successful scientific theories needn't have fundamental concepts in common and that the history of scientific discovery is full of sudden, unexpected shifts away from previously dominant paradigms, Gadamer helps us to recognize a similar sort of incommensurability that exists among successful interpretations and urges us to avoid attributing the success of an interpretation to its achievement of objectivity. The point, for Rorty as for Kuhn, is not to deny that a theory or an interpretation can be successful but to reject the most common way of speaking about what accounts for their success, namely, in terms of the degree to which they conform to unchanging rules of reason and accurately reflect objective nature.

According to this line of thinking, then, it is wrong to conceive of truth as what lies beyond interpretation because truth is nothing but the effect of a powerful interpretive act as in the case of some new revolutionary scientific theory. It is *constructed* in and by such acts. If this is so, then we can easily account for Gadamer's suggestion that the truth that emerges in a work of art does not easily permit comparison with other, external claims to truth or allow itself to be measured against some objectivity external to it. While we tend to think that what art and conversation aim at is "objectivity," a reflection of how things are in themselves, their disclosive power is grounded in nothing external to the interpretive act itself. Any truth they present is a reflection only of the power of the interpretive activity itself and not of anything that we could refer to and with which we were already familiar prior to this activity.

The constructivist theory of truth that Rorty attributes to Gadamer is in many ways compatible with what Caputo calls the project of "radical hermeneutics"[17] and what Theodore George calls "postmodern hermeneutics."[18] It does not look for bases of truth external to the actual singular event (e.g., the artwork or dialogue) in which truth appears. It conceives of truth not as the accomplishment of an objective belief or representation nor as an event whose validity can be grounded by referring to something outside of the event itself. The truth of Homer's Achilles, on this view, is not in its accurate representation of the real Achilles but in the ability of Homer and his audience to construct the character of Achilles in a way that is convincing and agreeable to them. The efficacy of a conversation about justice is not a matter of capturing justice as it is in itself but of *constructing together* an account of justice that is agreeable to the interlocutors.

This tradition of post-Gadamerian hermeneutics has been fruitful and illuminating for readers of Gadamer in several respects. It helps us to understand Gadamer's resistance to thinking about truth as correspondence to objective reality in the context of a much larger and longer humanist struggle. Moreover, as Caputo points out, it helps us to see the relevance of Gadamer's thought for understanding how it is possible to arrive at agreed-upon truth when there are substantial, even seemingly "incommensurable" differences between social groups from different cultural, historical, and linguistic backgrounds—something that is essential for deliberative democracy and, as Caputo points out, for interfaith dialogue.[19]

Moreover, as counterintuitive as the constructivist theory of truth is for many, there is certainly something to be said in favor of it, practically speaking, as an orientation toward truth. After all, it is very easy for us to adopt ways of understanding as a society that repeat and take for granted patterns of interpretation that have been passed on through social custom, and, as we will explore in more depth in the later chapters, it is beneficial to be able to recognize the way that this sort of socially immersive understanding can constrain how we approach certain topics. It is helpful to be able to track, for example, how we have "constructed" certain divisions—say, between social and natural sciences, sex and gender, East and West—that have come to inform how we tend to think about and organize things today. Revealing the contingency of these divisions, it can well be argued, is necessary for honestly evaluating them. It forces us to consider the merits of such divisions rather than believing that they must be acceptable because they are natural, intuitive, necessary distinctions in reality. Taken as such, constructivism is a helpful analytic tool for demonstrating how the ways that we interpret and understand things often do more than simply reflect a preexistent reality. Additionally and more positively, it can help us appreciate what is at stake in the interpretive activities that we undertake together. If art or conversation has anything close to the power to autonomously determine for us what something is, these activities must be given the greatest care. This is what Gianni Vattimo means when he argues that "nihilism," which he understands as the deconstruction of beliefs that have long served to rationalize existing structures of power, leads organically to a greater appreciation of the importance of dialogue. As Vattimo puts it, "Nihilism becomes hermeneutics: a thought that knows it can aim at the universal only by passing through dialogue, agreement, or *caritas*. . . . '*Veritatem facientes in caritate*': translated into the terms of today's philosophy, this Pauline motto . . . means that truth is born in agreement and from agreement, and not vice versa, that we will reach agreement only when we have all discovered the same objective truth."[20]

Although neither postmodernism nor nihilism is typically associated with Enlightenment humanism, Vattimo's is, in one sense, an exemplary case of Enlightenment humanist thinking. It is a normative argument on behalf of those beliefs that we have arrived at through human dialogue and shared forms of reasoning rather than those whose alleged justification is to be forever inscrutable to us. It is an argument, moreover, that the most relevant justificatory conditions that a belief can meet or fail to meet are those internal and not external to the epistemic agents involved, those that can be deduced from the actual conduct of these epistemic agents and, in particular, from the forms of agreement, however tentative, that they must inevitably come to as members of a society. Indeed, Rorty, Caputo, and Vattimo each have deep commitments to the modern liberal political tradition (Vattimo even served in the European Parliament) and very much see the interpretive process that constructs truth as the deliberative democratic process through which agreements are reached in modern liberal democracies.[21] In these ways, postmodern hermeneutics is like other forms of Enlightenment humanism in aiming to substitute arbitrary forms of authority with the authority of human freedom as determined through dialogue and human reasoning.

In recent decades, the proponents of postmodern hermeneutics have been far from alone in making such an attempt. As we shall see in the upcoming chapters, social epistemologists also tend to locate justificatory conditions in rules internal to communities of epistemic agents, and many of them (e.g., feminist epistemologists) do so in response to political concerns similar to Vattimo's. This group too—some of whom are inspired by the same turn against logical positivism that inspires Rorty—are concerned with how political power makes certain ideas appear self-evident and conceives of them, qua *foundations*, as beyond the possibility of justification or contestation.

That being said, not all readers of Gadamer conceive of the hermeneutic theory of truth as a constructivist doctrine in this way. Recently, Günter Figal has challenged this version of hermeneutic theory, highlighting the importance of the referential character of interpretive activity that Rorty, Caputo, and Vattimo each deny. In his *Objectivity: The Hermeneutical and Philosophy*, Figal argues that every hermeneutic experience is, in fact, oriented toward something that "stands over and against" (*entgegensteht*) the interpreter, placing a demand upon them. Interpretation is first prompted, after all, as Figal points out, "when something is not sufficiently clear in one's inner experience."[22] The photographer, for example, feels claimed by some subject or scene that draws them in, compelling them to investigate its meaning. Dialogue between two people forms around some topic that interests them but leaves them with questions, unsure of how to think through the matter. What claims us at the onset of such experiences, inspiring us to first undertake interpretation is, as Figal says, "like a promise that, in the moment one turns to devote one's attention to it, one believes can be fulfilled."[23] Such experiences point to the way in which these interpretive activities are oriented toward something that transcends the activities themselves, toward a reference that they do not simply construct. Moreover, as the interpretive activity unfolds, it remains oriented, Figal says, toward this reference that functions as a measure for the efficacy of the interpretation. The photographer, for instance, comes to feel that they have managed to capture what initially claimed them about a particular scene. The interlocutors may feel that their conversation at some point starts to steer away from what they initially hoped to clarify. In such ways, interpretive activity remains bound to what Figal calls the "objective" (*das Gegenständliche*): "what is there in such a way that one may come into accord with it and that yet never fully comes out in any attempt to reach accord."[24]

According to Theodore George, Figal's account of the referential dimension of interpretation initiates an alternative tradition of post-Gadamerian hermeneutics—alternative to the postmodern version offered by Rorty, Caputo, and Vattimo. This alternative, as George describes it, understands hermeneutics as a form of realism. It is grounded in the idea that "hermeneutical experience is substantive, that it refers us to something outside of ourselves, something that our attempts to understand and interpret can make accessible, but that nevertheless remains exterior to all such attempts."[25] Hermeneutic realism differs from the postmodern account outlined above in that it does not hold what is disclosed by interpretation to be entirely an effect of the interpretive activity—an emergence of meaning *ex nihilo*. What emerges in interpretation is not the expression of some singular event nor the will of a subject—individual or communal. For hermeneutic realists, what emerges in interpretation belongs to a reality that exceeds the interpretive event itself—the being of the subject matter. As Figal argues, this belonging is evident in the way that we praise successful interpretive works:

> When a musical performance is successful, one's enthusiasm holds not only for the activity of the interpreters, but, rather, always also for the respective presence of the work. . . . The joy in the discoveries one makes in a careful reading of a text is always also a joy of being into the matter [*Sache*]. And,

> when one succeeds in devoting one's attention to a picture in peace and with open eyes, one is rewarded for it with a special pregnancy of the visible.[26]

For the hermeneutic realists, it is our desire to witness such a transformation of the invisible into the visible, the abstract into the concrete, that attracts us both to fine art and to the art of discourse. Thus, what we seek in these activities is not something that has no reference at all in the lifeworld that is familiar to us but the disclosure of hidden dimensions of this world. Gadamer, for his part, is quite clear on this in his discussion of aesthetics. The truth of a work of art occurs in the event of recognition—where some reality comes to be recognized in a new, more comprehensive way. Put otherwise, what comes forth in a work of art has the character of nondifferentiation. It is not a construct without a referent but the truth of something already familiar.

This recognitive dimension of aesthetic experience, on the other hand, is hard to reconcile with the emphasis on incommensurability that we find in postmodern hermeneutics. For Rorty, for example, successful interpretations may very well have neither common referent nor common fore-conceptions. Rather than say that different works represent some subject matter—say, justice—in different ways and to different degrees, Rorty suggests that we be "nominalists" and hold that it is only in name that their referent is the same. For Figal, on the other hand, while interpretation is necessary for bringing clarity and for getting at the truth of matters, the matters that we find clarified through our interpretive efforts are not simply the effect of these efforts. Their reality is not reducible to an act of subjective construction—be it the product of individual genius or of an agreement reached through democratic deliberation.

The tradition of hermeneutic realism may, moreover, be understood as an attempt to demonstrate that attending to the role that interpretation plays in the discovery of *what is* does not mean that one is necessarily an "antirealist." It is often assumed, after all, that one who attends to the role of interpretation in the process of understanding must be abandoning not only epistemology, as we saw earlier, but also any notion of reality as something with which we must grapple in the course of our lives. This is, in part, the legacy of a distinction drawn in the past between realism and idealism. Figal's focus on the "objective" and "substantive" dimensions of interpretation contest this legacy by making clear that these concepts describe precisely the demands of the numerous interpretive activities in which people frequently engage.

Figal's emphasis on the referential dimension of interpretation is an important corrective to the project of postmodern hermeneutics that, in the interest of legitimating the value of interpretive understanding, ends up misconstruing what happens in any one interpretation. After all, as we have seen, one who takes the doctrine of nondifferentiation to mean that reality is unilaterally constructed by a given interpretive activity will have a hard time accounting for the experience of finding an artwork suddenly illuminate a subject we were already familiar with or the interlocutor's experience of having a conversation resolve the nagging question that motivated them to engage in the conversation in the first place. The constructivist theory simply cannot account for the interpreter's familiarity with and ability to refer to the subject matter prior to the interpretive activity.

Similarly, the postmodern theory faces great difficulty when trying to account for why, after a successful work of art or a successful conversation, one would undertake *further* interpretation of the subject matter at later points. On the constructivist model, the task of interpretation would be fully completed with the reception of a given work of art, a given conversation, and so on. After taking in Homer's presentation of Achilles, an audience needn't ever ask about the reality of Achilles again. Homer's Achilles would have to be the final and complete truth of Achilles, as the subject matter is constructed by Homer in such a way that it can have no reference to anything in comparison with which it would show up as lacking. Gadamer, for his part, clearly conceives of interpretation as an ongoing process, though. As he says, "the discovery of the true meaning of a text or work of art is never finished; it is in fact an infinite process" (TM, 309). Figal's account, in contrast to postmodern hermeneutics, offers us a way to make sense of both aspects of interpretation's relationship to truth. It suggests that, on the one hand, successful interpretation brings about a determinate clarification, and that, on the other hand, despite the determinacy in such moments, the disclosure of any reality through interpretation is an ongoing process. For the hermeneutic realist, no matter how successful an interpretation is, it never exhausts all that there is to say. Accordingly, for Figal, the event of truth is twofold: in it, an object both comes to self-presentation and, at the same time, is held to some degree in reserve.[27]

In offering an account of hermeneutic *realism* and of hermeneutic *truth*, this tradition of post-Gadamerian hermeneutics is helpful in directing philosophical hermeneutics away from the rocky shores of the anti-epistemological tradition of hermeneutics according to which truth is just what participants in a discourse community happen to agree upon. Briefly, however, I would like to caution against two ways in which hermeneutic realism may be interpreted. First, I worry about the idea that, in order to do justice to the ongoing character of interpretation, we need to posit that, even with successful interpretation, something is held in reserve. This would seem to reintroduce a Kantian distinction between the phenomenal and noumenal that Gadamer seeks to avoid. I propose instead a different model of the twofold character of truth, whereby, on the one hand, successful interpretation brings about a determinate clarification but, on the other hand, because of the inexorable historicality of interpretation, this clarification comes to appear as partial as soon as a more comprehensive interpretation is developed. Truth, on this model, then, refers both to the self-presentation of the object that occurs through a successful act of interpretation but also to the overall process that encompasses the series of such acts as historical consciousness unfolds. Second, those who, in response to the postmodern line, would emphasize the importance of "objectivity" and "realism" for hermeneutics must be careful to distinguish the meaning of these terms from meanings that Gadamer went to great lengths to avoid. For Gadamer, interpretation is integral to much of the reality that we seek to understand. If, in response to the excesses of postmodern hermeneutics, we find ourselves advocating for a realism that conceives of reality in every instant as something that exists in opposition to the subject in every respect, we would then be accepting the very dualism that Gadamer's account of truth and understanding seeks to unsettle. Gadamer cautions us about such a conception of reality in his 1960 essay "The Nature of Things and the Language of Things." There he describes how natural concerns about the rise of subjectivism and, specifically, about the rise of neo-Kantian idealism have led thinkers like Nicolai Hartmann to dismiss transcendental philosophy entirely and to conceive of reality as that which exists in complete indifference to human spirit. For Gadamer, it is easy in a world where so much is constantly being rewritten by codes of technological rationality "to understand such a polemical renunciation as an appeal to the nature of things" (PH, 74). Yet such a position is suspicious in his eyes in that it accepts the very opposition that underlies the theory of idealism—that theory Hartmann's "realism" intends to reject. Instead of challenging the idea that it is simply the impress of the subject that is at work in interpretation, it looks for reality beyond the interpretive domain. Another theory of reality emerges, however, when we take the subject as existing fundamentally in relation to being. This possibility emerges, however, only when we are willing to rethink the dualistic metaphysics typically taken for granted in discussions of mind and reality. Only then, Gadamer argues, can we think about the "nature of things" independently of the way they are narrowly construed by instruments of technological rationality.

Having explored Gadamer's theory of truth, we can now understand clearly why it is that the hermeneutic investigation into understanding leads Gadamer to rethink the nature of two things with which hermeneutics has rarely been associated, namely, truth and reality. Gadamer sees that the tendency to think about understanding as a purely subjective affair is bound up with the tendency to think about reality as entirely independent of the subject and of truth as the state in which an epistemic agent manages to capture this independent reality. One cannot rethink the nature of understanding without reconsidering these two common conceptions. At base, Gadamer's reconceptualization of truth and reality stems from his challenge to the dualistic metaphysics that has long informed investigations in epistemology. Modern epistemology takes for granted the framework of skepticism. It assumes that the ways in which we come to know the world are fundamentally sources of error that prevent us from beholding being-in-itself. This starting point is not a self-evident one, however. It was not an intuitive starting point, for example, for either classical philosophy or Gnosticism and its status as received wisdom was directly challenged by the emergence of Critical philosophy in the late eighteenth century. As we have seen in this chapter, however, Gadamer thinks the problem with this starting point and with the dualistic conceptions of truth and reality that it enables becomes especially clear when we reflect on the nature of aesthetic experience. We have a tendency to think that what issues from aesthetic experience has only subjective validity. For Gadamer, though, it is truth that is at issue in aesthetic experience. Art makes visible what is invisible. What appears to the audience in art, if it is successful, is being-in-itself and not the artist's or the audience's take on it. This is not to say that what emerges in one aesthetic experience amounts to the final word. As Figal's hermeneutic realism makes clear, effective interpretation leaves room for further disclosure. Yet it is this process of disclosure—each disclosure taking place in the interplay between the interpreter and the interpreted—that, for Gadamer, most warrants the name "truth."

Having now explored the arguments that Gadamer gives on behalf of his hermeneutic theory of understanding, I want to next consider a set of supporting arguments for this theory that can be found in other epistemological traditions that are rarely compared with the tradition of philosophical hermeneutics. Each of these epistemological traditions, like Gadamer's hermeneutics, emerges as an attempt to rethink the Enlightenment tradition of epistemology and to reimagine what a theory of understanding looks like that takes seriously how much inquiry is undertaken from a historically and socially *situated* position. In the next two chapters, I consider these developments as they have taken place, first, in the development of social epistemology (chapter 4) and, second, in the development of feminist epistemology (chapter 5). In the final chapter (chapter 6), I take stock of how Gadamer's hermeneutics is compatible in many ways with these other, more recognized epistemological traditions and how philosophical hermeneutics can, in fact, offer guidance on certain debates that have taken place within them. At the same time, I argue that many of the arguments developed in the service of social and feminist epistemology provide new ways of clarifying and appreciating the epistemological dimension of Gadamerian hermeneutics. With the aid of arguments developed in the context of social and feminist epistemology, then, I hope to address lingering questions that may remain at this point about the virtues of Gadamer's account. One may still wonder, for example, if Gadamer does not go too far in his exploration of understanding by reconceiving epistemological and metaphysical concepts as fundamental as truth and reality. One may wonder too whether the theory of understanding Gadamer offers allows concepts like "understanding" and "truth" to retain the *normative* function that they have traditionally had—a normative function that has long been central to philosophy's self-understanding. As these are questions that both social and feminist epistemology have had to answer in their own defense, the answers they have developed promise to shed helpful light for those interested in the prospects of hermeneutic epistemology.

Part 2
Gadamerian Hermeneutics and Social Epistemology

Chapter 4

The Central Question of Social Epistemology
What Does It Mean to Recognize Epistemic Practices as Social Practices?

> Thus the world is the common ground, trodden by none and recognized by all, uniting all who talk together.
>
> —Gadamer, *Truth and Method*, 462

In part 1, we examined Gadamer's exploration of understanding. We saw how this exploration leads him to recognize the way the event of understanding unfolds to a subject who is historically and socially situated. This insight emerges for Gadamer, we have seen, as a question for and a challenge to the model of knowledge introduced by the Enlightenment—a model that I have referred to as the transcendence model of knowing. For Gadamer, one needn't engage in inquiry as a blank slate free of social and historical baggage, for it is always in a particular social and historical context that understanding occurs. This claim, moreover, does not entail that the understanding that so occurs is *merely* subjective, unnecessary, and ultimately arbitrary. This holds only if we accept the way that the transcendence model of knowing and its counterpart, the immanence model, conceive of knowledge as a historically and culturally neutral apprehension of objective facts. When one examines the conditions in which understanding occurs, however, Gadamer finds that it is necessary to reconceive both the process of understanding and the object sought in this process along with a number of related epistemological concepts. In this, Gadamer makes a significant contribution to the theory of what we seek when we endeavor to understand something, what this accomplishment means when it occurs, and what allows it to take place. As such, Gadamerian hermeneutics makes a significant contribution to epistemology. However, as we have seen, this claim is a contentious one in that some commentators have taken Gadamer as rejecting epistemology and traditional epistemological aspirations entirely.

Gadamer, however, is not alone in his attempt to reconceive the process of understanding and the nature of the truth that emerges from it. Over the past several decades, one finds in the field of epistemology a growing awareness of the ways in which human reasoning is situated within social practices and historical circumstances and, with this awareness, a growing problematization of the transcendence model of knowledge that became firmly entrenched with the Enlightenment. While interest in social criticism remains robust, it is increasingly awkward for philosophers to see human thought processes, including the second-order processes by which people evaluate the rationality, justifiability, and credibility of given claims, as emerging in isolation from circumstances of history, culture, and social class. In response, many have attempted to reconceive the process of understanding as socially and historically situated and, in some cases, to reconceive the nature of truth that can emerge from these processes.

This development within recent epistemology has been contentious insofar as it threatens to unsettle a branch of philosophy that has long enjoyed a privileged status and has often in the modern period even been regarded as synonymous with the discipline itself. For while epistemology is still regarded as one branch of philosophy (alongside metaphysics and normative philosophy), epistemological questions have very often been regarded as the most radical, fundamental kind of questions one can ask. Epistemological questions are taken as philosophical questions par excellence because they are the expressions of absolute openness—the kind of questions that are supposed to presuppose nothing. Moreover, despite the significant ways in which major figures in the history of philosophy (e.g., Aristotle, Hegel, and Heidegger) have challenged this point, it is still generally accepted that one must tackle epistemological questions first if one is to make progress in any other branch of philosophy. On this view, one can make little progress in understanding the nature of reality (metaphysics) or arriving at the best ethical or political judgment in a certain situation (normative philosophy) without first asking: *How can I know for sure?* Thus, it is easy to imagine that effectively tackling any philosophical question first requires that one sort out the general rules for arriving at the most justified beliefs possible and that, if one tries to tackle any question before the question "How can I know?," one will inevitably find oneself back at this one. If, however, understanding human reasoning involves an exploration of the social and historical circumstances in which it takes place, this suggests that epistemological questions are not as radically presuppositionless as commonly thought and that they cannot come prior to but must be bound up and contemporaneous with some kind of historical and social analysis.

This recent development in epistemology, then, has not only problematized the priority that epistemology as a field has enjoyed throughout the modern period but has also brought to the fore questions about its aims and its scope. Indeed, standard introductions to the subject now include substantial discussion of debates about what counts as epistemology, what sorts of questions epistemology should be attempting to answer, and what kinds of questions are properly epistemological. While debate on these questions continues, there is broad agreement among those involved in the recent shift that epistemology should include a range of investigations previously excluded from the field. Alcoff captures this point well, for instance, when she says that "no absolute separation should exist between the way in which we actually justify our beliefs and the way in which we *should* justify them," clarifying that "all prescriptive proposals must be grounded firmly in current, actual practices since these alone can circumscribe the possible."[1]

As we shall see in the chapters remaining, this development in the way that philosophers are thinking about knowledge, understanding, and truth is in no way limited to small segments of the discipline. It is not a development limited to hermeneutics or phenomenology or even to the Continental tradition of philosophy. For decades now, it has been an important part of the conversation in analytic epistemology and in social movements whose members have found themselves grappling with questions of an epistemological nature. The next chapter of this book (chapter 5) will examine the latter more closely and, in particular, the emergence of this epistemological orientation within feminist thought. The present chapter will examine this shift as it has emerged within analytic epistemology, where it is referred to as a shift to "social epistemology." What both parts will make clear are the significant parallels between these recent developments in epistemology and Gadamer's own project to rethink the nature of understanding. By drawing out these parallels, I hope to show that Gadamer's own effort in *Truth and Method* at rethinking the nature of understanding anticipates important developments that would soon come to alter the landscape of epistemology and that it, indeed, contains insights that can provide guidance on matters of debate within these new branches of epistemology.

In this chapter, I shall focus, first, on introducing social epistemology as an epistemological orientation that emerges as a challenge to certain core components of the Enlightenment model of knowing, particularly, the treatment of socially situated forms of reasoning as untrustworthy. I go on to discuss an important contention regarding the implications of challenging the Enlightenment model of epistemology—one that Hilary Kornblith refers to as the tension between weak and strong versions of social epistemology's "replacement thesis." Whereas, for advocates of the strong version, rethinking Enlightenment epistemology means abandoning altogether traditional epistemic concepts like truth, justification, objectivity, normativity, and critique, advocates of the weak version argue that at least some portion of these concepts and procedures can and should be left intact by the social epistemological turn, albeit, in most cases, with a modified meaning. Recognizing the distinction between these two forms of social epistemology is important, since it allows us to see that the shift to social epistemology is not, in itself, a renunciation of all traditional epistemological concepts and aspirations, as it is sometimes understood to be. To bring this possibility more clearly into view, the chapter concludes by offering a closer look at how one social epistemological approach, namely, virtue epistemology, retains a normative dimension and at the character of the normativity that it offers.

The Emergence of Social Epistemology

It has become somewhat common within modern culture these days to recognize the ways that one's reasoning about things can be shaped by the circumstances in which one lives. The emergence of this sort of self-consciousness is not a very recent development. One essential feature of late modernity, after all, is the tendency of people to understand their own nature by relying on information uncovered by the natural and social sciences (and in the twenty-first century, especially insofar as that information has been operationalized by social and information technologies). Modern people rely a great deal on biology, neuroscience, psychology, and anthropology, for example, to understand who they are and what they should strive for in their lives. And while epistemological questions have traditionally enjoyed a kind of priority that required them to be answered without reliance upon information from the empirical sciences, beginning in the twentieth century, people have increasingly relied upon the empirical sciences to answer even epistemological questions. This pattern reflects, on the one hand, significant social changes happening during this period, namely, the increasing entrenchment of technologically rational forms of social organization and the impact of this change on university research. That said, we also find the case for this approach formulated explicitly in the early and mid-twentieth century by leading figures in analytic philosophy. Both Rudolf Carnap and W. V. O. Quine, for instance, found the idea that epistemological investigations should precede empirical scientific investigations untenable. According to them, epistemological questions must either be abandoned or radically modified. Carnap and Ludwig Wittgenstein proposed versions of the former: epistemological questions represent the sort of philosophical questions that should be abandoned. By contrast, Quine proposed that, rather than abandoning epistemology entirely, "epistemology, or something like it, simply falls into place as a chapter of psychology and hence of natural science."[2] Quine's "naturalized epistemology" thus emerges as a way of granting more priority in the treatment of epistemological questions to scientific investigation into the natural, psychological conditions in which thought occurs. As such, it reflects a much broader development taking place in the twentieth century, namely, the increasing self-consciousness that human beings have of the situated nature of their thought.

The development of social epistemology in recent decades can also be understood as part of this broader pattern. While important precursors to social epistemology can be sought in Quine's argument for a naturalized epistemology, social epistemology becomes, for the most part, consolidated as an approach to epistemology a few decades later in the late twentieth century with the work of Steve Fuller, Hilary Kornblith, Alvin Goldman, C. A. J. Coady, Frederick Schmitt, and Philip Kitcher as well as the work of a number of philosophers, like Alcoff and Sandra Harding, who saw their contributions to social epistemology, at least in part, as the result of their attempts to think through the project of feminist epistemology. As Frederick Schmitt defines it, social epistemology is "the conceptual and normative study of the relevance of social relations, roles, institutions, and relations to knowledge."[3] Essential to the approach of social epistemology is, first of all, the insight that our habituation into socially meaningful practices plays a large role in human reasoning. While Enlightenment thinkers presented reasoning as a purely cognitive process during which one must rely on one's own mind and not any learned social habits, social epistemologists argue that reasoning requires immersion in these habits. Like Gadamer, they find the Enlightenment model of reasoning too individualistic and too narrowly cognitivist. Moreover, like Gadamer, they take their task to be an examination of actual epistemic practices that occur in our everyday social lives and reject the epistemological approach according to which such practices are regarded with suspicion.

Indeed, while Enlightenment thinkers took the reliance of one's thought upon a historical and social milieu to be an obstacle to rational, enlightened thinking, social epistemologists such as Alcoff and Kitcher argue that abstracting reason from the social practices in which it is embedded is a mistake. The mistake arises, on the one hand, because of a tendency that Kitcher refers to as the "individualistic reduction" according to which knowledge "can be obtained by relying only on sources whose credentials have been individualistically checked."[4] The spirit of this principle is captured well by numerous mottoes for the Enlightenment: from Kant's version of the motto ("Have the courage to use your own understanding") to the motto of the British Royal Society, *Nullius in verba* ("Take nobody's word for it"). According to this view, to rely too much on others—be it a tradition or a community of knowers—is not to have thought through the matter for oneself and therefore not to have reached any kind of knowledge of real value. By contrast, social epistemologists see the social dimension of reasoning as essential to it. Alessandra Tanesini, for example, explains that we come to adopt epistemic norms that are "implicit in practices and in the habits we develop when we are inducted into them."[5] For Tanesini, a good reasoner cannot rely exclusively on sources that have been individualistically checked but will also be informed by the epistemic norms that are embedded in practices into which they have been socialized. Enlightenment epistemology has conceived of reasoning, for the most part, as too individualistic a process.

It has also conceived of the process, social epistemologists claim, as too narrowly cognitivist—as comprised of a series of mental representations produced by an individual knower. It denies the status of knowledge to any kind of tacit understanding that one has by virtue of learned social habits. Moreover, it denies epistemic value to any thoughts, even those that have come to take clear propositional form, that are in any way the effect of one's immersion in a social and historical lifeworld. A version of this argument can be found articulated by Jon Elster in the distinction he draws between rational beliefs and socially caused beliefs. Elster argues: "Generally speaking, a belief is rationally caused if (i) the causes of the belief are reasons for holding it and (ii) the reasons cause the beliefs qua reasons, not in some accidental manner. Conversely, they are shaped in the wrong way if irrelevant causes enter into their formation or they are irrelevantly shaped by relevant causes. Among such irrelevant causes we may cite the interest or position of the believer: socially caused beliefs are not rationally caused."[6] While Elster's argument here is aimed primarily at explaining why a belief should not be regarded as rational on the basis of the social-political standpoint of the person who believes it (a challenge to standpoint theory), he formulates well the cognitivist principle that social epistemologists like Tanesini are challenging, that is, that a belief's emergence from social practices excludes it from being rational. As Elster puts it, socially caused beliefs are not rationally caused. They are ideological—beliefs one possesses by habits acquired through some form of social conditioning. On this view, a great many of the beliefs we hold are the product of social causation, and nobody immersed in a society is immune to this pattern of belief formation. Nobody entirely transcends their social situation. At the same time, each of us is capable of arriving at some beliefs through the causation of reasoning, and one is rational precisely to the extent that one arrives at one's beliefs through this type of causation rather than the other. Elster accepts, then, a cognitivist model of reasoning: one has arrived at beliefs rationally when it is reasons rather than causes that have led one to those beliefs.

The analytic distinction between the social causation of belief and the rational, cognitive causation of belief is a helpful one and one that can be traced far back in history to at least the medieval scholastic distinction between *ratio cognoscendi* and *ratio essendi*. To explain why a certain belief that one possesses is justified or why others should share this belief, it is not enough to simply describe the causal chain of events in society that led one to hold the belief. We may recall here Simone de Beauvoir's response to her philosophical colleagues in France who would tell her that she believed some particular point because she was a woman.[7] She recalls her constant response: "I believe it because it is true." What is the difference that Beauvoir insists upon at this moment? At minimum, she insists that she holds the belief due to reasons that, if articulated, should compel others to hold it as well. This is, in fact, why she is so annoyed with the suggestion that her gender is the sole reason for her making the claim. While her historical and social situation are not irrelevant to her acceptance of certain beliefs, the reasons she finds for them have a normative quality to them. They lead those who consider them toward a certain position or at least away from certain positions. Indeed, the significant social activity of giving reasons to and receiving reasons from others hinges on the idea that the forms of reasoning at work in such deliberative activity are ones that have a normative force and thus that others can be compelled by.

Social epistemologists challenge the cognitivist model, however, by arguing that reasoning is frequently embedded in social practices and that such forms of reasoning are not irrational simply on account of their social embeddedness. On this point, they find inspiration in a number of twentieth-century figures—particularly, Ludwig Wittgenstein, Wilfrid Sellars, John McDowell, and Robert Brandom—who account for reasoning precisely in terms of social practices. More recently, Alessandra Tanesini argues that it is through practices into which we are socially habituated, and in particular through the normative attitudes that we develop on account of these practices, that we are primarily familiar with epistemic norms.

> The trained scientist, for example, knows how to go about making an experiment. She is sensitive to the norms implicit in experimental practice. Her sensitivity will be expressed by endorsements of propositions about rules of conduct, but it will also involve bodily "habits." These habits are dispositions to behave in particular ways, which exhibit normative assessments. They are dispositions which invest behavior with a normative significance. . . . When one acquires a new habit of this kind, one has acquired a new range of normative attitudes. The learning process does not have to be mediated by beliefs. Rather, one is tempted to say that, by means of training, embodied individuals become endowed with new normative responses.[8]

Tanesini problematizes the cognitivist model by arguing that social habituation can and often does give rise to the sort of epistemic attitudes and activities that cognitivists find important but that they believe cannot be socially caused. What the cognitivist values and what they fear is lacking in a person with socially caused beliefs is, after all, *the capacity for that person to function in an evaluative, that is to say, a normative way.* The cognitivist's assumption is that, insofar as one's dispositions come from social habituation, these dispositions will lack any evaluative quality. As Tanesini describes it, though, the scientist is not merely imitating some learned behavior or parroting some learned set of beliefs. She acquires not simply behavioral patterns but normative attitudes that allow her to make evaluative determinations about what is and is not appropriate in the design of an experiment. And she does this, Tanesini argues, without having at any moment to quit her training, suspend her embodied know-how, and consult evaluative principles in a purely cognitive way. That the description does not contain such a moment—where consideration of epistemic norms is made independently of socially acquired habits—is a source of distress for the cognitivist. What Tanesini is trying to demonstrate, however, is that it is unnecessary to posit this as an independent step and an independent capacity when trying to account for how one comes to exercise evaluative judgment. We needn't imagine that the scientist, for example, must put aside her social habituation in order to think in a purely individualistic and purely cognitive way about how to design her experiment. She may be able to articulate the principles of good experimental design pretty well if asked, but, for the most part, she allows herself to be guided by the norms implicit in the practice in which she was trained. In this, Tanesini demonstrates what is wrong with the idea that something one knows through social habituation is of no epistemic value.

That such an idea needs to be rethought is further supported by studies in developmental psychology on social cognition. These studies show that there are a number of cognitive abilities that emerge precisely through social connections. If the social connections are absent, so is the cognitive ability. One particularly important milestone in this development is the capacity for joint attention, a capacity that typically emerges in human beings around the age of nine months and that allows one to focus with another individual on the same object and to regard the object as something that they apprehend in common. The development of joint attention is a vital step in cognitive maturation.[9] With the development of joint attention, one starts to recognize a lifeworld that one has in common with others and as containing aspects that are disclosed to one by, for, and with others. One needs to have achieved the milestone of joint attention in order to develop language skills and, more generally, in order to engage in the kind of interpretive activity that hinges on mutual understanding with others.[10] In this way, social connections are vital to cognitive development. Moreover, these accounts of cognitive development help further substantiate Tanesini's claim that social habituation into embodied social practices provides us, not simply with a rigid set of rules for future behaviors, but with normative attitudes and evaluative capacities. When children learn to clue into social practices, they are not simply learning to imitate these practices in a rote, mechanical way. They are clueing into norms that allow them to be the sort of reflexive epistemic subject that manages these practices well.

For social epistemologists, this sort of attunement to social context makes up a much larger part of the process of understanding than we normally recognize. While traditional epistemology holds that serious inquiry requires putting aside habits and beliefs acquired through the development of a shared lifeworld, social epistemologists argue that socially attuned forms of judgment play a necessary role in the process. The interpretation of data, for example, takes place in a social, historical, and linguistic context. These contexts are partially what make the data meaningful in one way or another. The diagnosis of certain physiological developments depends on culturally informed ideas about health and illness. Likewise, one makes sense of various indicators of economic health based on culturally informed ideas about human flourishing. Moreover, the hypothesis that one might generate about any of these phenomena is not, despite what we are often taught, the first step in the research process. One needs to be clued into some context of shared meaning to develop a hypothesis or ask an appropriate question that might guide research. For the most part, when we rely on such cultural contexts to analyze data, we do so without conscious awareness of the role that they play. On this point, social epistemologists and hermeneutic phenomenologists agree: interpretation happens very quickly and without the mediation of conscious belief. One simply perceives the slowing of metabolism as a diminishment of health or the increase in consumer spending as a sign of economic health. Alongside the more reflexive normative attitudes that Tanesini describes, then, our social habituation also affords us with a number of these interpretive habits that become second nature to us.

These interpretive habits can certainly lead to problems, and, for some social epistemologists, like Sandra Harding, the task is to become aware of their influence in order to be able to better evaluate their appropriateness. Others, like Alcoff, argue that it is futile to imagine that we can eradicate completely the dependence of thought upon such contexts. After all, we would make little progress in our understanding of the world if we had to wipe the slate clean each time we read a new article, encountered a new claim, heard a new testimony, or made a new observation. Understanding requires that we inevitably rely on background knowledge that we come to acquire through social acculturation and on the testimony of others to whom we learn to grant a default trust. And even if some part of what we take for granted proves later to be problematic, we cannot proceed otherwise. It is simply not the case that good epistemic practice is entirely a matter of individual, nonsocial cognition. Alcoff argues that this, in fact, follows naturally from the principle of coherence: the principle that, in order for one to be justified in regarding a claim as true, it must cohere with other claims that one believes to be true. "Belief formation," Alcoff writes, "generally involves judgment calls about relevance, plausibility, coherence, consistency, and credibility. What I already know and believe will have a privileged place in my judgments by affecting my determinations of coherence, consistency, and plausibility, and this is in fact good epistemic practice."[11]

Social epistemologists thus challenge traditional epistemology by demonstrating that thinking requires habituation into social practices and familiarization with specific social contexts, and that such thinking can be and often is reflexive and evaluative. They thus reject the strict opposition that traditional cognitivist epistemology draws between rationally caused beliefs and socially caused beliefs. In so doing, social epistemology also raises questions about the proper scope of epistemology as a field. While traditional epistemology draws a sharp distinction between normative and descriptive treatments of knowledge and locates the task of epistemology exclusively in the former, social epistemologists argue that inquiry into how people come to inhabit a shared lifeworld and how this lifeworld functions in the background as they form beliefs and epistemic attitudes constitutes a legitimate and important part of the field.

The Question of Normativity in Social Epistemology

Social epistemology's attempt to shift the aim and scope of the field has been controversial to say the least. Some take social epistemology to be a conscious attempt to abandon epistemology's responsibility to evaluate and critique the processes by which beliefs are formed. Others argue that, regardless of whether social epistemology intends to abandon this responsibility or not, what it proposes effectively undermines the normative function of epistemology by undermining the autonomy of epistemological inquiry. Many worry, in other words, that the turn to social epistemology—like the turn to naturalized epistemology—undermines the unique normative role that epistemology (and, by extension, philosophy) has traditionally played.[12] Is epistemology to be nothing more than a description of how we arrive at beliefs? Is it no longer to be in the business of evaluating the legitimacy of those beliefs or the principles followed when arriving at them? Moreover, if it does somehow retain an evaluative function such that it is able to say that some beliefs and principles are more justifiable than others, must it not qualify such evaluative claims as true only relative to a given social context?

Social epistemology is not alone in prompting this sort of anxiety about the possibility of relativism. Some version of this tends to emerge whenever there is attention paid to the situatedness of reasoning with particular social and historical circumstances. In highlighting the role that our historical and linguistic circumstances play in our process of understanding, Gadamer's hermeneutic account of understanding has given risen to similar concerns. It too has often been said to entail epistemological relativism and to be incompatible with the important philosophical task of normative critique. We will return to this comparison in the last chapter.

Now, there are certainly some who take the descriptive task of social epistemology to replace the normative task of traditional epistemology. This is not surprising given the influence of Quine, who sought very explicitly to replace traditional philosophical questions with ones that could be answered through naturalistic investigation. It is also not surprising given the default trust that in recent decades most people in the modern world put in the empirical sciences regardless of whether those sciences have grappled with normative issues. Finally, this version of social epistemology finds some traction in social movements that aim to reveal the extent of the social privilege that some have by showing how patterns of belief formation are constrained by power relations. According to this approach to social epistemology, the conclusions that we arrive at can hold, at best, relative to the historical and social circumstances that we find ourselves in, and, because there is no way of removing oneself entirely from such circumstances, there is no form of reasoning that one can rely on ultimately to adjudicate between competing and conflicting accounts. One is inevitably bound to thinking within a limited horizon of socially defined epistemic norms. Traditional epistemological aspirations are completely unattainable. There is no general, unchanging sets of rules for reasoning that would allow us to arrive at certain or even the most justified beliefs, for those epistemic norms that appear most fundamental and necessary are but reflections of the most firmly entrenched power structures. Rather than trying to figure out how one can know for certain, then, one would be better off understanding the reasons why, in a given society, people believe what they do and how mechanisms help to ensure that certain epistemic norms and not others are kept in circulation. On this view, then, the best understanding of reality can be achieved not through traditional epistemology but through psychological and sociological investigations into the causes of belief.

Do all approaches to social epistemology, though, entail an abandonment of all evaluative responsibilities? Does this follow inevitably from social epistemology's basic claims? Most social epistemologists think not. For them, social epistemology is compatible with many of the normative, evaluative responsibilities traditionally understood to be the domain of epistemology. They argue, however, that normative questions about knowledge (e.g., "How ought we to arrive at our beliefs?") cannot be answered independently of descriptive ones (e.g., "How do we arrive at our beliefs?"). This is what Kornblith calls the *"replacement thesis" of social epistemology*—a thesis that rejects the view that the first type of question can be answered independently of the second. Kornblith goes on, however, to describe two different versions of this thesis. According to one version that Kornblith calls the "strong version," the first type of question dissolves entirely into the second. It has no validity except insofar as it is taken as the kind of question that descriptive psychological or sociological investigations on their own can answer. Kornblith argues that this first version essentially abandons the tasks of evaluating and justifying beliefs. The second version, which Kornblith calls the "weak version," however, does not. It holds questions of justification and evaluation to be important and avoids the naturalistic reductionism of the strong version. It simply argues that questions of justification and evaluation require consideration of the actual ways in which people arrive at their beliefs and thus proposes that the material circumstances of belief formation studied by empirical disciplines must be factored in when we go to answer normative epistemological questions. Kornblith summarizes the distinction between the two versions:

> The question at issue is the autonomy of epistemology. Are there legitimate epistemological questions that are distinct in content from the questions of descriptive psychology? Advocates of the strong version of the replacement thesis answer this question in the negative, advocates of the weak version answer in the affirmative. The consequences of the strong version of the replacement thesis for the study of epistemology are clear: epistemology must go the way of alchemy and be absorbed into another science. . . . If the weak replacement thesis is true, epistemologists need not fear that they will be replaced by descriptive psychologists.[13]

In the strong version, then, social epistemology is about putting aside the normative questions that epistemology traditionally investigates and replacing these questions with those that can be adequately answered by purely descriptive means. In the weak version, social epistemology involves not just describing the social and psychological processes by which beliefs and epistemic norms tend to emerge but also critically examining these processes.

Normative Social Epistemology

Naturally, it is the weak version of social epistemology that has been attractive to those philosophers interested in normatively evaluating the epistemic attitudes and habits that we may exercise as social beings. The interest of these *normative social epistemologists*, after all, is not just in describing these practices but in determining where they go astray. For Alcoff, for example, social epistemology is identifiable by two equally important concerns: "the need for a normative theory of knowledge that can offer an epistemic account of how evaluative distinctions between competing claims should (and can) be made, and the need for an account of knowledge that is self-conscious about the interconnections between knowledge, power, and desire."[14] Likewise, Miranda Fricker's highly influential project in *Epistemic Injustice* aims not just to describe how habits of interpretation and belief formation reflect power imbalances in a society but to identify the conditions necessary for just and responsible epistemic practice. Indeed, Fricker finds shortcomings in the "postmodernist spirit" that reduces reason to an effect of power while neglecting the normative task of helping to distinguish justified and unjustified epistemic practices.[15] Charles Mills makes a similar appeal when he argues that, rather than making such decisions on the basis of a distinction between rationally caused and socially caused beliefs, we should rely on "an internal distinction between different varieties of social causation, according to their likelihood of producing positive or negative epistemic consequences."[16]

How do social epistemologists conceive of the basis for such a distinction? Among the most popular approaches to the problem today are various types of what analytic philosophers call "internalism," which takes factors internal to epistemic agents (e.g., attitudes, habits of mind, ethical comportments) as the basis for determining the justifiability of a given belief.[17] Although the debate between "externalism" and "internalism" is relatively recent, the question of how essential factors internal to epistemic agents are for knowledge has long been considered by philosophers. It arises in several ways, for example, in the Platonic dialogues, most notably in the context of the exploration between knowledge and right opinion (e.g., *Meno* 97d). In contemporary epistemology, theories of pure internalism arise in response to problems perceived with pure externalism, that is, with the idea that things external to the epistemic agent (e.g., correspondence of their belief with objective facts or with evidence) are ultimately what matter in terms of determining the justification of their belief. Contemporary articulations of these problems recall the treatment of the problem in Plato's dialogues: internalists point out that it would be absurd to say that someone knows something when they have merely been lucky in guessing and that the very practice of critically examining our beliefs entails examining the strength of the justification that we possess for them.

While not all normative social epistemologies are internalist, internalism has a natural compatibility with social epistemology. Instead of grounding the evaluation of a claim on the extent to which it corresponds with a reality or body of evidence the access to which is always mediated by one's social and historical situation, internalism grounds evaluations in the processes going on within an epistemic subject, whatever their historical and social situation. One might say, for example, as virtue epistemologists do, that beliefs that one has arrived at through the exercise of epistemic virtues such as attentiveness, self-examination, concern for coherence, and intellectual courage are more justified than those one has arrived at without such virtues.[18] This internalist, virtue epistemological approach to determining the justifiability of claims is compatible with the idea that our reasoning is socially and historically situated. In this way, it offers an approach to normativity that pairs naturally with social epistemology.

One particularly popular form of virtue epistemology today is the one offered by epistemic justice theorists. Epistemic justice theorists argue that there are social habits that one may fall into that encourage them to either deny credibility to certain speakers (what Fricker calls "testimonial injustice") or exclude them from the process of meaning-making ("hermeneutical injustice") solely on account of their social position. These habits, they argue, harm us in our capacities as knowers. They cut us off from potentially important sources of knowledge. Importantly, epistemic justice theorists argue that these habits are ones that, for the most part, we fall into without intending any slight. As an example of hermeneutical injustice, Fricker describes the state of things before the concept of sexual harassment was developed. Before the development of the concept, one may have registered a co-worker's or one's own experience of a supervisor's unwelcome advances as nothing more than a slightly awkward, slightly embarrassing affair. For Fricker, to say that there was a hermeneutic injustice taking place in this situation is to say that there was "a lacuna where the name of a distinctive social experience should be"[19]—one that reflects the way that some are marginalized from collective processes of interpretation (what Fricker calls "hermeneutic marginalization").

Like other virtue epistemologists, epistemic justice theorists distinguish between those habits and attitudes that, when present in an epistemic agent, increase the justification of their beliefs and those that, when present, diminish justification. Formulated in this way, epistemic justice theory is clearly an internalist theory. José Medina describes, for example, various forms of epistemic vice that, when prevalent in a society, will severely limit the shared enterprise of reasoning within it. These vices include, for example, epistemic arrogance (the tendency to believe that what one has already considered regarding a topic is sufficient and needs no further examination or development), epistemic laziness (the tendency not to seek out any information that might complicate or raise questions regarding one's current understanding of a topic), and epistemic closed-mindedness (the tendency to hastily dismiss any accounts that challenge the sufficiency of one's understanding regarding a particular topic). These epistemic vices together and in relation to one another make up the condition of active ignorance—a way of actively contributing to one's ignorance on a topic in a way for which one is oneself, as an epistemic agent, partially responsible.

Epistemic justice theory's relationship to internalism is complicated, however. It differs from other virtue epistemologies in conceiving of epistemic vices as bound up with dysfunctional social relations. Epistemic vices do not happen in a vacuum; they have, in some sense, an external counterpart. They have, as Medina says, a systematic character, meaning that they are "produced by—and are at the same time productive within—a complex system of social relations and practices in which unfair disparities among groups are maintained."[20] Thus, to use the example of the epistemic vices just described, one is more likely to be epistemically arrogant, lazy, and close-minded about structural racism in a society if one belongs to a social class whose power would be unsettled by recognizing the practical importance of the many studies and testimonies of structural racism that exist today. One is more likely to fail in one's understanding when one clings to fore-conceptions that are narrow-sighted reflections of social power. Such analyses make epistemic justice theory a peculiar combination: a virtue epistemology with a distinctively critical character.

In truth, epistemic justice theorists are divided about whether one can formalize a set of epistemic virtues and vices that will permanently hold as normative criteria or whether these "internal" factors should be understood as having their ground in forms of social inequality that must be analyzed independently of the criteria. For some, determining whether a particular epistemic habit enables or is enabled by a system of social injustice constitutes the *entire* method by which we determine whether the habit is justified. Epistemic habits that emerge within societies where power relations encourage systematic forms of ignorance are *necessarily* unjustified. Justified beliefs are those, on the contrary, that emerge within a society where there are just social relations free of misrecognition and arbitrary social inequality. In this case, the analysis of social inequality constitutes what Catherine Elgin calls a "perfect procedural epistemology"[21] for determining the justifiability of one's epistemic habits. Some critical social epistemologists, however, offer an alternative to this perfect procedural approach by insisting that the justness of a given epistemic habit must itself be, in part, determined by consulting the normative ideals implicit in social epistemic practices, however unjust they may be. Medina offers a particularly strong version of this method. In *The Epistemology of Resistance*, he begins with concrete situations that appear plainly to be forms of epistemic injustice and attempts to deduce from these situations the normative ideals of good epistemic practice that have been violated in them. Medina sees this method as consistent with his commitment to "the priority of the nonideal." As he sees it, "The methodological commitment to the priority of the non-ideal is a commitment to the priority of real in-justices over ideal justice. If our normative theories should start where we are, in medias res, we should start our theorizing by reflecting on the details of the actual injustices that surround us, rather than by speculating about what perfect justice might be."[22] Medina's approach differs from the one previously described in that it does not make a formal ideal of social justice the single factor determining the justifiability of an epistemic practice. Rather than relying upon either a transcendental notion of understanding or of justice, Medina attempts to derive his idea of both from a reflection upon concrete instances of failure—of misunderstanding and injustice—and in this way to arrive at normative epistemic ideals. Moreover, his approach differs from that of a perfect procedural epistemology in that he does not claim at any point during these reflections to arrive at a perfect procedure for determining the justifiability of epistemic norms once and for all. His method corresponds instead to what Elgin calls an "imperfect procedural epistemology"—an epistemology that aims not at rules for arriving at certainty but that "construes justification as inherently provisional."[23] According to this approach, responsible epistemic practice cannot be formalized into a procedure that guarantees understanding if followed. It simply makes it more likely that understanding will occur. Being as self-aware as possible about the interconnections between knowledge and power and avoiding bad habits like epistemic arrogance are helpful forms of self-edification but they are no guarantee of understanding. They merely make the achievement of understanding more probable.[24]

For many normative social epistemologists, this version of internalism that regards epistemic virtues as indications of probable justification is a particularly comfortable one, as it allows them to maintain a specific sort of realist orientation that has been dominant in the field of analytic philosophy for over a century. This is an orientation that regards the targeted object of understanding as a reality that is beyond and ontologically separate from any means one has of grasping it. It is also an orientation that prefers to think about normativity in terms of achieving justification rather than truth. This orientation is reaffirmed when epistemic virtues are seen simply as indicators that the agent's belief is more *justified*, more *likely* to be true, than a belief held by one without these virtues. It is an orientation that is valued, in part, because it is regarded as indispensable for a commitment to fallibility. Many epistemologists interested in identifying dysfunctional forms of social cognition are attracted to this approach. While wanting to learn something about good epistemic practices from such dysfunctional cases, they refrain from drawing too perfect and too final an articulation of these ideals from any given case—ensuring that further exploration and discovery about reality is always possible. On this model, then, there is no reason to claim that the historical and social situation in which an attempt at understanding occurs discounts it from being knowledge. What matters is the epistemic virtue and vice demonstrated by the subject regardless of their historical or social situation. This is, thus, one way of affirming the social situatedness of epistemic agents while retaining a way of normatively evaluating their beliefs.

Let us recall why it is that some have considered this combination to be impossible. For many, epistemology is a search for what we can be certain about and the principles by which we can attain such certainty. It is a project launched in response to the challenge of skepticism that aims to determine what we can really know given the deep dependence of our thinking upon social customs. On this conception, the social epistemological turn appears to be problematic indeed. Instead of pursuing what can be known independently of a social and historical lifeworld, it resigns itself to describing social systems of belief formation. Instead of drawing conclusions about what can be known with certainty, it settles on what beliefs are justified given the normative ideals implicit in the epistemic practices of a community. For one who regards epistemology as an account of what can be known through purely cognitive means and without reliance on social customs, the social epistemological turn appears to be a clear retreat from the core aspirations of epistemology.

As we have seen, though, social epistemology need not entail an abandonment of epistemology. It is, however, at its heart, an attempt to reinterpret the field—to reimagine its meaning, parameters, and operations. As such, social epistemologists understand themselves to be reconceiving rather than denying the basis for evaluating the justifiability of claims. They hold that beliefs and epistemic norms acquired through social habituation are not inherently untrustworthy. They can certainly be problematic, but they are not categorically so. This starts to become apparent when we realize, first, just how much we rely upon others and what we share with others when we engage in reasoning. When we consider whether or not to accept a claim, we inevitably consider the degree to which it is coherent with those background beliefs that we possess on account of our socialization. While it is certainly possible to become locked into arbitrary, restrictive habits of interpretation, it is wrong to think that the particular social situation in which one finds oneself is necessarily an impediment to understanding. Since the social origin of a belief is not a reason to regard it as unjustified, we need, according to normative social epistemologists, a different measure for distinguishing justified and unjustified beliefs. Above all, social epistemologists claim, we must consider whether there are, in a person's reasoning, problematic habits that reflect distortions in the system of social cognition.

That we should be able to articulate the ideals that allow for such a distinction is not surprising though, since, as Tanesini's analysis of normative epistemic attitudes suggests, our embeddedness in social life gives rise not only to certain habits of interpretation but also to more reflexive and evaluative epistemic norms. These reflexive and evaluative norms are what allows us to reflect on and to critique our own epistemic habits—even those that are widely taken for granted in our societies. The capacity for such criticism naturally develops as we apply these norms in practice. Thus, while traditional epistemology is right to emphasize the importance of our capacity for critical reflection, social epistemologists help us to see how we come to develop this capacity naturally insofar as we are social beings and practical agents in the world.

In the final chapter, we will consider how understanding the social epistemological turn can provide greater clarity regarding the nature of the epistemological contributions of Gadamer's hermeneutics and why these contributions have often been overlooked. We will find important parallels between Gadamer's account of understanding and the social epistemological account of knowledge introduced in this chapter. We will also consider whether it suffices to think about Gadamer's hermeneutics as an internalist epistemology and how his hermeneutic account of truth problematizes the internalism upon which much normative social epistemology depends. First, though, it will be helpful to look more closely at another recent development in epistemology that, like social epistemology, attempts to take into account the way in which inquiry is socially and historically situated and thus parts ways from the transcendence model of knowing. In the next chapter, then, we will explore how the development of feminist epistemology provides further reason to rethink the traditional scope of epistemology and to reimagine understanding as it occurs for a socially and historically situated subject.

Chapter 5

Feminist Contributions to Social Epistemology

> It is not enough just to be more rigorously empirical in adjudicating such controversial knowledge claims with the expectation that biases that may have infected the "context of discovery" will be eradicated in the purifying processes of justification. Rather, the scope of epistemological investigation has to expand to merge with moral-political inquiry, acknowledging that "facts" are always infused with values, and that both facts and values are open to ongoing critical debate.
>
> —Lorraine Code, "Taking Subjectivity into Account," 42

Despite recent developments in epistemology explored in the last chapter, it is still quite common for claims of understanding that draw upon a social and historical situation to be regarded with suspicion. This is nowhere clearer than in those cases where members of a social group present a critical intervention into some prevailing discourse by reflecting on their experiences and their historical consciousness as a social group. One need only think about the backlash in the United States and elsewhere today against accounts (historical, legal, sociological, economic, biological, etc.) that draw in some way from recent developments in social consciousness. These include, for example, in the United States, attempts to tell the story of the nation-state in a way that does not assume the perspective of colonizers or slaveholders, attempts to think about constitutional law that do not hold the founding fathers to be infallible, attempts to gauge economic health in a way that gives due priority to the overall well-being of workers, attempts to understand sexuality in a way that does not take it as simply an effect of a reproductive drive, and so on. For many, both the fact that such accounts can be said to be motivated by the interests of some social group and the fact that some members of that group are situated in a way that makes them personally invested in their truth is enough to deny their validity. Regardless of whatever forms of warrant the arguments have, many dismiss them as idiosyncratic worldviews creeping into the established space of valid reasoning.

Although the interests of many social groups today are subjected to this sort of epistemic marginalization, this is nowhere clearer than in the treatment of arguments drawing from the historical-social situation of women, that is, in the treatment of feminist inquiry. There is, after all, a long, well-documented history of regarding women's interests in particular as merely private and not representative of general human interests. Relatedly, women have also long been regarded in various mythologies of gender as acting on the basis of emotion and personal attachments rather than reason.[1] For these reasons, it is common even today for those who engage in feminist inquiry to be undermined in their attempts to share their results and to argue for their validity. Where feminist inquiry appears in a context where the epistemic attitudes and interests they are challenging are already well established to the point of being invisible, the reaction to feminist inquiry tends to be especially hostile.[2] The attempt to introduce it as a form of reasoning in such spaces is, even today, often dismissed as an effect of the subject's socialization or their personal psychology and thus not as a form of reasoning that others are responsible for taking seriously. If, for example, one points out the troublesome history behind some part of a well-established social custom or argues that one's community as a whole might be better off replacing this custom with something else, one is likely to be laughed at and dismissed as an eccentric with whimsical ideas.

In this way, feminist argumentation is often regarded, as Sara Ahmed puts it, as "a removal from the world rather than engagement with the world."[3] Rather than being treated as a genuine, good-faith attempt to make sense of things, it is often dismissed as no more than the expression of a personal, idiosyncratic tendency—a dismissal that, when consistent, constitutes a form of "gaslighting."[4] Consider the following personal anecdote that Ahmed shares from her life to illustrate this point.

I remember one time we were talking over the family dinner table about the film *Kramer vs. Kramer*. I remember questioning how the mother is demonized. I make that point, that rather obvious feminist point, which is hard not to make once you have acquired a feminist tendency. And then: the noise, the noise! "Oh, you can't just let us enjoy this lovely sweet film"; "Oh, can't you see how special the relationship is between the father and the son, how cruel she is." "Oh, you are always looking for problems," and so on. Feminists: looking for problems. It is as if these problems are not there until you point them out; it is as if pointing them out makes them there. . . . You sense that an injustice follows pointing out an injustice. Another dinner ruined. So many dinners ruined.⁵

Many feminists are especially accustomed to their interpretations being treated in this way as nothing more than expressions of personal psychology or idiosyncratic interests. They are told that they are too sensitive or too angry, and that's why they think this way. They are told that they are paranoid, and that's why they notice things others do not. These are ways of denying their analysis real epistemic relevance. Treated as the effect of some particular emotional disposition or psychological condition, their attempts to expand understanding may be dismissed as having no legitimate role in honest, truth-seeking inquiry. Here gaslighting functions as ways of avoiding taking the feminist's analysis seriously as a claim to truth. In denying the contribution any real normative relevance, those who engage in this sort of dismissive behavior suggest that there is no reason to take seriously the feminist's remarks.

What results from this gaslighting is a kind of harm that is both social and epistemic. It produces, on the one hand, forms of social marginalization whereby those who undertake feminist inquiry are left out of the evolution of social rituals that give people a sense of belonging and that produce social bonds upon which one is often, at least in part, materially dependent. It produces, on top of this, epistemic injustice whereby such inquirers are harmed in their capacities as knowers and in which the community misses out on new insight.⁶ In not being recognized as making a valid contribution to the discussion, in being told that their interpretation is *just* a subjective and distorting take on reality that occurs as they turn away from things just as they are, these attempts to contribute to the broader development of understanding are subject to the sort of injustices with which, as we saw in the last chapter, Fricker and other epistemic justice theorists are concerned.

Epistemic justice theory is one of several projects within the broader movement of social epistemology that attempts to challenge, at the theoretical level, the epistemological assumptions on display in the sort of dismissive behavior just described. According to social epistemologists, one's understanding does not need to achieve "the view from nowhere" in order to be valid. Indeed, they argue, a significant portion of what we know comes from our immersion in a shared lifeworld and from research and inquiry that, in its design and execution, remains immersed in it. For social epistemologists, dependency on such know-how is not, in itself, a relevant basis for denying justification to a belief that emerges in these conditions or to the reasoning that leads one to it. This is not to say that all beliefs and forms of reasoning that emerge from any kind of social cognition are well justified. It's just that the social and embodied dimension of some cognition is not a valid basis upon which to deny it credibility. This realization, as we saw in the last chapter, gives rise to the project of normative social epistemology, which aims to examine other ways of distinguishing between legitimate and illegitimate forms of reasoning where the epistemic subject is reliant upon others and on inherited social forms of meaning.

While feminist inquiry continues to be dismissed by many in the broader sphere of public reasoning, it should be no surprise that feminist epistemology, the theoretical formulation and defense of feminist inquiry, has been at the forefront of normative social epistemology. Both are, after all, attempts to reconceive the process of understanding so that efforts to draw from one's experiences as an embodied and socially situated epistemic subject are not unduly marginalized. Moreover, many of the most significant publications in feminist epistemology immediately predate the most significant publications in social epistemology.[7] Just before the release of C. A. J. Coady's *Testimony: A Philosophy Study* (1992) and Frederick Schmitt's edited volume *Socializing Epistemology: The Social Dimensions of Knowledge* (1994), Sandra Harding published her highly influential study on *The Science Question in Feminism* (1987) and Donna Haraway her equally influential article "Situated Knowledges: The Science Question in Feminism and the Privilege of Partial Perspective" (1988). As these titles suggest, many early works in feminist epistemology emerged out of attempts to think about the role of social, historical, and political consciousness in the production of science. Grounded by a concrete set of political aspirations and concerns, feminist philosophy of science starting in the 1980s began to critique aspects of the model of scientific practice (e.g., its presumptive disinterestedness and ahistoricality) still largely taken for granted at the time even after Thomas Kuhn's *The Structure of Scientific Revolutions* (1962) and, importantly, began to formulate alternative concepts and models for scientific and epistemic practice in light of these critiques. Indeed, according to Frederick Schmitt, alongside naturalized epistemology, early feminist philosophy of science was one of the two most significant inspirations for the development of the social epistemological movement.[8]

Given the influence of British empiricism on the development of Anglo-American philosophy and of Quine's naturalized epistemology on the development of the predominantly Anglo-American tradition of social epistemology, feminist engagements with the philosophy of science have been particularly influential for the social epistemological turn. There were, however, important precursors to feminist philosophy of science to be found in earlier feminist theory. Already in *The Second Sex* (1949), Simone de Beauvoir explores the way in which one's experience being gendered in a gender-stratified society can encourage one to develop certain epistemic habits and not others. Beauvoir explains, for example, how being gendered as a woman in a highly patriarchal society discourages one, on the one hand, from noticing the way that many aspects of our world reflect the intentions of the historical human beings who have organized the world in particular ways and encourages one, on the other hand, to develop a more embodied, prereflective understanding of the mundane activities that go into shoring up the stability of many aspects of the social world.[9] In the 1970s, there was a good deal of attention within the popular feminist movement to the idea that our ways of thinking about the world can be affected by our gendered experience and, it was now argued, could also be reformed by becoming more critically aware of the gendered history of our epistemic habits. This was the theory underlying the well-known "consciousness-raising" activities in the movement during this time. In the early 1980s, several feminist theorists would start to formulate in more explicitly philosophical terms the theory underlying the concept of feminist consciousness. Notable among these contributions was Nancy Hartsock's formulation in the early 1980s of feminist standpoint theory, which, indebted to Marxist critical theory, explores the genesis of the "feminist standpoint" and its epistemic relevance as a tool for understanding aspects of social reality, and Sandra Bartky's "phenomenology of oppression," which presents consciousness of oppression, such as feminist consciousness, as an important source of understanding.[10] Beyond feminist philosophy of science, then, the feminist theoretical traditions of feminist phenomenology and feminist critical theory have also made significant contributions to understanding the epistemological relevance of gendered experience.

In this chapter, I want to consider how some of these works in feminist epistemology have contributed to the formulation of a theory of knowledge that does not unduly marginalize *situated* understanding, that is, understanding that draws from the experiences and interests of particular social groups. There have been several different attempts at such a formulation within feminist epistemology, and, as I will explain, these attempts have been of varying success. Echoing the neotraditionalist response to the critique of Enlightenment epistemology presented earlier (in chapter 2), some feminist theorists have conceived of membership within a social group as bestowing upon an epistemic subject a fixed, immutable set of epistemic norms that are entirely incommensurable with other social groups. By contrast, I want to argue on behalf of a version that conceives of the historical-social situation in which an epistemic subject is embedded as an opportunity for *interpretation* and to explore how we might gauge the validity of such interpretations. To do this, I will examine the way that the virtue epistemological account of normativity provides a way of accounting for the epistemic relevance of feminist inquiry as well as the significance that many ascribe to *comprehensiveness* in particular as an indicator of justification.

The Feminist Epistemological Concept of "Situated Knowledge"

Like hermeneutic phenomenologists and social epistemologists, feminist epistemologists take it that the ways in which we, as epistemic subjects, are situated in culture and history often affect how we tacitly make sense of things and do so in ways that are generally difficult to recognize. This claim has been axiomatic for feminist epistemology since its inception and, in this particular field, is referred to as the doctrine of "situated knowledge." It is what, for the feminist epistemologist, justifies the search for particular interests and perspectives, such as androcentrism, that shape inquiry in ways of which the epistemic subjects involved are usually unaware as well as the search for alternative interests and perspectives that may replace the problematic ones unearthed. Moreover, because it is difficult to become aware of how one's situation affects what one takes for granted in one's understanding, most feminist epistemologists interpret this doctrine to mean that an extra effort of some kind is necessary to help minimize the risk of failing to recognize the potential limits of the partial perspective built into one's tacit understanding.

The doctrine of situated knowledge has been central to feminist engagements with scientific inquiry. It underlies the arguments feminist theorists have presented against the notion that, when done properly, scientific inquiry is value-neutral and that it proceeds unconditioned by the social, historical, and political contexts in which research is designed, undertaken, and interpreted. One especially influential version of the situated knowledge doctrine is the version articulated by Donna Haraway in the abovementioned article "Situated Knowledges: The Science Question in Feminism and the Privilege of Partial Perspective." In the article, Haraway proposes a theory of knowing that is unconditionally perspectivist. She argues that all subjects in all of their attempts at understanding make sense of the world through a dynamic set of partial perspectives—perspectives she conceives of as interpretations and translations of reality. These interpretive perspectives are not the direct result of social group identity for Haraway (e.g., the direct result of identifying or being identified as a woman) but of a much more complex intersection of dynamic modes of embodiment and the particular things with which, through these various modes, we interact. Haraway argues that a naturalistic, ecological, systems-based approach to science requires that we understand any particular scientific inquiry as emerging from and reflecting the partial perspective that can be attained from intersecting conditions of this kind and that we actively seek out understanding from other situations, particularly those that we have reason to believe are subordinated by the interpretations that we generally take for granted. Haraway describes this sort of approach as "feminist science" and argues that this approach offers its own version of objectivity, one that "privileges contestation, deconstruction, passionate construction, webbed connections, and hope for transformation of systems of knowledge and ways of seeing"[11] and that is, thus, "about limited location and situated knowledge, not about transcendence and splitting of subject and object."[12] Haraway's doctrine of situated knowledge, then, is both a descriptive and a normative social epistemology. It posits that all initial orientations toward understanding are partial because it is impossible for an embodied, historical, socially situated agent to occupy all epistemically relevant situations at once, and it is normative because it lays out a program for the sciences through which they might avoid the problems that arise when a partial perspective is mistaken as an exhaustive and neutral account.

An earlier and slightly different iteration of the idea can be found in Sandra Harding's feminist philosophy of science to which Haraway is directly responding in her article. Picking up on insights into the social and historical character of science developed by Kuhn and others, Harding argues that each part of the scientific process can be conditioned in meaningful ways by the implicit meanings, values, and interests of those involved. While avoiding Haraway's theory of unconditional perspectivism, Harding argues that it is urgent to recognize that each step of scientific inquiry *can* be and often is situated in these ways. She points out that we typically think of science, when it is pursued in good faith, as transcending the normal social and historical conditions that characterize our everyday thinking and, in turn, understand it to be inherently neutral of values and political orientations. Harding argues, however, that this is a misguided and even dangerous presumption. For Harding, the presumption that real science is completely politically neutral can be just as problematic as explicit attempts to deploy science for ethically and politically nefarious purposes. This is because the presumption prevents us from recognizing instances where a particular set of values or interests has, rather than intruding into a preexisting scientific project, constituted the nature of that project and preliminarily determined the horizon of background assumptions, questions, and methods relevant to it. Consequently, the same harm comes from either allowing a scientific program to be suddenly redirected toward nefarious purposes or from failing to recognize the nefarious values and purposes that have constituted aspects of a scientific program from the very beginning. Yet the former is an easily recognizable error, while the latter is not. The error that is more difficult to recognize lies in what Harding calls "objectivism": "Objectivism defends and legitimates the institutions and practices through which the distortions and their often exploitative consequences are generated. It certifies as value-neutral, normal, natural, and therefore not political at all the policies and practices through which powerful groups can gain information and explanations that they need to advance their priorities."[13] In response to this problem of objectivism, Harding proposes that responsible scientific practice requires recognition of and reflection on the perspectives and interests that, because of their constitutive role, are likely to be taken for granted and left unquestioned.

For Harding, Haraway, and others,[14] the need for feminist research programs in science stems from this conception of responsible scientific practice and from the fact that many of the questions, concepts, and interests guiding scientific inquiry still bear the imprint of centuries of women's subordination. For these thinkers, it is rather simple. If we want to understand the world as fully and clearly as we can, we need to actively correct the androcentric biases that scientists today inherit from science past. It is not enough to have the sincere intention to proceed without this bias. What is needed are deliberate research programs that will go looking for the situated experiences out of which new questions, concepts, and evidence might emerge. It might involve, for example, seeing what new evidence comes to light when primatologists work with a concept of sexuality that does not assume that only intimate activities occurring during a female primate's ovulation period should count as "sexual activity"[15] or when social scientists work with a concept of divorce that centers on the separation of parental roles from spousal roles rather than the breaking up of a family.[16] A feminist research program in economics, on the other hand, might involve seeing how new aspects of economic and social stability come to light when we take into account the degree of compensation and support that those involved in reproductive labor, including childrearing, have in the society.[17] Such research projects are explicit attempts to reorient questions, concepts, and interpretive frameworks in order to catch sight of what is otherwise easily lost or obscured by the tacit forms of understanding currently operating in the discipline (e.g., in biology, behavioral science, or economics).

What sort of validity do the results of such critical reflections have? Does undergoing such a reflection mean that the questions and beliefs that emerge in response are guaranteed in their validity and that they need never be problematized themselves? For Harding, the answer is no. Undergoing such reflection does not mean that there will be no tacit understanding or prereflective orientation in the perspectives and interests that are left to guide us afterward. One must be willing to undergo this self-critique again when needed. The need for this vigilance is ongoing. Nevertheless, Harding argues that, despite the ongoing nature of this process, the understandings that emerge from it have an important form of validity. All else being equal, they are more justified than—or, as Harding sometimes puts it, "less false"—than those that do not. For Harding, then, validity clearly does not mean having the final and infallible word. As she states: "We do not have to be claiming to approximate the one true story about nature or social relations in order for it to make sense to argue that our account is less false than some specified set of competitors to it."[18] In the next two sections, we will examine more closely the theory of epistemic normativity that is implied here. First, though, let us consider another version of the situated knowledge doctrine that has occasionally appeared in feminist epistemology.

In their enthusiasm for reorienting inquiry toward a substantially different set of questions, concepts, and frameworks, some theorists interpret the task of feminist epistemology to involve identifying ways of understanding essential to women and substantially different, often opposite, from prevailing epistemic norms that they found to be androcentric. This sort of argument was especially popular in the 1980s and early 1990s and was buttressed by studies in psychoanalysis and developmental psychology that examined differences between the ways that boys and girls tend to develop. It was during this time that feminist care ethics, for example, developed as a new approach to moral theory—one that was, in part, explained as an attempt to examine morality as it appears to those who undergo the social and cognitive development typical of girls rather than tacitly privileging that typical of and expected of boys.[19] The epistemological analogue to such work was to be found in the work of Andrea Nye and Genevieve Lloyd. For Nye and Lloyd, important parts of the prevailing epistemic model, like the emphasis on science, logic, and reason, are androcentric in that they privilege what they regard as "masculine" epistemic norms that have historically served to epistemically marginalize women.[20] By laying bare the androcentric dimension of these norms, these theorists suggest, one then arrives at an alternative set of epistemic norms—norms that they regard as "feminine." These are then thought to provide an alternative *situation* from which inquiry can proceed, although, in this case, there is significantly less confidence that this situation is accessible to those immersed in the epistemic norms characteristic of "masculine" forms of development. On this version of the situated knowledge doctrine, then, feminist inquiry has primarily descriptive but quite limited normative relevance.[21] It is, like the strong version of social epistemology, an attempt to replace the search for truth with a story about how beliefs and even epistemic ideals differ from social group to social group. It provides a historical or developmental account to explain why different epistemic ideals seem to have more validity for certain social groups. It does not offer an argument for why any of these ideals *ought* to compel epistemic subjects in general.

Skepticism about Feminist Inquiry

Earlier, we considered some of the ways that feminist inquiry is marginalized in everyday social interactions. Often dismissed in this sphere as inquiry based on merely idiosyncratic interests and personal psychology, many learn to regard feminist inquiry early on as something that they can largely disregard in the process of developing their beliefs about the world. Put another way, they learn to treat feminist inquiry as having no normative relevance—no place in the search for truth. For some theorists, this attitude is not unjustified, as it manages to recognize, at some level, problems that they believe genuinely plague feminist epistemology and the forms of feminist inquiry it attempts to defend.

Susan Haack, for example, criticizes the general project of feminist epistemology on two fronts. First, she argues that the very concept is "designed to convey the idea that inquiry should be politicized,"[22] an idea that, for Haack, is a dangerous threat to honest inquiry. For Haack, one is not inquiring in good faith if one begins with commitments that will shape the direction of the investigation and what comes to light through it. Inquiry should begin from a position of complete openness—free of any kind of political bias. As she puts it:

> I would say that inquiry really is best advanced by people with a genuine desire to find out how things really are, who will be more persistent, less dogmatic, and more candid than sham reasoners seeking only to make a case for some foregone conclusion; except that, since it is a tautology that inquiry aims at the truth, the sham reasoner is not really engaged in inquiry at all. This should remind us that those who despair of honest inquiry cannot be in the truth-seeking business . . . they are in the propaganda business.[23]

For Haack, feminist epistemology is suspect in that it attempts to replace the universality and neutrality of scientific inquiry with an inquiry that is structured around a particular political interest. Honest inquiry, for Haack, depends on putting aside one's interests. Here Haack's criticism echoes the reactionary response of many on the right today who regard attempts to conduct research—historical, legal, biological, sociological, economic, and so on—on the basis of unduly marginalized interests as illicit interventions into a process that they consider neutral. Yet, as Harding argues, the force of this criticism rests on the validity of the assumption that the research methods and designs that feminist inquiry is poised to intervene on are, in fact, neutral with respect to political interests. The truth is, however, that research projects frequently reflect the situations in which the inquiring subjects were embedded early in the development of their research and in ways of which they and those who later engage in the project often remain unaware. While what comes to light through research is not completely bound by the possibilities set forth by the questions and interests of the original investigators, they can and often do constrain what such research can discover. Thus, for Harding, in understanding a particular body of research, one must consider whether there are interests that have played a constitutive role and yet do not appear to operate as any kind of "angle" or interest at all. The doctrine of situated knowledge, as Harding articulates it, just serves to remind us that such reflection is often necessary if we are not to be biased (or "closed") in ways of which we are unaware.

Haack's criticism of feminist epistemology, though, is not limited to a concern about the adulteration of neutral inquiry with political interests. She also criticizes feminist epistemology for trading the pursuit of truth for a description of how one particular social group understands things. When it is not advancing a theory on the basis of a particular political interest, she fears, feminist epistemology is advancing the idea that women have a distinctive "woman's way of knowing" that is generally foreign to and inaccessible to men. Haack regards this claim as a perversion of the goal of early feminists to demonstrate that women are not fundamentally different from men and that they are, in fact, just like them in every aspect that is essential to being human.[24] To suggest that attempts to understand are situated relative to different genders is, Haack fears, to give up on the pursuit of truth altogether. It is to replace the pursuit of truth with a description of how things appear within this or that closed horizon. This concern, we should recognize, is identical to that introduced in the earlier chapters in response to Gadamerian hermeneutics and to that introduced in the last chapter in response to the social epistemological turn. It is a concern that situating epistemology must necessarily entail abandoning normative epistemology.

To be sure, it is easy to sympathize with Haack's frustration in response to the arguments of Nye, Lloyd, and others that have taken the goal of feminist epistemology to be the articulation of ways of knowing that are specific to women. There are several problems with this version of feminist epistemology. First, even where different epistemic attitudes are, in fact, generally observable as broad, statistically significant patterns among men and women (which they sometimes are), it is nevertheless inductively problematic to reach conclusions about the *essential* characteristics of each gender on the sole basis of generalizations made from this difference. Broad, statistically significant differences between women's epistemic habits and men's epistemic habits may very well be an effect of social and economic arrangements that, though persistent, are attributable to some external, contingent set of causes. Second, to shore up these claims about different epistemic worldviews, these theorists often invoke a strictly binary concept of gender according to which a given epistemic practice must be considered either masculine or feminine—these two qualities being regarded as mutually exclusive. Although Haack's appeal to the putative virtue of gender-blindness appears much more questionable today,[25] her comments remind us that dividing humanity up into two genders that are thought to have completely opposed worldviews is an old habit that in itself warrants reorientation. Finally, versions of feminist epistemology that suggest that there is no way of deciding between what are determined to be incommensurable epistemic norms can indeed be said to undermine the normative relevance of feminist inquiry. If other genders cannot possibly grasp the epistemic habits purportedly essential to women's lives, then they could be no more transformed by the presentation of these habits than women, on this account, could be compelled by logic and science. Such applications of the situated knowledge doctrine run into serious trouble.

Is feminist epistemology really limited to such essentializing claims about women's epistemic habits and how they differ from men's, though? Must the social situations and the historical subjects from which feminist inquiry proceeds be understood as closed and unrelated horizons in this way—one perspective among others with which it stands in absolute opposition? One clue as to the insufficiency of this approach arises when we shift our way of conceiving of the "situation" relevant to feminist epistemology: from the way of thinking inherent to a social group (women) to the interests and other theoretical orientations that become clarified to socially embedded subjects through the development of a highly *interpretive* feminist consciousness. Let us explore in more depth, then, what it means to think about the historical-social situation out of which feminist inquiry emerges in this way.

The Interpretive Dimension of Feminist Consciousness

Feminist research, as we have seen, has been portrayed as the interruption of methodical forms of understanding caused by a prioritization of personal or political interests—a way of asserting one-sided subjective interests in a realm that should be neutral of particular interests and worldviews. According to this portrayal, feminist research is a set of preestablished answers in the guise of real inquiry. This impression seems even more plausible when feminist research is collectively undertaken, requiring that those participating solidify the interests, aims, and principles that will guide their research. Yet this collective and organized feminist inquiry is precisely what takes place at the level of culture when millions of people start to help one another to examine gender roles differently. It is also the kind of feminist inquiry that takes place at the institutional level when, for example, a group of researchers must coordinate and seek support for some feminist research project in, say, pharmacology or anthropology. Thus, despite its rigorous defense by epistemologists like Harding, the organized and institutionally supported feminist research most typical in the sciences can easily appear to casual observers to be a way of adulterating inquiry with idiosyncratic perspectives and dogmatic political interests. But is feminist inquiry really nothing more than an assertion of one group's subjective interests onto reality? To explore this question, let us leave behind for the moment the conversation in feminist philosophy of science and explore feminist inquiry at a more fundamental, phenomenological level.

Let us begin by considering the basic sort of experience—personal, embodied, prereflective—out of which feminist questions and feminist interests emerge. Feminist inquiry emerges with the development of an attunement that is oriented toward certain subject matters and alive to what we can learn about them. It is an attunement that encourages the development of questions and, through these questions, the development of certain forms of awareness (i.e., of the things that have historically led to the subordination of women, of the nature of this and related forms of injustice, and of the capacity we have in our human communities to challenge these injustices and reform the world accordingly). The basic experience of feminist inquiry, then, is not the application of a fixed worldview or a set of subjective interests but a living form of inquiry that takes place as people engage with the world in a reflective and questioning way. Sara Ahmed captures this point well when she writes:

> Living a feminist life does not mean adopting a set of ideals or norms of conduct, although it might mean asking ethical questions about how to live better in an unjust and unequal world (in a not-feminist and antifeminist world); how to create relationships with others that are more equal; how to find ways to support those who are not supported or are less supported by social systems; how to keep coming up against histories that have become concrete, histories that have become as solid as walls.[26]

On this conception, then, feminism is at its very heart a commitment to questioning in a way that is deeply engaged with and in constant reference to the lifeworld. A feminist is passionately committed to exploring theoretical and practical questions that are often, for them, genuine, personal, and urgent and to seeking out good answers to them. In this sense, feminist inquiry is truth-seeking inquiry oriented toward what is unfamiliar, which it makes an honest attempt to clarify. Yet here there is no pure separation between the questioning subject and the matter they wish to understand. The relationship between these two is, rather, an interpretive one. One finds oneself struck by parts of the social world in which one is immersed but that appear troublesome. The nature of the problem is familiar in one way but not another. It is familiar as a problem that one keeps running up against but also awaits elucidation through interpretation. Here one's life experiences play two roles in the inquiry. What one seeks to understand, on the one hand, belongs to the realm of one's life experiences, yet this elucidation also requires that one draw from one's experiences. In drawing from one's experiences, one does not simply apply them to the matter at hand in a way that overdetermines what will come to light. Rather, as Ahmed's remarks here suggest, the "text" of feminist experience lives in its interpretive application. Like a written law, one cannot understand it apart from its application. This is the hermeneutic circle that characterizes a feminist interpretation.

To put the point another way familiar to hermeneutic thinkers, feminist inquiry requires a way of understanding the part through the whole and the whole through the part. It requires that one attend to the concrete situations out of which questions and problems related to gender first appear, but it also requires that one strive for a more comprehensive understanding of these things by considering the broader patterns of social organization to which they belong. This part of feminist interpretation may involve, for example, recognizing the challenges that women around the world regularly face—from lack of reproductive autonomy to deflated wages to higher vulnerability to domestic abuse—as part of a pattern the enabling conditions of which can be understood.[27] In trying to reconstruct the whole of which these phenomena are parts, the feminist does not automatically chalk the phenomena up to instances of bad luck ("Her boss is just a jerk") or to the result of individual psychology ("She just isn't as ambitious as him"). They see the particular situation in terms of a general trend—not as a singular, chance event. They see the situation too as emerging out of causal conditions in the past—not as suddenly occurring in some historical void.

In her description of "feminist consciousness," Sandra Bartky describes in detail the development of this sort of interpretive comportment, arguing that it is this development that, above all, makes one a feminist. This is an interpretive comportment (or, as Bartky, puts it, "consciousness") that is not only attuned to questions and problems that emerge within concrete experience but to patterns of injustice. To be a feminist, for Bartky, is to be generally attuned to the world in this way. As Bartky puts it:

> Women have long lamented their condition, but a lament, pure and simple, need not be an expression of feminist consciousness. As long as their situation is apprehended as natural, inevitable, and inescapable, women's consciousness of themselves, no matter how alive to insult and inferiority, is not yet feminist consciousness. . . . Women workers who are not feminists know they receive unequal pay for equal work, but they may think that the arrangement is just; the feminist sees this situation as an instance of exploitation and an occasion for struggle. Feminists are no more aware of different things than other people; they are aware of the same things differently.[28]

For Bartky, it is the interpretive dimension of feminist consciousness—prior to and foundational for any project in feminist science—that makes it so epistemically valuable. This is because feminist consciousness allows one to begin recognizing certain things that would be difficult, if not impossible, to recognize without it. It reveals questions and connections otherwise hidden. This is one reason why it is such a transformative experience for the one who undergoes it. As the feminist becomes "aware of the same things differently," a number of things that one once found familiar and unremarkable start to appear conspicuous and questionable to one. This might include certain social customs, parts of the socioeconomic order, habits at home, commonplace behaviors at work, and so on. For example, someone who lives in a social community where marriage is taken to be one of the most important milestones in life and weddings among the most significant cultural events may find themselves more aware of the problems with these customs. When thinking about marriage, they might not be able to ignore the history of the institution and its connection to women's subordination. If they attend a wedding, they will have to exert a tremendous effort not to notice the parts of the ceremony that stem from a time where it was a legal transfer of a woman's person from one man to another man (e.g., the ritual of the father giving away the bride and the bride taking the name of the man, the virginal white of the wedding dress, the need for legal witnesses, and so on). Similarly, someone who grew up in a culture where a certain segment of the population is expected to perform significant reproductive labor that is unrecognized and leaves one especially vulnerable to abuse might have a harder time turning a blind eye to the ongoing exploitation of the earth's own reproductive resources and humanity's failure to replenish the earth in exchange for what it takes. What becomes conspicuous and which questions these things raise will vary to some degree, depending on the customs and institutions in which different people find themselves absorbed. In each case, though, the feminist is one who has become "aware of the same things differently." They are, like others, socially embedded in customs that they have learned to take for granted but, unlike many others, are also burdened with an awareness of how these customs belong to broad and historical patterns of subordination.

As I have described it, feminist consciousness is similar to a helpful concept developed by sociologist C. Wright Mills. Mills calls the "sociological imagination" the ability to situate personal biographical events in the context of larger social and historical processes. For Mills, sociological imagination is essential to understanding the world in which we live. In his words:

> Men do not usually define the troubles they endure in terms of historical change and institutional contradiction. The well-being they enjoy, they do not usually impute to the big ups and downs of the societies in which they live. Seldom aware of the intricate connection between the patterns of their own lives and the course of world history, ordinary men do not usually know what this connection means for the kinds of men they are becoming and for the kinds of history-making in which they might take part. They do not possess the quality of mind essential to grasp the interplay of man and society, of biography and history, of self and world.[29]

Feminist consciousness, the fundamental attunement out of which organized forms of feminist inquiry develop, grasps this interplay. Indeed, one of feminism's greatest accomplishments is its problematization of the traditional dichotomy between the personal and the political and the tendency to define the political (and normative) domain in opposition to that of private life. On this model, personal life affairs, particularly those associated with the domestic sphere, are not considered important matters for political concern, as they are considered merely private affairs. As Virginia Held has argued, this dichotomy, where it exists, is especially disempowering for women, as women have historically been regarded as having their natural place in the private realm, which according to this dichotomy is of no serious political concern.[30] In response to this, feminists in the twentieth century—particularly during the second wave—began to operate under the principle that "the personal is political." In so doing, feminists were, in effect, committing themselves to the ongoing development of the sociological imagination whereby they would recognize the interplay "of biography and history, of self and world." To grasp this interplay as a feminist came to mean, on the one hand, making sense of certain developments in one's family, one's community, and one's own personal life in terms of broader narratives about the history of gender. In turn, it entailed understanding these broader dynamics not as impersonal truths about the world but as pressing, personal issues for oneself and for others in one's life that one can begin to understand by *interpreting* the particular social and historical *situations* in which one finds oneself.

This account of feminist consciousness as interpretive, then, gives us a way of understanding the doctrine of situated knowledge that avoids some of the problems described earlier. On this account, the doctrine does not mean that every epistemic agent is limited to understanding only in terms of the epistemic habits and worldview specific to their social group nor that these worldviews are mutually exclusive. Although this account takes developing awareness of the limitations of one's current perspective as a virtue, it does not hold that it is impossible to improve one's understanding because one is locked into a closed system of beliefs and epistemic habits. Moreover, it carries forward an important tenet of the humanistic tradition, namely, that the things that touch us personally in our lives tend to send us on a quest for their meaning. In other words, it echoes that idea of understanding explored earlier within the context of Gadamer's thought, namely, as bringing clarity to what is already in some sense familiar.

So far in this chapter, we have explored how feminist inquiry is an engagement with the world oriented toward understanding and why it is, nevertheless, often denied epistemic relevance. We have seen how this denial emerges not only as a theoretical argument put forward by philosophers concerned with the encroachment upon epistemology by politically interested subjects but also as a more everyday habit within certain communities where feminists are subjected not only to hermeneutic but also social marginalization. These explorations should encourage us to take a second look at the reasons—implicit and explicit—for marginalizing feminist inquiry today. For many, feminist epistemology does not sincerely engage in the task of coming to knowledge, because it offers only a description of certain epistemic tendencies characteristic of a particular social group (women)—tendencies that have legitimacy only for this particular social group and not for anybody outside of it. So too, it is thought, does feminist inquiry play at best an ancillary role in the process of coming to know. That a number of people are struck with the importance of a particular question or concern related to gender in society does not mean, on this view, that this question or concern has an especially important role to play in the production of knowledge. At best, it may incidentally lead us to recognize evidence that we did not previously recognize. At worst, it may distract us from evidence by making it so that our observations are constantly mediated by a limited set of questions and concerns. As we have seen, though, this characterization misconstrues the genesis of feminist questions and concerns. It overlooks the way that these questions and concerns emerge not from some closed sphere of subjectivity but from a continual engagement with the world, that is, from an attempt to make sense of the phenomena that one encounters that are not reducible to unilateral effects of subjectivity. What is disclosed through the development of feminist consciousness, then, is not simply the effect of an isolated subjectivity, as the term *consciousness* might suggest. Another way to put this is in terms of what the account of feminist consciousness suggests about the nature of the "situated knower" that is misconstrued by the criticism. According to the account above, the knower is "situated" not in the sense that they are limited to the finite set of fore-conceptions into which they are socialized. They are situated in that their inquiry is bound up with social and historical conditions that are to be taken up in the interplay of interpretation that Mills describes as sociological imagination and Bartky describes as the development of feminist consciousness. It does not therefore make sense to deny epistemic relevance to what is disclosed by feminist consciousness on the grounds that it is subjective rather than objective, legitimate from the perspective of one social group but not others.

What can we say, though, more *positively* on behalf of the claim that feminist inquiry contributes to the pursuit of knowledge and leads to more justified beliefs? As with social epistemology, the argument that feminist epistemology provides for its normative relevance requires that we rethink what it is that makes a given claim or interpretation justified or true. In what follows, then, I examine an argument for the normative basis of feminist inquiry that naturally follows from this account of feminist consciousness.

The Epistemic Virtues of Feminist Inquiry

The virtue epistemological conception of normativity introduced in the previous chapter provides us with a natural way of understanding the normative basis of feminist inquiry. It is not only the case that feminist inquiry avoids the subjectivism that has on occasion been taken as the basis for denying it epistemic relevance. Insofar as it entails a number of positive epistemic virtues, on the virtue epistemological conception of normativity, the development of feminist consciousness plays a clearly positive role in our process of coming to know. Based on what we have come to understand about feminist consciousness, let us now consider some of the epistemic virtues that it entails.

Most of the epistemic habits that feminist consciousness entails will be readily recognized as epistemic virtues, that is, as habits internal to an epistemic subject that make the subject's beliefs justified. For example, feminist consciousness encourages one to ask tough but relevant questions. More specifically, it encourages one to track the development of questions (above all, about our habits and policies related to gender) where the conditions that make possible the posing of such questions have started to deteriorate. At an even more basic level, feminist consciousness also helps one to pay attention to things that one might otherwise overlook. It heightens one's awareness of phenomena near and far. Near are the phenomena in our personal lives that feminists pay attention to and try to explain but that otherwise tend to be regarded as the effect of merely personal preferences. Far are the phenomena taking place in various parts of the world not directly inhabited by the feminist subject that would otherwise tend to go unnoticed by most in their community. This heightened awareness of phenomena is, in part, a result of the feminist's attentiveness to certain patterns in human conduct and social organization that result in larger patterns of gender inequality. Yet, as we have seen, feminist consciousness is not about simply seeing the same thing everywhere. It is not about recognizing similarities to the detriment of recognizing relevant differences. Instead, it demonstrates the virtue of allowing new evidence to impact the patterns that are tracked.

Such habits of mind are easy enough to recognize as valuable epistemic habits, as they conform well, up to a certain point, with the epistemic norms of empiricism. They emphasize the importance of being attentive to new evidence issued from experience and of developing questions that can allow this new evidence to appear. They emphasize keeping theoretical and interpretive models flexible enough so as to respond to this evidence. In this, they map fairly well onto what we tend to think of today as good "critical thinking skills," remaining consistent with the norms of empiricism and its concomitant conception of the realities we investigate as existing independently of our biases. Appeal to such epistemic virtues and the concept of reality they imply is widespread in feminist epistemology. Lorraine Code, for example, argues that the doctrine of situated knowledge "is constrained by a realist, empiricist commitment according to which getting [the circumstances in which knowledge is produced] as right as possible is vital to effective action."[31] Haraway too insists on a feminist epistemology that demonstrates "a no-nonsense commitment to faithful accounts of a 'real' world."[32]

Not all of the epistemic virtues that feminist epistemologists consider important for the process of understanding, though, function in this way. Consider, after all, the value that some feminist epistemologists have put on striving for *the most comprehensive* possible understanding of a situation. While, for the traditional empiricist, the raw, unmediated facts one gains from experience have the highest epistemic credibility, feminist philosophers have argued repeatedly that there is something problematic about the tendency to accept any experience, observation, or data that an empirical study presents as the basis for its conclusion as a "given." As Harding puts it, the problem with such an approach "is not that it is too rigorous or too 'objectifying,' as some have argued, but that it is not rigorous or objectifying enough; it is too weak to accomplish even the goals for which it has been designed, let alone the more difficult projects called for by feminisms and other new social movements."[33] For Harding, an appeal to an immediate experience or fact has little epistemic credibility if removed from any consideration of the broader contexts of meaning to which it belongs.

What are these broader contexts of meaning? For Bartky, we have seen, these are dimensions of the lifeworld of which some fact or experience that one may encounter comprises a part. For Harding and others, getting a handle on the contexts of meaning through which a fact emerges requires not simply an account of those forms of social life that *causally* condition it but also the values and interests embedded in that lifeworld that serve as its anterior conditions. Achieving more comprehensive understanding can also mean, then, taking into account the way that a given discovery is conditioned by the questions we have become accustomed to asking and the discourse through which we have become accustomed to thinking about the topic. We may call these the "discursive conditions" of a given fact or experience. Helen Longino, for example, argues for the importance of recognizing the particular questions and values that tacitly shape either a given investigation or the evidence that emerges from it.[34] Like Harding, she argues that understanding is more justified when it takes into account the role that such discursive conditions play in what is "given" or discovered. In these ways, feminist epistemologists hold comprehensiveness to be an important criterion of justification. For these theorists, taking into account these conditioning factors does not mean doubting the validity of the inquiry, evidence, and so on that is conditioned but understanding it in a more comprehensive context.

Some theorists have argued that there are ways of being positioned within the social system of understanding that make one more likely to notice the role played by these contexts of meaning and thus more likely to develop a more comprehensive understanding of social reality as a whole. This is the way that feminist standpoint theorists understand the epistemic advantage of the development of feminist consciousness.[35] According to feminist standpoint theory, this form of consciousness tends toward more comprehensive forms of understanding, because it takes reality not as a static, ahistorical entity that can be captured in simple statements of fact but as the result of a process. This process is what feminist standpoint theorists using the theoretical framework of the Marxist tradition understand as the ongoing process of social production that organizes individual social relations in a particular way.[36] For Nancy Hartsock, the degree to which one's understanding is comprehensive of social reality as a whole is the most important measure of understanding. Quoting Lukács, Hartsock argues:

> Although it may be possible to describe an event without understanding it as part of a historical process, . . . "intelligibility of objects develops in proportion as we grasp their function in the totality to which they belong." The philosophical importance of the whole in giving meaning to the parts calls attention to the links between the facts as they are given to us and their mediated meaning, or put in a different way, to the links between their isolated meanings and their social significance. Indeed, it calls attention to their status as manifestations or expressions of the whole of social relations. It requires one treat "things"—even simple commodities—not as objects but as manifestations of the social relations of a society.[37]

In arguing that objects are intelligible to us "in proportion as we grasp their function in the totality to which they belong," Hartsock suggests that such contextualization is both necessary and sufficient for understanding. This is a stronger claim than most feminist epistemologists tend to make. Most feminist epistemologists, like most critical social epistemologists, conceive of critical reflection and critical contextualization as what Elgin calls an imperfect epistemological procedure. In other words, they conceive of the justificatory character of these processes in internalist terms. This is largely on account of the commitment that feminist epistemologists have to fallibilism and even to the fallibility of those theories of reality that emerge from a given critical reflection. What Hartsock's version of standpoint theory suggests, however, is that when it comes to objects of investigation that are bound up with larger processes of meaning, this mediation also characterizes the objects themselves. The objects, in themselves, are not immediate "givens." They are complex phenomena that bear the imprint of the questions, interests, and historical horizons of the epistemic subjects that have participated in them. As such, to understand them in this greater context is to understand them as they are objectively.[38] The dispute here is over the question of what exactly is gained epistemically as one develops a more comprehensive understanding of a given phenomenon. The dispute is grounded in a tension between internalist and externalist currents in feminist epistemology and, indeed, in critical social epistemology in general. We will return in the next chapter to consider whether this tension is irresolvable or whether Gadamerian hermeneutics might point to a possible resolution.

While this tension represents one question still very much in dispute among feminist epistemologists, its existence should not overshadow where there is an emerging consensus in the field. I have argued here that there is an emerging consensus among feminist epistemologists that the doctrine of situated knowledge does not entail an abandonment of normative epistemology. Like most other social epistemologists, feminist epistemologists offer an account of justification consistent with a theory of epistemic subjects as situated. This account, on the one hand, fits into the broader virtue epistemological approach introduced in the last chapter. Moreover, feminist epistemologists have argued effectively for the importance of a particular epistemic practice that is often overlooked by other virtue epistemologists, namely, that of understanding things in terms of the social conditions and contexts of meaning that set them forth. They have contributed, in other words, not only to the investigation of what it means to understand but to an examination of the general character of many of the things we seek to understand. In these ways, feminist epistemology helps further social epistemology's critical reflection upon the Enlightenment model of knowing, demonstrating how inquiry that emerges from socially and historically situated subjects contributes greatly to the advancement of understanding.

Chapter 6

Gadamer's Hermeneutic Conception of Understanding as Social Epistemology

> The normative image of human beings, which, however incomplete and vague, lies at the basis of all human social behavior, not only does not allow itself to be wholly eliminated in research but also should not be wholly eliminated.
>
> —Gadamer, "Theory, Technology, Praxis," 29

In the previous two chapters, we saw how important developments in epistemology in recent decades have contributed to an increased interest in the role that social and historical context play in the process of understanding. In highlighting the important role that these contexts play both in determining how we *tend to* arrive at beliefs and how we *should* arrive at them, social epistemologists and feminist epistemologists challenge the transcendence model of epistemology that first took root in the Enlightenment and that has been reinforced in new ways by technological rationality. Yet, as I have argued, there has been limited consensus among these movements about the extent to which they are meant to replace the classic targets of epistemology: justified belief, objectivity, normative evaluations, and so on. Certainly, many recently developed versions of epistemology—from Quine's naturalized epistemology to postmodern feminist epistemology—have argued for a shift away from these pursuits and have proposed to replace them with descriptions of how belief arises in particular conditions—natural or social. As we have seen, though, many involved in the development of these alternative epistemologies take the normative pursuits of traditional philosophy seriously and argue that things like objectivity and justified belief need not be abandoned in light of the increased awareness about the contexts in which belief formation takes place. Instead, they attempt to reconceive these traditional epistemological goals.

In this final chapter, I want to return to the anti-epistemological reading of Gadamer introduced in part 1 to consider how it fares when we start to look at Gadamer's hermeneutic account through the lens of the social epistemological turn. What I hope to demonstrate is that Gadamer's account of understanding is not a retreat from the search for truth or from the responsibility of justification but that it, like much of social epistemology, is an attempt to reconceive these important touchstones. In addition, I want to show how putting Gadamer's hermeneutics into dialogue with social epistemology can help shed light on internal debates within social epistemology and its feminist varieties explored in the previous two chapters. If I am right, and if Gadamer's revised concepts of objectivity, justification, and truth offer an improved and meaningful alternative to the technologically rational model of knowledge dominant today, then Gadamer's account of understanding may have an important role to play in helping us to appreciate the value of those forms of social and historical cognition that are obscured today by the dominance of technological rationality.

The Hermeneutic Fork

In part 1, we considered the anti-epistemological reading of Gadamer offered by Richard Rorty, John D. Caputo, and others. According to this reading, Gadamer's hermeneutic account of understanding should not be considered an epistemology because it does not attempt to determine the method by which we can arrive at certain knowledge and, in fact, offers an account of how attempts at such certainty fail. On this reading, Gadamer's point is that one who understands a text understands only what it says to them and to their time. One who understands a historical development understands only its meaning for the present. An interpretation sticks not when it is correct but simply when it coheres with the expectations and schemas that the interpreter brings to the hermeneutic encounter. On this reading, then, Gadamer's focus on the role that situated interpretation plays in the way we make sense of the world amounts to an argument for the impossibility of ever reaching truth, justification, objectivity, or normativity and an argument to replace these traditional epistemological targets with the humbler goals of self-edification and self-coherence.

In part 1, we explored some of the important dimensions of Gadamer's thought that such a reading overlooks. We saw how, for example, it fails to account for Gadamer's criticism of the immanence model. Gadamer's point is not that one must resign oneself to understanding only a version of truth that fits the parameters of one's or one's tradition's limited preconceptions, for the horizon in which understanding occurs is not fixed. As one applies preconceptions in the process of understanding, they become subject to revision. There is no reason, then, to think that Gadamer's attention to the role of fore-conceptions in the process of understanding is meant to indicate the limits of the truth or normativity that is yielded by that process. As we saw in part 1, then, the anti-epistemological reading of Gadamer misconstrues his account of interpretation by neglecting to acknowledge how, for Gadamer, interpretation can bring forth not merely a subjective construct but a subject matter in its truth. It presents Gadamer, instead, as a postmodern nominalist, overlooking the sort of realism that is to be found in his hermeneutics.

Having explored the rationale behind the social epistemological turn, we can now appreciate another way in which the anti-epistemological reading of Gadamer falls short, namely, in its narrow conception of epistemology. For it, all epistemology is Enlightenment epistemology, an enterprise that seeks to examine the conditions in which one can know with certainty that a claim is necessarily or objectively true. According to the anti-epistemological reading, epistemology as a whole considers reliance upon social norms or upon trust in others as reasons to doubt that one has achieved justified knowledge. Gadamer's hermeneutic account of understanding is certainly no epistemology in this sense and, indeed, it is on the basis of rejecting such an enterprise that he speaks in *Truth and Method* of "overcoming the epistemological problem" (TM, 244). What the anti-epistemological reading of Gadamer misses, though, is the extent to which the Enlightenment model has come under significant scrutiny by many epistemologists over the past several decades. Indeed, those who would exclude Gadamer's account of understanding from the domain of epistemology are typically begging the question of what counts as epistemology. Alcoff explains the nature of the mistake as follows:

Gadamer's arguments are often excluded from epistemology only because of an excessively narrow and dogmatic account of the necessary presuppositions for epistemology, and that this account ends up begging the question against Gadamer's counterarguments. That is, the fact that Gadamer's theory of understanding eschews method, correspondence, or an intrinsic conception of truth, meaning, and reality cannot mean that it is not a theory of knowledge at all, if Gadamer proposes alternative views about the nature of inquiry. . . . If we can define epistemology as a discipline that asks and answers questions about the possibility of knowledge, truth, and justified beliefs, and as a project that does not merely describe processes of inquiry but offers an evaluation of them, then it is clear that Gadamer does have an epistemology.[1]

Brice Wachterhauser offers a similar explanation of why Gadamer is so often excluded from the canon of philosophers who have made significant contributions to epistemology. While all hermeneutic theorists recognize that one's thinking is always mediated by traditions that one did not oneself author, they differ in how they conceive of the status of this mediation. For some, recognizing this point means that we must give up on traditional philosophical aspirations like, for example, reaching universal truth or holding truly justified beliefs that have normative force. For others, the upshot of this hermeneutic insight is the way it highlights the need to reconceive some of these traditional philosophical aspirations. As Wachterhauser puts it, "The hermeneutic fork divides those within the hermeneutical movement who think that hermeneutics, properly understood, implies the demise of traditional philosophy and those who do not. It is a difference between an essentially destructive, debunking program and a critical, constructive program."[2] Wachterhauser explains that Gadamer has often been interpreted as belonging to the first camp. The anti-epistemological reading of Gadamer interprets his hermeneutics as a debunking program that implies the demise of traditional philosophical pursuits. Recall that, in chapter 1, we encountered a couple of different versions of this argument. On the one hand, the argument comes from anti-epistemological thinkers like Richard Rorty, who considers epistemology as a whole misguided and regards Gadamerian hermeneutics as helpful for dislodging epistemology from what he regards as its undeservedly privileged position within philosophy.[3] On the other hand, one finds the anti-epistemological reading also advanced by theorists who are friendly to epistemology but who criticize Gadamer's hermeneutics for its neglect of fundamental epistemological responsibilities. According to Emilio Betti and E. D. Hirsch, for example, Gadamer's description of the process of understanding falls short in failing to account for truth and objectivity beyond interpretation and for how interpretive understanding might reach them if, as Gadamer suggests, it is always bound up with linguistic and historical preconceptions. If an act of understanding is mediated in this way, it simply cannot, on this view, give us the truth of the object.

As Wachterhauser points out, these readings that position Gadamer on the anti-epistemological side of the "hermeneutic fork" have been particularly influential. What many in the analytic philosophical tradition, for example, know about Gadamer's hermeneutics is what Rorty says about it. For such readers, Gadamer's hermeneutics is an attempt to shift philosophical concerns away from truth and knowledge. In part 1, I provided some reasons as to why I think this reading is mistaken. In what follows, I want to add to my criticism of the anti-epistemological reading by tracing out how the development of the social epistemological turn provides us with new ways of thinking about the epistemological dimensions of Gadamer's hermeneutics.

Gadamerian Hermeneutics as Social Epistemology

As the last two chapters have made clear, Gadamer is not alone in attempting to rethink the nature of understanding. In recent decades, social epistemologists and feminist epistemologists have been successful in getting a number of philosophers to rethink several aspects of the traditional model developed during the Enlightenment. Let us consider some of the ways in which their efforts parallel Gadamer's own interventions.

First, like Gadamer, social epistemologists have argued that immersion in a social-historical lifeworld is an irreducible part of our cognition, providing us with, among other things, a set of background beliefs and attitudes with which new understanding must cohere. As we saw in the last chapter, this idea is also central to the doctrine of situated knowledge developed by Sandra Harding, Donna Haraway, and other feminist epistemologists. Echoing Gadamer's critique of the "prejudice against prejudice," Harding argues that we must get out of the habit of thinking that it is only behind unjustified beliefs and bad science that we will find preconceptions and interests playing a constitutive role. For Harding, like Gadamer, preconceptions are a means not only of misunderstanding but of any understanding at all. While some feminist philosophers worry that Gadamer's stance on the inevitability of fore-conceptions is unnecessarily conservative in regarding tradition as impossible to escape,[4] many find recognition of their inevitability refreshing in light of longstanding feminist concerns about the way implicit biases can shape the context of discovery in research in ways that normally go unacknowledged. As Lorraine Code puts it:

> A central objective for feminist philosophers, theorists, and activists is to interrogate the androcentricity and other centricities that, often silently or covertly, inform and indeed saturate the Western social, intellectual, political, cultural order. Feminists need to know these centricities well if they are to achieve and enact transformative understandings. When prejudgments and the constitutive effects of situatedness are cloaked by a veil of unknowing, unacknowledged and/or systematically disavowed as this "prejudice against prejudice" requires, the intellectual labor of examining and contesting them is arduous indeed. Thus feminists can find cautious inspiration in the place prejudices and foreknowledge openly occupy in Gadamerian hermeneutics: they are *there* from the beginning, explicitly part of what any conversation, any understanding is about.[5]

Second, like Gadamerian hermeneutics, social epistemology has sought to reconcile this insight into the inevitability of fore-conceptions with some account of how it is that they can come to be modified. Gadamer, in fact, regards such modification as a necessary condition for understanding to take place. Where understanding occurs, Gadamer argues, some portion of a subject's fore-conceptions are put to the test and are revised, expanded, and developed in light of what they encounter. Gadamer therefore does not endorse the idea that, because fore-conceptions play an inevitable role in socially and historically situated acts of understanding, understanding is therefore inevitably confined to a fixed and finite horizon. His doctrine of the inevitability of fore-conceptions "does not mean that we are enclosed within a wall of prejudices" (PH, 9). Likewise, most social epistemologists who find value in acknowledging the constitutive role of implicit biases also in some way or another address how it is possible to revise these biases. Many feminist epistemologists, as we have seen, prescribe certain epistemic practices that facilitate the recognition and evaluation of hidden biases and interests. Harding, for example, proposes that, in order to bring to light and evaluate such hidden elements, one must make a conscious effort to "start one's thought, one's research project, from *outside* those conceptual schemes and the activities that generate them . . . from the lives excluded as origins of their design—from 'marginal lives.'"[6] Those who propose and engage in such strategies clearly do not imagine their own thought to be limited to the fore-conceptions that they expect to disrupt.

Harding's articulation of this practical and theoretical orientation makes clear a *third* point of similarity with Gadamer's hermeneutics. While Gadamer, for the most part, does not intend his philosophical hermeneutics to prescribe an orientation for research in the way that Harding intends, both argue that understanding requires, to some degree, that a subject undergoes a process of self-reflection whereby some of their fore-conceptions are revised or restructured to the point of seeming almost displaced. Gadamer describes, for example, how understanding a text or following along in conversation requires that one not simply apply one's fore-conceptions in a unidirectional way. One starts, for example, with an expectation of what will be said and how one will incorporate or respond to it; however, if one hopes to understand the text or the conversation, one must allow these expectations to be revised as they proceed. For Gadamer, then, understanding requires that some of these background expectations that initially enable the inquiry are put at risk. Similarly, Harding's proposal to generate research questions by starting from the standpoint of marginalized lives envisions a process of understanding that attempts to reorient itself by focusing on what has been historically marginalized. For Harding, as for Gadamer, this is seen as a necessary step toward ridding understanding of arbitrary omissions and, thus, toward making understanding more comprehensive. Such ongoing reorientation is especially valued by that portion of feminist theory for which ongoing critical self-reflection is paramount. Judith Butler, one of the most influential critical feminist theorists and a student of Gadamer's at Heidelberg, appeals often to the importance of ongoing critical self-reflection. As Butler envisions it, feminism not only begins with an attempt to shake up certain sedimented ideas and habits related to gender but evolves as the subject of feminist inquiry evolves and some of its own foundational preconceptions become revised and expanded.[7]

As this comparison suggests, Gadamerian hermeneutics has particular resonance with critical social epistemology, since the latter, more than other forms of social epistemology, emphasizes the importance of putting at risk many of the beliefs and attitudes one has by virtue of one's immersion in a social-historical lifeworld. Yet there are two points on which they would appear to differ. First, while critical social epistemologists would seem to consider revision of fore-conceptions necessary only in those cases where some socially rooted bias is obstructing further discovery, Gadamer seems to treat it as essential to any and all acts of understanding. To say, after all, that all understanding involves a "fusion of horizons" would seem to suggest that every act of understanding requires a critical revision of some set of fore-conceptions. On Gadamer's view, one is not really understanding a text if reading it prompts no reflection upon or revision of one's current beliefs, attitudes, or habits, that is, if it is only passively absorbed. In acts of genuine understanding, subjects rely on historical and social fore-conceptions to make sense of what they encounter but, at the same time, allow these fore-conceptions to be revised and expanded. Likewise, good interpretation strives both to understand the object's relevance to the present horizon of interpretation and to allow it to expand and defamiliarize parts of this horizon. Gadamer puts this at one point in terms of the way that understanding involves recovering a question within the horizon of the present. To understand a text, he explains, we must gain a sense for the question to which it offers an answer and appreciate it as a living question. "For the text must be understood as an answer to a real question" (TM, 382–83). Silja Freudenberger takes this argument to imply the claim that one is not justified in believing any set of claims that one has not subjected to this sort of reflexive questioning—a claim that she believes fails to account for how much scientific knowledge today depends on accepting and not retesting a substantial body of findings generated by scientists past.[8] Put another way, if Gadamer's argument is that one cannot claim to understand anything except that which one has reconstructed as a response to a living question, then this argument would seem to lie in some tension with the social epistemological axiom that one's own individual testing of claims is not a requirement for justified belief.

While it is tempting to imagine the testing of one's fore-conceptions as an activity undertaken by a subject who has, for the sake of epistemic responsibility, consciously and heroically suspended their reliance on social cognition, this neglects one of the most compelling parts of Gadamer's argument, namely, that it is usually at a prereflective level and as a normal part of the process of application that the critical revision of fore-conceptions takes place. While Freudenberger is right, then, that scientists must rely on a substantial set of theories developed by their colleagues in the past and cannot consciously set out to test and revise each of them, how exactly these theories are understood is something that we can expect to undergo revision over time. These revisions need not be consciously registered as deliberate revisions. This is why Gadamer prefers to think about such change as happening from within a single horizon.[9] Moreover, we should keep in mind that Gadamer's description of the fusion of horizons is not offered as a formal principle. It describes only what must occur in those cases when there is dissonance between fore-conception and object and not what must occur regardless of what shows up in the encounter. Insofar as we begin the journey of understanding (as individuals or as societies) as *ungebildet*, there will inevitably be much need for such revision. Yet we misunderstand the point if we think of this need for revision as a general, formal necessity. It is at least *possible* that attitudes and beliefs that one brings with one to examine a certain subject turn out to be completely adequate for understanding it and will be revised very little through their application. This is logically possible but extremely rare.[10] On the other hand, to the extent that what one seeks to understand contains dimensions not already accounted for by one's current fore-conceptions, understanding will require the revision and expansion of these fore-conceptions.

This leads us to a second significant point on which Gadamerian hermeneutics and social epistemology might appear to differ. While some readers have argued that Gadamer puts too much emphasis on critical reflection in the process of understanding, others argue that he does not emphasize this enough and is unnecessarily conservative in downplaying the limits of tradition and safeguarding it from any serious critique.[11] If this is the case, then, there would seem to be a tension between philosophical hermeneutics and any critical examination of the social process of understanding such as that found in feminist epistemology. We turn to consider this concern in the next section.

Rethinking Normativity with Gadamer

As we saw in chapter 4, one of the biggest challenges that social epistemologists have had to face since the development of the movement is the charge that the social epistemological turn amounts to an abandonment of normative criteria. According to this charge, if we accept the social epistemological account of understanding, it seems that we have no way of distinguishing between better and worse, correct and incorrect claims. Since the publication of *Truth and Method*, a number of commentators have made the same criticism of Gadamer, arguing that, because Gadamerian hermeneutics cannot furnish such evaluative criteria, it lacks a properly epistemological dimension. These concerns, which make up part of the anti-epistemological reading of Gadamer, come from two main directions: those who say that Gadamer gives no real attention to subjectivity—viewing any individual interpretation as lacking any reality ontologically separate from the object being interpreted, and those, on the other hand, who say that his account of understanding implies a pure subjectivism. The first amounts to a concern that his account would leave no room for comparing competing interpretations or critically evaluating them, since all interpretations would be ontologically inseparable from the matter at hand. The second concern is that, on his account, any understanding that occurs is, at best, only compelling for a particular subject with a given set of historical preconceptions and is thus not true in a universal sense. One of the first and most influential articulations of the second criticism came from a theorist introduced in part 1, Emilio Betti. For Betti, Gadamer's hermeneutics does not provide a reliable criterion to make such evaluative distinctions. Instead, it "enables a substantive agreement between text and reader . . . to be formed without, however, guaranteeing the correctness of understanding," adding that, for this, "it would be necessary that the understanding arrived at corresponded fully to the meaning underlying the text as an objectivation of mind."[12] According to Betti, Gadamer makes some attempt to address the basis for normativity but fails, since coherence is not a sufficient criterion for making normative distinctions. For Betti, one needs above all a way of measuring an interpretation's correspondence with reality. Karl-Otto Apel expresses similar concerns about a neglect of normativity in Gadamer's hermeneutics, arguing that it "made something like a normatively controlled progress in understanding appear totally inconceivable."[13] In place of Gadamerian hermeneutics, Apel calls for a normatively and methodologically relevant hermeneutic that would allow us to distinguish between better and worse interpretations.

    A number of more recent commentators have renewed these concerns about the fate of normativity in Gadamer's hermeneutics, arguing that Gadamer's hermeneutics is irreconcilable with the normative tasks of epistemology. Michael Forster, for example, argues that Gadamer's argument for the formative role of preconceptions in inquiry problematically implies that historical situatedness is "epistemically insurmountable, that it is impossible to abstract from one's own specific pre-understanding."[14] For Forster, while this insight might therefore be helpful as a description of what happens in certain interpretive contexts such as taking in a performance or listening to a conversation, it falls short of explaining the phenomenon of understanding in its specifically normative dimension. Like Forster, Kristin Gjesdal argues that the normative dimension of the German philosophical tradition is derailed with Gadamer and twentieth-century hermeneutics. Gjesdal focuses mostly on the first of the two concerns about normativity in Gadamer's hermeneutics described above. The mistake, as she sees it, lies in Gadamer's insistence on the ontological unity of the situation in which inquiry takes place and the object of inquiry—a commitment that prevents him from recognizing the possibility of critiquing fore-conceptions and of arriving at reliable normative criteria. We will turn soon to consider the question of what, if any, general normative criteria for judgment can be distilled from Gadamer's hermeneutics. First, though, let us consider the claim that Gadamer's hermeneutics neglects the importance of critical reflection.

For Gjesdal, Gadamer "systematically denounces the relevance of critical reflection to the hermeneutic enterprise."[15] Is it really the case that recognizing the historical and social situatedness of inquiry entails neglecting the role of critique in understanding, though? As we saw in chapter 4, for most social epistemologists, the answer is no. It is simply that the ground of critique must be reimagined. What the above comparison with social epistemology makes clear is that Gadamerian hermeneutics offers a similar response to the challenge. It is not that there is no basis for critical reflection, fallibility, or evaluative distinctions among interpretations in Gadamer's theory of understanding. It is just that, as Gadamer demonstrates, it is not necessary to deny the situatedness of inquiry in order to account for these important phenomena. We have already seen the way in which Gadamer's theory of interpretive understanding allows for evaluative distinctions and recognizes interpretations as fallible—important components of what we might call *hermeneutic normativity*. Let us say more about how Gadamer conceives of the critical and reflexive dimension of understanding, though, since, just as in the case of social epistemology, Gadamerian hermeneutics has at times been presented as undervaluing the importance of a critical relationship to tradition.

Recall that social epistemologists argue that one needn't remove oneself from systems of social cognition in order to critically revise them. Likewise, for Gadamer, one does not need to stand outside of one's historical situation in order to encounter something that brings aspects of one's present horizon into question. While, for Gadamer, attempts at understanding always take place within historical situations, this should not be understood in terms of a one-way causality, where the interpreting subject is simply the effect of a given set of social norms. What takes place in the application of social norms or preconceptions is a more reflexive, bidirectional process for Gadamer. As a community relies on historical consciousness to make sense of different moments in the past, that historical consciousness changes and develops over time.

As we saw in chapter 2, Gadamer understands tradition in a similar way. As tradition is carried forward over time, it is inevitably applied in a series of new concrete circumstances, and it develops through these applications. In Hegelian terms, a tradition is an instance of concrete universality: it operates as a universal only insofar as it evolves through its actual applications.[16] Wachterhauser explains this crucial point in terms of the way that traditions persist through ongoing ad hoc revision:

> We belong to history (or tradition) long before it belongs to us, says Gadamer. Such traditions of inquiry form and shape us as epistemic agents long before we can even begin to turn around and shape them. . . . Nevertheless, when we do "turn around" and begin to act on the traditions that have formed us, this is still a significant act of freedom. One way to illustrate both this dependence on tradition and our freedom within it is to remind ourselves that one of the most common ways in which a tradition evolves is by the ad hoc revision of the norms that constitute the tradition itself. Such revisions show us how better to capture the goal of the norm itself in the particular epistemic context in which we happen to find ourselves.[17]

If one overlooks this aspect of Gadamer's account of tradition, then it would be easy to conclude that his account entails that, because it is always embedded in a tradition, understanding cannot engage in serious critical reflection. This is the conclusion drawn by Forster and Gjesdal in their criticisms of Gadamer, each of whom neglects the way in which Gadamer views traditions as horizons in development.

A comparison with social epistemology on this point can be instructive, however. After all, there is a significant point of affinity here between Gadamer's argument for the ever-evolving norms that constitute a tradition and the social epistemological analysis of normative ideals as explored in chapter 4. Influenced by the turn to naturalized epistemology, social epistemologists take seriously the way that we come to acquire beliefs and habits of epistemic reasoning through processes of socialization. While some fear that this means that, as reasoners, we are always just imitating epistemic norms in a rote, mechanical way, others like Alessandra Tanesini argue that the application of such learned habits in the course of our lives requires more than rote imitation. It requires judgment and thus the ad hoc revision of these norms as they are applied in the concrete circumstances that one faces as an epistemic agent.

Yet Betti and other critics worry that the claim that understanding happens through application reduces understanding to the effect of purely subjective associations. Any development in understanding, on this view, would then be a purely one-sided development—a development entirely within the subject. We have already seen how the tradition of hermeneutic realism, with its emphasis on the referentiality of understanding, debunks this criticism. Also helpful here is David Liakos's argument about the distinctive character of what he calls "hermeneutical application," which he argues requires both "first-person" and "third-person" comportments.[18] Liakos's argument for the necessity of both components echoes the argument presented in chapter 1 about the personal dimension of understanding and why the presence of this dimension does not mean that an act of understanding is merely subjective. Moreover, his use of the terms *first-person* and *third-person* is quite helpful here in capturing a common internalist intuition about what an interpretation needs to possess in order to be justified or epistemically responsible, namely, that it must show openness and diligence in examining the matter at hand by putting some of one's fore-conceptions at risk. The idea that a good interpretation has a third-person orientation captures this ideal more precisely than the more familiar externalist notion that the most relevant normative criterion consists in correspondence with evidence or facts. In hermeneutical interpretation, then, it is not that the first-person dimension is irrelevant (as it is in what Liakos calls "objectifying application"); it is only that it requires a third-person comportment as well. There is certainly a mediation that occurs in understanding a law, a text, or a part of history. However, Liakos explains, "this mediation must always respond to and draw upon the actual content of the target of understanding. To be sure, these statements cannot be divorced from their historical effects. But the item of interpretation nevertheless stands over and against us and issues its claim to meaning."[19] If this is right, then the hermeneutic application of one's social and historical fore-conceptions is not unlike what happens with the application of feminist consciousness as described in the previous chapter. Each is a way of engaging the world such that one's horizon is being regularly transformed through that engagement.

Does this resolve Apel's concern about the need to recognize progress in understanding, though? If ad hoc revision is built into the hermeneutical applications that are a regular feature of our everyday understanding, then it does not seem as though the presence of such revision could itself provide a criterion for distinguishing between better and worse, more and less legitimate interpretations. Horizons are regularly undergoing ad hoc revision as they are applied to new contexts of understanding, and, as we saw in chapter 2, for Gadamer, this applies to those horizons that we call "traditions." Yet not all attempts to understand by fusing horizons are equal. If we want to be able to compare the strength of attempts at understanding, we will need another criterion. In those cases where what we seek to understand is the "effective history" of a text, historical event, and so on, though, the answer cannot be a purely externalist criterion, since what we seek to understand in such cases is not incidentally related to our own social-historical horizon.

In light of this problem, let us recall Alcoff's procedural argument for coherence explored earlier in chapter 2. According to Alcoff's argument, an act of understanding can be evaluated by considering the extent to which it projects relevant ideas from the contemporary lifeworld but is also able to adjust these ideas when they either fail to cohere themselves or fail to make sense of the object as a coherent whole. Recall Alcoff's example of how, in order to understand the Martian in the garden, we must rely on our background fore-conceptions to project a coherent meaning for the things the Martian points to and, as we are given further opportunities to clarify the creature's meaning, must refine and correct our initial projection. As Alcoff explains, one is unsuccessful in one's attempt to understand if either, after seeing the Martian point at a couple of things, one arrives at a final, definitive verdict on what the Martian means or if one hastily concludes that the Martian's attempt to communicate is unintelligible. Likewise, understanding a whole essay by finding a few passages and, on their basis, either regarding the essay as nonsensical or as saying only what is already predictable or evident for us amounts to a very low grade of understanding. In such cases, the encounter does not bring to light what is questionable or in need of refinement about the current horizon but reinforces its self-evidence. The object either coheres with it or is unintelligible. In both cases, understanding proceeds from a social-historical lifeworld and looks to make sense of the object from within this horizon, but the orientation toward the lifeworld is different in these two cases. For one, the lifeworld is that understanding which always emerges from and yet is constantly tasked with elucidating and refining. Conversation, reading, and the like are, for this sort of understanding, opportunities for *Bildung* and *Selbstbildung*. For the other, these encounters are ways of receiving information to be filed into and processed through the ideas and customs that are already at hand.

The procedural argument for coherence explains the benchmarks we are striving for when we try to understand something and that we employ in order to distinguish between better and worse attempts at understanding. To put it in the internalist terms used by value epistemologists, it identifies those epistemic habits and attitudes that one may adopt that make it more likely for their interpretation to be successful. Gadamer tells us, for example, that it is "constantly necessary to guard against overhastily assimilating the past to our own expectations of meaning" and that we must always try, on the contrary, to "listen to tradition in a way that permits it to make its own meaning heard" (TM, 316). As Cynthia Nielsen and David Utsler have argued, such attitudes effectively function as epistemic virtues for Gadamer, providing, as they say, "an orientation toward the other that facilitates an occasion for one's prejudices to be challenged so that they might be corrected and one's understanding expanded."[20]

From Justified Belief to Truth

With this comparison to internalism in mind, one might think that Gadamer would speak more in terms of "justification" than "truth"—for example, justified rather than true interpretations and justified rather than true applications. Yet Gadamer does not hesitate to call interpretations that meet these criteria "true," and, as we saw in chapter 3, truth is one of the most important concepts in *Truth and Method*. We might think that the language of "true" is more appropriate for those philosophers with an externalist epistemology who use it to describe the correspondence of a proposition or a propositional belief with some external reality. For Gadamer, though, one who approaches the matter at hand in a way that maximizes comprehensive coherence is doing more than following good epistemic protocol for arriving at justified beliefs. Successful interpretation does not just make it more *probable* that one might think on the matter at hand without distortion. It is not simply more justified. Such interpretation is, instead, an occurrence of truth itself. The mediation that occurs in successful interpretation, Gadamer says, "lets the true meaning of the object emerge fully" (TM, 309).

Here is where, I think, we start to see the limits of the comparison between Gadamerian hermeneutics and internalist forms of normative social epistemology such as epistemic justice theory. As I argued in chapter 4, the latter preserves a firm ontological separation between understanding and truth, regarding a given attempt to understand as only more or less likely to get at the immediate truth that is, for an undistorted cognition, there to behold. Gadamer, however, questions the very need to begin with this separation.

As we have seen, Gadamer's insight here is that, in most cases, what we want to understand is not something totally indifferent to our interpretive horizons. When we go to understand a written law or a historical event, what we go to understand is its "effective history"—the meaning that it has for us today. Likewise, when we understand what is being said in a conversation, what we understand is not just the hidden intentions and private associations of our interlocutors but what is being said in the conversation. Thus, as Gadamer puts it, "what is so understood is not the Thou but the truth of what the Thou says to us . . . the truth that becomes visible to me only through the Thou, and only by letting myself be told something by it" (TM, xxii). While understanding always occurs in a situated way, for Gadamer, then, his version of this theory does not posit truth as some *Ding an sich* always just beyond what becomes concretized through human understanding. It regards as "true" those attempts to understand that achieve success in interpretation in the way just described and as "truth" the entire development of interpretation as it unfolds through such attempts. As we saw in chapter 3, this aspect of Gadamer's theory of truth is indebted to Hegel's idea of truth as the way a universal becomes concretized through *Bildung*—an idea that he credits with helping him to think the basic experience of hermeneutics.[21] In this way, Gadamer does not abandon the concept of truth but argues that it must be rethought as something that actually occurs through increasingly comprehensive events of human understanding.

This argument about the nature of truth is largely neglected in epistemology even after the social epistemological turn. As we have seen, most social epistemologists argue that ethical epistemological principles must be taken into consideration when determining the justifiability of a given system of social cognition. For many, such principles constitute at best, though, an imperfect procedure of justification. They function primarily to indicate where some form of epistemic justice is preventing us from gathering or taking seriously information about the world, particularly information offered by testimony. One who does not critically reflect on how their understanding of a topic may be mediated by aspects of their particular social and historical situation is, on this view, more likely to be looking at the topic in an overly narrow way and is more likely to hold unjustified beliefs. While this approach takes seriously the way that understanding is historically mediated, it falls short of assigning to such events of mediation a truly positive, necessary role in the process of understanding. For Gadamer, by contrast, these events of mediation are essential to the way understanding must unfold. Accordingly, the alternative that Gadamer provides is one that assigns more weight to historical, social, and linguistic situations, as it is through these situations that true understanding is able to develop.

Now this contrast I am drawing may appear quite controversial in light of the places where Gadamer presents what is achieved through interpretive understanding as a *qualified* success in some sense. Gadamer says, for example, with regard to the hermeneutic situation that we find ourselves in: "The illumination of this situation—reflection on effective history—can never be completely achieved; yet the fact that it cannot be completed is due not to a deficiency in reflection but to the essence of the historical being that we are. *To be historically means that knowledge of oneself can never be complete*" (TM, 312–13). The last sentence of the passage would seem to suggest that hermeneutics is, above all else, about the finitude of human understanding. Yet Gadamer cautions us not to see a deficiency here. As I read it, the comment reminds us not to measure what emerges from the process of understanding by comparing it to some "god's eye view." After all, Gadamer criticizes this ideal of completely unsituated knowing throughout his work.

A Gadamerian Theory of Hermeneutic Demarginalization

With the above contrast in mind, let us return to consider a question that arises in critical social epistemology regarding the ideal of striving for the most comprehensive possible account of social reality and the role of resolving forms of hermeneutical injustice in working toward this ideal. Let us now see what light might be shed by examining this question with the aid of Gadamer's theory of the process of understanding. Recall that hermeneutical injustice occurs when members of some disadvantaged group are prevented from contributing to the process by which the interpretation of some part of social experience is generated, that is, when they are hermeneutically "marginalized." Recall that, for Fricker, to qualify as hermeneutic marginalization, their exclusion from interpretation of this part of social experience cannot be random but must be on account of some specific form of political disempowerment generated by some kind of systemic inequality. This kind of exclusion is evident, for example, in the situation where, prior to the development of the concept of sexual harassment, one finds oneself at a loss for ways to effectively communicate about routinely receiving unwanted sexual advances by a supervisor in one's workplace. Hermeneutic marginalization can also occur when discourse on a social experience is constituted in such a way as to exclude certain possibilities because of their potential disruption of forms of social inequality. Take, for example, the collective hermeneutical resources we have for understanding experiences of sexual violation. Currently, these resources direct us to understand such experiences in terms of certain dichotomies determined largely by the punitive interests of the criminal justice system and, to a lesser extent, civil courts—for example, to describe the interaction as strictly consensual or strictly nonconsensual, to regard it as either criminalizable rape or entirely ethically unproblematic. As such, experiences of sexual violation that are not easily described in such terms tend not to factor much into how we as a society think about the kinds of harm that can occur in sexual interactions or about the way that sexual interactions can be affected by power relations. Here too, then, there is "a lacuna where the name of a distinctive social experience should be"[22]—one that constitutes an injustice for those who, in the face of the lacuna, are less capable of making sense of and advocating on behalf of their experiences.

Now, while all critical social epistemologists agree that identifying such sites of hermeneutic marginalization is important, there is less agreement on what exactly occurs in and is gained by identifying and resolving such marginalization. Fricker distances her own position on this question from the classic version of standpoint theory as formulated by Nancy Hartsock, for whom the *only* way of truly understanding social realities is through the resolution of systemic hermeneutic marginalization. Following the process ontology characteristic of the Hegelian-Marxist tradition, Hartsock argues that, in order to understand a given social reality, one must reconstruct those interpretations of it that help to make sense of that reality's total constitution but that, for ideological reasons, are excluded or considered inessential. For Hartsock, these exclusions are not incidental to the reality that we seek to understand, since true understanding occurs through their remediation.[23] By contrast, for Fricker, this process of remediation—even if consistently pursued—is not necessary for true understanding. Such corrections are, for Fricker and epistemic justice theorists, epistemologically but not ontologically significant.[24] They remove a bias but do not provide any positive clue into the phenomenon we wish to understand. To say that they do, Fricker worries, is to overstate what is gained from the practice of critiquing forms of hermeneutic marginalization.[25]

Fricker is not alone in her concerns about the ontological weight that standpoint theorists ascribe to corrections of hermeneutic marginalization. Indeed, for most feminist epistemologists, to address the systemically marginalized interpretations of social reality is to engage in what, following Catherine Elgin, we referred to in chapter 4 as an "imperfect epistemological procedure." Put simply, it is to move the needle in the right direction. It is a way of arriving at *more justified* beliefs about that reality, where justification is understood in purely internalist terms. One who has negated the undue marginalization of certain interpretations, on this view, has managed to achieve a subjective condition more amenable to understanding the social reality at hand. For Harding, recall, it is in this sense that we can speak about what results from the practice of demarginalizing interpretations not as "the one true story about nature or social relations" but as "less false" than what results without such demarginalization.[26] Haraway too resists drawing ontological conclusions from what is disclosed through such demarginalization, echoing Harding's words of caution that what is achieved should not be considered the "one true story." For Haraway, achieving the "one true story" is neither possible nor desirable. Rather, she argues, the aim of feminist epistemology should be to encourage ongoing critical reflection on the conditions in which inquiry takes place so that, as an epistemic subject, one has done one's due diligence to minimize the chance that the inquiry is unduly constrained by any number of powerful biases. It is this version of standpoint theory—as the methodology of an ongoing critical practice—that Haraway endorses. In her words: "There is no single feminist standpoint because our maps require too many dimensions for that metaphor to ground our visions. But the feminist standpoint theorist's goal of an epistemology and politics of engaged, accountable positioning remains eminently potent."[27]

Harding and Haraway, like many feminist epistemologists, set out very specifically to avoid offering an account of situated knowledge that amounts to a version of relativism. They embrace the task of normative epistemology and in no way limit their arguments, as some feminist theorists have previously, to descriptions of "women's ways of knowing."[28] At the same time, like most other critical social epistemologists, they tend to remind us of the ultimately provisional character of even our most demarginalized theories and, on account of this, to conceive of these theories as justified on the basis of the reflective epistemic practices that have led to them. While some acknowledge the importance of striving for *comprehensive* understanding, those feminist epistemologists whose concerns focus mostly on epistemic practices in the sciences tend instead to argue for methodological principles and epistemic virtues that grant one's understanding, on internalist grounds, richer justification. Yet one might wonder if it is necessary in this case to treat the results of demarginalizing interpretations as having only subjective validity in this way or if, on the other hand, there might be some less qualified sense in which to describe what is disclosed through demarginalizing interpretation as *true*.

Based on what I have argued here and in chapter 3, I contend that Gadamerian hermeneutics can offer such a conception. For Gadamer, critical reflection upon fore-conceptions is not just a formal method that one consciously takes up to rid oneself of bias so that one can better grasp reality. Where we recognize the inadequacy of some fore-conception for understanding the matter at hand, such reflection is an integral moment in the truth of the subject matter itself. This was the theory of truth gleaned from Gadamer's treatment of the ontology of art in chapter 3. For Gadamer, the truth that unfolds in the work of art always takes place as an experience of recognition within an audience. In recognizing what is presented in the artwork, some portion of the audience's fore-conceptions must be revised and expanded. As Gadamer says, what is presented—be it the subject of a portrait or the story enacted on the stage—"manifests itself as what it is only when it is recognized. As recognized, it is grasped in its essence" (TM, 114). On Gadamer's account, then, the truth that comes to presentation in such hermeneutic encounters is an event that refers to and corrects something that the spectator already knows.[29] The correction that occurs and the horizon in which it occurs belongs to the horizon of the subject matter itself. As in classic standpoint theory, here too the correction has both epistemic and ontological relevance.

Does this claim, however, entail that there is no need for further examination of the subject matter? Does it imply that the correction in fore-conceptions that the spectator undergoes leaves them finally with the "one true story" in such a way that discourages further reflection? These are, after all, the worries that some feminist epistemologists have expressed about treating the process of demarginalization as a perfect epistemological procedure. In Gadamer's theory, though, the fact that truth occurs at such sites of correction does not imply that what is disclosed at any one of these sites has the final word. As I have argued (in chapter 3), for Gadamer, truth has a twofold meaning. It refers, on the one hand, to what emerges determinately and concretely at the moment where a fusion of horizons takes place and, on the other hand, to the unfolding of such moments in the larger development of history and thought. We thus say that an excellent interpretation of a text is true in the fusion of horizons it enacts but not that no other fusions are in order. The interpretation itself may well one day start to appear to readers as quite narrow, and, in this case, it will then be important—regardless of how canonical it has become—to put the account that it offers at risk so as to demarginalize aspects of the text that have become conspicuous. It is with the latter possibility in mind that Gadamer says that "the discovery of the true meaning of a text or work of art is never finished" but "is in fact an infinite process" (TM, 309). Yet, for Gadamer, to engage in this process means nothing less than "understanding what is there" (TM, 279).

I have argued in this chapter that Gadamer's philosophical hermeneutics offers an account of what it means to understand that parallels in many ways descriptions of the phenomenon offered by social epistemology. Rather than conceiving of understanding as a transcendence of one's historical and social lifeworld, Gadamer's account is one that affirms the social and historical situation of epistemic subjects. Indeed, while Gadamer does not refrain from attempting to describe the experience and the task of understanding as it appears to individuals, understanding is ultimately, for Gadamer, a development of self-recognition within historical consciousness. Insofar as we are accustomed to thinking about attempts at understanding as discrete, individual efforts to grasp an objective reality unrelated to any fore-conceptions, Gadamer's emphasis on the role of self-recognition in understanding will strike us as strange. Yet, as I have tried to demonstrate throughout this book, it is also an account that helps us to make sense of a very familiar dimension of everyday human existence. In the vast majority of cases, what we find ourselves striving to understand is not something completely unfamiliar and new but something that is already meaningful within the shared lifeworld to which we belong. We become curious because we want to know more about the world to which we belong. Social epistemologists, too, argue that the majority of what we come to understand about the world comes from social cognition—whether it is our reliance on background concepts that we possess through our sociality to interpret new information or our consulting of normative ideals implicit in learned epistemic habits. Like social epistemologists, Gadamer is aware of the fact that such attempts to conceive of understanding as situated will seem problematic to those who take the Enlightenment model of epistemology as the only viable model. Moreover, both have had to respond to the concern that situating understanding in any kind of social or historical consciousness entails epistemological relativism or, at the very least, that it denies that account of reality that we must necessarily take recourse to if we are to critique and evaluate the fore-conceptions that we bring with us as social and historical subjects. On this point, I have argued that there is a striking concordance between the social epistemological claim that there is a reflexive relationship between normative ideals and their application in the know-how of an epistemic subject and Gadamer's argument that the preservation of a tradition or any sort of historical horizon requires that it be cultivated and transformed as it is applied. While the exercise of this sort of critical capacity does not itself guarantee the legitimacy of revised judgments and habits that it yields, it does present a powerful challenge to the assumption that the beliefs and habits that one possesses in part by virtue of one's immersion in a social form of life are necessarily uncritical.

While there is a growing consensus that social epistemology cannot be merely descriptive but must also address normative questions and concerns, there is much debate still on how to do this. Some see forms of virtue epistemology as best suited to provide a new ground for normative distinctions while others argue that what is of foremost importance is securing an objective account of social totality that can be referred to in gauging the degree to which a given account has achieved comprehensiveness. These are, of course, just a couple of the responses generated to the challenge so far. As the normative dimension of social epistemology continues to be developed and refined, those working in the field or in closely related fields like feminist epistemology should find Gadamerian hermeneutics helpful on certain points. While there are many other philosophers to turn to in order to better understand the power relations that give rise to problems like gaslighting and hermeneutic marginalization, I have suggested that Gadamer's hermeneutic theory of truth can be helpful in making clear why any society that affirms the need for ongoing critical self-reflection in order to avoid such problems should understand itself as a society committed to the pursuit of truth.

There are some philosophers today and even some readers of Gadamer who are content to move on from the terms *truth* and *knowledge*. Ours is, however, not a social-historical situation that permits us to abandon these terms. I mean this in two ways. First, these terms continue to have a powerful persuasive effect on people in the twenty-first century—a power that is, unfortunately, often abused. Strategically, those who would prefer a world where knowledge is understood to be what human beings achieve together, as an evolving historical consciousness, through a shared exploration of their world rather than a presentation of fact immune to any historical contextualization or critical questioning would do well not to abandon these terms. As a Gadamerian, though, I do not think that our obligation to these words is solely strategic. For Gadamer, the language that is passed down to us connects us to a history that we have no choice but to engage if we are to understand our present. Gadamer recounts a message that he used to tell students to help them develop this appreciation for the relevance of the language that we inherit. "You must sharpen your ear, you must realize that when you take a word in your mouth, you have not taken up some arbitrary tool which can be thrown in a corner if it doesn't do the job, but you are committed to a line of thought that comes from afar and reaches out beyond you" (TM, 574). Even if there were not strategic reasons for wanting to bring more clarity to the nature of truth and knowledge today, concern for them is rooted in our linguistic, which is to say, our historical being. It is out of this sincere commitment to acknowledging and engaging our intellectual tradition that Gadamer embarks on the inquiry into understanding that lies at the heart of his project of philosophical hermeneutics.

Notes

Introduction

1. Lorraine Code, "Taking Subjectivity into Account," in *Rhetorical Spaces: Essays on Gendered Location* (New York: Routledge, 1995), 29.

2. Hans-Georg Gadamer, *Truth and Method*, trans. Joel Weinsheimer and Donald G. Marshall (London: Bloomsbury, 2013), 308. [Hereafter abbreviated parenthetically as TM.]

3. John Caputo invokes a distinction along these lines when he presents *Truth and Method* as ontological rather than epistemological in its orientation. "For Gadamer hermeneutics is not an epistemological-methodological inquiry but an ontological inquiry into being and truth." John D. Caputo, "Gadamer and the Postmodern Mind," in *The Gadamerian Mind*, ed. Theodore George and Gert-Jan van der Heiden (London: Routledge, 2022), 436.

4. Likewise, in the foreword that Gadamer writes for the second edition, he clarifies that, in writing *Truth and Method*, he "did not intend to produce a manual for guiding understanding in the manner of earlier hermeneutics" (TM, xxv).

5. Gadamer acknowledges the criticisms of the work published by Apel and Betti in the foreword he writes for the second edition.

6. Michael Forster, *German Philosophy of Language: From Schlegel to Hegel and Beyond* (Oxford: Oxford University Press, 2011), 312.

7. Rorty continues, "What metaphysicians call moving closer to the true nature of an object nominalists call inventing a discourse in which new predicates are attributed to the thing previously identified by old predicates, and then making these new attributions cohere with the older ones in ways that save the phenomena." Richard Rorty, "Being That Can Be Understood Is Language," in *Gadamer's Repercussions: Reconsidering Philosophical Hermeneutics*, ed. Bruce Krajewski (Berkeley: University of California Press, 2004), 24.

8. Gadamer cautions that one cannot simply consult the self-understanding of the human sciences as a means of discovering the sense of truth and knowing

at issue in them (TM, 91). This is, in large part, because of the influence that the model of the natural sciences has had on these areas of inquiry.

9. Linda Martín Alcoff refers to these two arguments as Gadamer's "procedural argument for coherence" and his "ontological argument for coherence." Linda Martín Alcoff, *Real Knowing: New Versions of the Coherence Theory* (Ithaca, NY: Cornell University Press), 47.

10. Frederick Schmitt defines social epistemology as "the conceptual and normative study of the relevance of social relations, roles, interests, and institutions to knowledge." Frederick F. Schmitt, "Socializing Epistemology: An Introduction through Two Sample Issues," in *Socializing Epistemology: The Social Dimensions of Knowledge*, ed. Frederick F. Schmitt (Lanham, MD: Rowman & Littlefield, 1994), 1.

11. It is not quite right to present feminist epistemology as a separate tradition from social epistemology, since, as Frederick Schmitt argues, feminist epistemology, specifically feminist philosophy of science in the 1980s, was one of two primary inspirations (alongside Quine's naturalized epistemology) for the development of the broader movement of social epistemology at the end of the twentieth century. Nevertheless, because feminist epistemology focuses especially on how understanding is mediated by gender roles and the historical traditions they carry with them and social epistemology is not defined by such a focus, and because the readership of feminist epistemology and of social epistemology have only partial overlap, I refer to them separately throughout the book.

12. Sandra Harding, *The Science Question in Feminism* (Ithaca, NY: Cornell University Press, 1986), 137.

13. Gadamer describes these two tendencies and the need for an alternative to them in his essay "Theory, Technology, and Praxis." He writes there that, in the face of the progress of technology, humanity "vacillates between the extremes of an affect-laden opposition to rational innovation and a no less affect-laden craving to 'rationalize' all forms and sectors of life, a development which more and more acquires the form of a panic flight from freedom." Hans-Georg Gadamer, "Theory, Technology, Praxis," in *The Enigma of Health: The Art of Healing in a Scientific Age* (Stanford, CA: Stanford University Press, 1996), 24.

Chapter 1

1. Martin Heidegger, *Being and Time*, trans. John Macquarrie and Edward Robinson (New York: Harper & Row, 1962), 190–91.

2. Martin Heidegger, "Phenomenological Interpretations with Respect to Aristotle: Indication of the Hermeneutical Situation," trans. Michael Baur, *Man and World* 25 (1992): 358.

3. For a helpful discussion of this point as it emerges out of Heidegger's engagement with Aristotle and as it informs the development of Gadamer's

hermeneutics, see James Risser, *Hermeneutics and the Voice of the Other: Re-reading Gadamer's Philosophical Hermeneutics* (Albany: State University of New York Press, 1997), 40–49.

4. I borrow the distinction between existential and transcendental phenomenology from Hubert Dreyfus's *Being-in-the-World: A Commentary on Being and Time, Division I* (Cambridge, MA: MIT Press, 1991).

5. See Catherine Zuckert, "Hermeneutics in Practice: Gadamer on Ancient Philosophy," in *The Cambridge Companion to Gadamer*, ed. Robert J. Dostal (Cambridge: Cambridge University Press, 2002), 201–24 and Carlo DaVia, "The Role of Aristotle in Gadamer's Work," in *The Gadamerian Mind*, ed. Theodore George and Gert-Jan van der Heiden (London: Routledge, 2022), 207–20.

6. While Heidegger presents the fore-structure of the understanding in *Being and Time* as manifest in three closely related modalities (*Vorhabe*, *Vorsicht*, and *Vorbegriff*), Gadamer tends to use one term, *Vorurteil*, to capture the same idea. Nevertheless, it is clear that he intends by *Vorurteil* what Heidegger has in mind in his articulation of the fore-structure of the understanding. To avoid the possible confusion caused by switching among these terms, I will primarily use the term *fore-conception* to refer to the general set of things that are apprehended in advance in interpretation and as a translation of Gadamer's term *Vorurteil*. It is important to keep in mind, however, that neither Heidegger nor Gadamer takes the ways that we engage in the world through anticipatory projections to be primarily a matter of mental representation. For both Gadamer and Heidegger, feeling and embodied know-how are also forms of understanding characterized by anticipatory projection. Thus, while I use the term *fore-conception* throughout the book, I recognize that the choice is an imperfect one. On the problems created by thinking about understanding primarily in terms of mental representation and on the place of Gadamer's work in the history of this problem, see Alexis Shotwell, *Knowing Otherwise: Race, Gender, and Implicit Understanding* (University Park: Pennsylvania State University Press, 2011).

7. It should be noted that, in some significant ways, Heidegger later abandons his early interest in the hermeneutics of facticity. Gadamer studied under Heidegger during Heidegger's early years in Marburg and Freiburg, however, and it was this early period of Heidegger's thought that interested Gadamer most and that was most influential for the development of his thought. William McNeill gives an account of Heidegger's turn away from existential phenomenology and the hermeneutics of facticity in the later part of his career in his recent book *The Fate of Phenomenology: Heidegger's Legacy* (Lanham, MD: Rowman & Littlefield, 2020).

8. Gadamer conceives of the hermeneutic relevance of "situation" as follows:

> We define the concept of "situation" by saying that it represents a standpoint that limits the possibility of vision. Hence essential to the concept of situation is the concept of "horizon." The horizon is

the range of vision that includes everything that can be seen from a particular vantage point. Applying this to the thinking mind, we speak of narrowness of horizon, of the possible expansion of horizon, of the opening up of new horizons, and so forth. . . . The task of historical understanding also involves acquiring historical horizon, so that what we are trying to understand can be seen in its true dimensions. (TM, 313)

    9. Georgia Warnke, *Gadamer: Hermeneutics, Tradition, and Reason* (Stanford, CA: Stanford University Press, 1987), 19.

    10. Emilio Betti, "Hermeneutics as the General Methodology of the *Geisteswissenschaften*," in *Contemporary Hermeneutics: Hermeneutics as Method, Philosophy, and Critique*, ed. Josef Bleicher (London: Routledge & Kegan Paul, 1980), 83.

    11. Betti, "Hermeneutics," 79.

    12. Betti, 78.

    13. Hans-Georg Gadamer, *Philosophical Hermeneutics* (Berkeley: University of California Press, 1967), 57. [Hereafter abbreviated parenthetically as PH.]

    14. Friedrich Schleiermacher, "General Theory and Art of Interpretation" in *The Hermeneutics Reader*, ed. Kurt Mueller-Vollmer (New York: Continuum, 1985), 74.

    15. Schleiermacher, "General Theory," 75.

    16. Günter Figal, *Objectivity: The Hermeneutical and Philosophy*, trans. Theodore George (Albany: State University of New York Press), 64.

    17. This theory of textual interpretation has its analogue in intentionalist theories of legal interpretation according to which the meaning of a law lies in the author's intended meaning. For a discussion of intentionalism in legal interpretation, see Ralf Poscher, "Hermeneutics, Jurisprudence, and Law," in *The Routledge Companion to Hermeneutics*, ed. Jeff Malpas and Hans-Helmuth Gander (London: Routledge, 2014), 451–65.

    18. Richard Rorty, *Philosophy and the Mirror of Nature* (Princeton, NJ: Princeton University Press, 1978).

    19. Rorty, *Philosophy*, 373.

    20. Caputo laments that "Gadamer has no taste for this destruction of metaphysics. His thought operates within fundamentally traditional constraints, although he has had the good sense to loosen their death grip and give them historical, contextual flexibility. He offers us the most liberal possible version of a fundamentally conservative idea. He allows as much movement and play as will not disrupt the ageless truths of the tradition or cause it too much difficulty." John D. Caputo, *Radical Hermeneutics: Repetition, Deconstruction, and the Hermeneutic Project* (Bloomington: Indiana University Press, 1987), 115.

    21. Caputo, *Radical Hermeneutics*, 113.

22. Caputo, 6.
23.

Gadamer refines the Hegelian thesis by insisting on the indefinite plurality of moves which the unchanging truth can make. For a while we take him to be on the side of movement, as indeed he is, up to a point. But at that critical point he bails out on us, invoking the doctrines of recollection and mediation, the age-old narcotics of metaphysics designed to let us sleep through the thunderstorm, to curb our restlessness, and assures us that it is always the same eternal truth which is on the move. (Caputo, 112)

24. I should mention that, in his recent *Hermeneutics: Facts and Interpretation in the Age of Information* (published in 2018), Caputo is less concerned to leave behind the discourse of truth than he was in *Radical Hermeneutics*. Likewise, he is less interested in critiquing the "metaphysics of truth" in Gadamer's thought and more interested in presenting the way Gadamer and other hermeneutic thinkers are rethinking truth and objectivity. When I refer in this book to Caputo's thought as an important contribution to postmodern hermeneutics, I am referring to the argument he presents in his *Radical Hermeneutics*.

25. According to the banking concept of education, "the scope of action allowed to the student extends only as far as receiving, filing, and storing the deposits" of information by teachers. Paolo Freire, *Pedagogy of the Oppressed* (New York: Continuum, 2000), 74.

26. Shaun Gallagher, *Hermeneutics and Education* (Albany: State University of New York Press, 1992), 187.

27. For another helpful analysis of the hermeneutic dimensions of education, see Paul Fairfield, "Dialogue in the Classroom," in *Education, Dialogue, and Hermeneutics*, ed. Paul Fairfield (New York: Bloomsbury, 2011), 77–89.

Chapter 2

1. To be precise, Gadamer's argument in *Truth and Method* is that this reflection is requisite in the human sciences (*Geisteswissenschaften*) and intrinsic to all objects taken up in these fields but not requisite for making certain discoveries in the natural sciences (*Naturwissenschaften*) (TM, 295). This does not mean that, for Gadamer, it is never appropriate or important to reflect on the historical situation of scientific inquiry but that there is an epistemic value of inquiry in the natural sciences that is distinct from the epistemic value of inquiry in the human sciences. While Gadamer prefers in *Truth and Method* to treat these two types of research separately, it should be noted that there is no formal

method for determining when an object of inquiry belongs to the domain of the natural sciences or the human sciences, and Gadamer does not shy away from bringing humanistic inquiry to bear on matters where competency is thought to lie exclusively with the natural sciences. This is the case, for example, throughout the later essays published in *The Enigma of Health: The Art of Healing in a Scientific Age* (Stanford, CA: Stanford University Press, 1996).

2. Gadamer takes this formulation directly from Heidegger's description of the hermeneutic circle in *Being and Time*. Heidegger writes, "In the circle is hidden a positive possibility of the most primordial kind of knowing. To be sure, we genuinely take hold of this possibility only when, in our interpretation, we have understood that our first, last, and constant task is never to allow our for-having, fore-sight, and fore-conception to be presented to us by fancies and popular conceptions, but rather to make the scientific theme secure *by working out these fore-structures in terms of the things themselves*" (emphasis added). Martin Heidegger, *Being and Time*, trans. John Macquarrie and Edward Robinson (New York: Harper& Row, 1962), 195.

3. Linda Martín Alcoff, *Real Knowing: New Versions of the Coherence Theory* (Ithaca, NY: Cornell University Press, 1996), 50.

4. For a detailed examination of the role of address in the hermeneutic conception of understanding and of its ethical dimension, see James Risser, *Hermeneutics and the Voice of the Other: Re-reading Gadamer's Philosophical Hermeneutics* (Albany: State University of New York Press, 1997) and Theodore George, *The Responsibility to Understand* (Edinburgh: Edinburgh University Press, 2020).

5. The hermeneutic circle, Gadamer claims, "is not formal in nature. It is neither subjective nor objective, but describes understanding as the interplay of the movement of tradition and the movement of the interpreter" (TM, 305).

6. Alcoff identifies both a "procedural argument for coherence" and an "ontological argument for coherence" in Gadamer's philosophical hermeneutics. According to the latter, coherence of horizons is a condition for any hermeneutic encounter whatsoever. The ontological argument therefore does not present coherence as a criterion for evaluating interpretations. Alcoff points out, however, that alongside the ontological argument, Gadamer also provides a procedural argument for coherence, and it is this argument that contains normative criteria for evaluating interpretations. See Alcoff, *Real Knowing*, 46.

7. Alcoff, *Real Knowing*, 47.

8. This form of justification will be unsatisfactory to one whose standard of justification is certainty. For a helpful explanation of why this form of justification is nevertheless epistemically valuable and even more valuable than the measure of certainty invoked by skeptics, see Brice Wachterhauser, "Getting It Right: Relativism, Realism, and Truth," in *The Cambridge Companion to Gadamer*, ed. Robert J. Dostal (Cambridge: Cambridge University Press, 2006), 52–78.

9. This claim should not be taken to mean that, for Gadamer, there is no sense in which objectivity is a measure for justified belief, as Emilio Betti suggests. For Gadamer, it is just that the *Sache* by which one tests one's fore-conceptions is not independent of interpretive interaction. Emilio Betti, "Hermeneutics as the General Method of the *Geisteswissenschaften*," in *Contemporary Hermeneutics: Hermeneutics as Method, Philosophy, and Critique*, ed. Josef Bleicher (London: Routledge & Kegan Paul, 1980), 76–80.

10. According to Fricker, the assumption that the pursuit of knowledge is entirely separate from the pursuit of virtue and self-knowledge makes it difficult to recognize and combat habits like epistemic laziness and meta-blindness. Miranda Fricker, *Epistemic Injustice: Power and the Ethics of Knowing* (Oxford: Oxford University Press, 2007), 43–59.

11. Central to Fricker's account and to the field of epistemic justice studies that it inspired is the insight that, although one's cultural-historical situation can encourage one to engage in epistemic injustice (for example, by denying epistemic relevance to the testimony of hermeneutically marginalized people), it is possible to correct this deficiency through the development of certain habits of mind referred to as "epistemic virtues" and "hermeneutic virtues." For an especially illuminating discussion of these virtues and what can encourage their cultivation, see José Medina, *The Epistemology of Resistance: Gender and Racial Oppression, Epistemic Injustice, and Resistant Imaginations* (Oxford: Oxford University Press, 2013).

12. Medina argues that color-blindness and gender-blindness are forms of epistemic vice for this reason. For Medina, these attitudes, common in our contemporary social world, involve a failure in self-knowledge. Medina, *Epistemology of Resistance*, 37.

13. Whitney Mannies, "Elements of Style: Openness and Dispositions," in *Inheriting Gadamer: New Directions in Philosophical Hermeneutics*, ed. Georgia Warnke (Edinburgh: Edinburgh University Press, 2016), 87.

14. Francis Bacon, *The New Organon*, ed. Lisa Jardine and Michael Silverthorne (Cambridge: Cambridge University Press, 2000), 39.

15. Jean le Rond d'Alembert, *Preliminary Discourse to the Encyclopedia of Diderot*, trans. Richard Schwab (Evanston, IL: University of Chicago, 1995), 77.

16. Bacon, *New Organon*, 40.

17. Immanuel Kant, "Answer to the Question: What Is Enlightenment?," in *Practical Philosophy*, ed. Mary J. Gregor (Cambridge: Cambridge University Press), 11.

18. For a compelling description of how the current devaluation of the history of philosophy reflects this Enlightenment ideal, see Charles Taylor, "Philosophy and Its History," in *Philosophy in History: Essays on the Historiography of Philosophy*, ed. Richard Rorty, J. B. Schneewind, and Quentin Skinner (Cambridge: Cambridge University Press, 1984), 17–30.

19. Gadamer's critique of the Enlightenment on this point echoes the critique that G. W. F. Hegel gives in the *Phenomenology of Spirit* in the section on "The Struggle of the Enlightenment with Superstition." See G. W. F. Hegel, *Phenomenology of Spirit*, trans. A. V. Miller (Oxford: Oxford University Press, 1977), 329–49.

20. Novalis, "Christianity or Europe: A Fragment," in *Early German Romantic Political Writings*, ed. and trans. Frederick Beiser (Cambridge: Cambridge University Press, 1996), 70.

21. Novalis had as much contempt for those who advocated for a rational interpretation of the Bible as he had for those who advocated for secularization. Similarly, fundamentalists today often hold special contempt for those members of their own religion or nation who embrace its historical, reflective character and critique aspects of the religion or nation on this basis.

22. This is one way of understanding the error in the rationale behind efforts by many Republican state legislators in the United States in recent years (including in Oklahoma, Arizona, and Florida) to eradicate curricula from schools that grapple with the moral failings of the nation, most notably in the context of critical race theory. Those behind these efforts insist that the story of American history has already been told and that attempts to tell this story in a new way are innovations that undermine the knowledge of this history implied by nationalist traditions. Gadamerian hermeneutics suggest, however, that there is no way of preserving the memory of the past except through a rational reflection that determines the meaning of the past and present in conjunction with one another.

23. Gadamer offers an extended example of this point in his discussion of the category of the "classical" (TM, 296–302). Classical works are not something, according to Gadamer, that can be properly understood by reconstructing the classic world as a closed horizon in the past, since "our understanding will always retain the consciousness that we too belong to that world, and correlatively, that the work too belongs to our world" (TM, 301). Catherine Zuckert offers the following helpful gloss on Gadamer's critique:

> Insofar as it treats the past as simply past, as the product of a set of circumstances and expressing an understanding of the world that cannot possibly be duplicated in the present, an exclusively historical or scholarly reading of a past text precludes the text from challenging the truth of our current conceptions, including the historical insight itself. We do not learn anything new, which is to say that we do not really learn anything at all, about ourselves or the part of the tradition that shaped us contained in the particular text. To expand our horizon, we must not only identify the way in which things from the past are different; we also have to ask how they can be combined with or otherwise affect our current understanding.

Catherine H. Zuckert, "Hermeneutics in Practice: Gadamer on Ancient Philosophy," in *The Cambridge Companion to Gadamer*, ed. Robert J. Dostal (Cambridge: Cambridge University Press, 2002), 205–6.

24. Gadamer makes this especially clear in his discussion of the hermeneutic significance of temporal distance. The hermeneutic object is familiar in one sense, belonging within the horizon of historical consciousness, but it is unfamiliar in another sense, being part of that consciousness that is not yet appropriated. In the hermeneutic object, one finds a "play between the traditionary text's strangeness and familiarity to us, between being a historically intended, distanced object and belonging to a tradition" (TM, 306).

25. Caputo captures the problem with such neotraditionalism well when he writes, "The misguided attempt to be literally loyal to the past makes the past into a monster, closes down the future and deprives tradition of its inherent ability to renew itself." John D. Caputo, *Hermeneutics: Facts and Interpretation in the Age of Information* (London: Penguin, 2018), 100.

Chapter 3

1. Hans-Georg Gadamer, "Art and Imitation," in *The Relevance of the Beautiful*, trans. Nicholas Walker (Cambridge: Cambridge University Press, 1986), 99.

2. "Testifying to order, mimesis seems as valid now as it was then, insofar as every work of art, even in our own increasingly standardized world of mass production, still testifies to that spiritual ordering energy that makes our life what it is." Gadamer, "Art and Imitation," 103.

3. As Gadamer explains, the nondifferentiation that occurs in art "does not imply a reference to an original as something other than itself, but means that something meaningful is there as itself." Hans-Georg Gadamer, "Poetry and Mimesis," in *The Relevance of the Beautiful*, trans. Nicholas Walker (Cambridge: Cambridge University Press, 1986), 121.

4. It is in opposition to certain dimensions of Kant's argument in his *Critique of Judgment* that Gadamer articulates his own theory about the relevance of aesthetic experience for truth. Gadamer takes issue with the opposition Kant draws between aesthetic judgments and theoretical judgments and argues, instead, for the relevance of aesthetic experience for the theoretical cognition of reality. For Kant, aesthetic judgment bespeaks the freedom of those subjects with the capacity for such judgment over and against the rules of theoretical cognition. While drawing directly from Kant's description of the free play that characterizes aesthetic judgment, Gadamer rejects Kant's claim that this free play is indicative only of subjective freedom, arguing instead that it is a dynamic internal to reality itself.

5. Johan Huizinga, *Homo Ludens: A Study of the Play-Element in Culture* (London: Routledge & Kegan Paul, 1949), 10.

6. Richard Palmer, *Hermeneutics: Interpretation Theory in Schleiermacher, Dilthey, Heidegger, and Gadamer* (Evanston, IL: Northwestern University Press, 1969), 168.

7. Understood through the lens of hermeneutics, academic lectures are not about the unidirectional transmission of information. What comes to be understood through the serious engagement of the students with the lecture is something that neither students nor professor can have certainty of in advance. When lectures facilitate such engagement from students and when what emerges through this interaction is considered epistemically relevant by the parties involved, they are remarkably effective alternatives to the banking model of education criticized by Freire as discussed in chapter 1.

8. For an account of the academic lecture as a hermeneutic event, see my "Play in Conversation: The Cognitive Import of Gadamer's Theory of Play," in *Language and Phenomenology*, ed. Chad Engelland (New York: Routledge, 2021), 248–63.

9. In *Truth and Method*, Gadamer writes that "language has its true being only in dialogue, in coming to an understanding" (TM, 462) and later in "The Boundaries of Language" that "language is realized not in statements but as conversation, as the unity of meaning that develops out of the word and answer." Hans-Georg Gadamer, "The Boundaries of Language," in *Language and Linguisticality in Gadamer's Hermeneutics*, ed. Lawrence Schmidt (Lanham, MD: Lexington Books, 2000), 16.

10. Dennis Schmidt explores, through Gadamer's hermeneutics, the capacity of art and dialogue to bring us out of ourselves and, in so doing, to establish new forms of community. See especially Dennis Schmidt, *Lyrical and Ethical Subjects: Essays on the Periphery of the Word, Freedom, and History* (Albany: State University of New York Press, 2005), 19–31.

11. In genuine conversation, Gadamer explains, "each person opens himself to the other, truly accepts his point of view as valid and transposes himself into the other to such an extent that he understands not the particular individual but what he says" (TM, 403).

12. Unlike the space of the work of art or the space of the game, the space in which conversation occurs is seldom delineated by clear and sacred boundaries. This is even more the case today as verbal exchanges increasingly take place in virtual environments and become separated from the physical spaces that people inhabit together. A discussion in a formal seminar, a book club, a group therapy session can still feel like a sacred space for conversation where participants can trust that others are there to seriously engage. In many other exchanges, however, including especially exchanges on the internet where there is no moderation, it is harder to establish and maintain firm parameters and thus to create a situation where there is this kind of default trust.

13. This describes what Hegel means by the "absolute method" that characterizes his own investigation in the *Logic*. In *The Science of Logic*, Hegel clarifies that absolute method does not proceed by way "of external reflection but takes the determinate from its subject matter, for it is itself its immanent principle and its soul." G. W. F. Hegel, *The Science of Logic*, trans. George di Giovanni (New York: Cambridge University Press, 2010), 741.

14. Darren Walhof, *The Democratic Theory of Hans-Georg Gadamer* (Cham, Switzerland: Palgrave Macmillan, 2017), 39.

15. Günter Figal, "The Doing of the Thing Itself: Gadamer's Hermeneutic Ontology of Language," in *The Cambridge Companion to Gadamer*, ed. Robert J. Dostal (Cambridge: Cambridge University Press, 2002), 108.

16. For Hegel's account of the logico-metaphysical unity between essence and appearance, see "The Doctrine of Essence," in Hegel, *Science of Logic*, 337–505.

17. If Rorty were right to attribute this theory of truth to Gadamer, however, this would certainly raise doubts about Caputo's claim that Gadamer conceives of events of truth and understanding on the model of Platonic *anamnesis* and thus makes a premature exit from the movement he calls radical hermeneutics. John D. Caputo, *Radical Hermeneutics: Repetition, Deconstruction, and the Hermeneutic Project* (Bloomington: Indiana University Press, 1987), 111–13.

18. Theodore George, *The Responsibility to Understand: Hermeneutical Contours of Ethical Life* (Edinburgh: Edinburgh University Press, 2020), 11–15.

19. John D. Caputo, *Hermeneutics: Facts and Interpretation in the Age of Information* (London: Penguin, 2018), 111.

20. Gianni Vattimo, "Nihilism as Emancipation," *Cosmos and History: The Journal of Natural and Social Philosophy* 5, no. 1 (2009): 20.

21. That Rorty associates the need to overcome epistemological foundationalism with the need to advance the cause of liberal democratic politics is clear when he writes that "hermeneutics does not need a new epistemological paradigm, any more than liberal political thought requires a new paradigm of sovereignty." Richard Rorty, *Philosophy and the Mirror of Nature* (Princeton, NJ: Princeton University Press, 2009), 325.

22. Günter Figal, *Objectivity: The Hermeneutical and Philosophy*, trans. Theodore George (Albany: State University of New York Press, 2010), 56.

23. Figal, *Objectivity*, 61.

24. Figal, 2.

25. George, *Responsibility to Understand*, 20.

26. George, 65.

27. A similar argument can be found in Gert-Jan van der Heiden's recent account of the twofold character of the "reserve/object" of testimony. Testimony, Van der Heiden argues, both requires of witnesses that they strive to recognize and understand what is being disclosed (rendering it an "object") but also that

they tend to the limits of what appears in the disclosure (regarding what is borne witness to as held in "reserve"). Gert-Jan van der Heiden, *The Voice of Misery: A Continental Philosophy of Testimony* (Albany: State University of New York Press, 2019), 127.

Chapter 4

1. Linda Martín Alcoff, *Real Knowing: New Versions of the Coherence Theory* (Ithaca, NY: Cornell University Press, 1996), 13.

2. W. V. O. Quine, "Epistemology Naturalized," in *Ontological Relativity and Other Essays* (New York: Columbia University Press, 1969), 82.

3. Frederick F. Schmitt, "Socializing Epistemology: An Introduction through Two Sample Issues," in *Socializing Epistemology: The Social Dimensions of Knowledge*, ed. Frederick F. Schmitt (Lanham, MD: Rowman & Littlefield, 1994), 1.

4. Phillip Kitcher, "Contrasting Conceptions of Socializing Epistemology," in *Socializing Epistemology: The Social Dimensions of Knowledge*, ed. Frederick Schmitt (Lanham, MD: Rowman & Littlefield, 1994), 112.

5. Alessandra Tanesini, "The Practices of Justification," in *Epistemology: The Big Questions*, ed. Linda Martín Alcoff (Malden, MA: Blackwell, 1998), 161.

6. John Elster, *Making Sense of Marx* (Cambridge: Cambridge University Press, 1985), 474.

7. Beauvoir's point is not that her experience as a woman has played no role in what she believes is true. Her response is meant simply to indicate that, whatever their origin, her beliefs have a normative dimension. To the extent that the warrant for the claims is strong, they should compel agreement from others, including those who are not women. Simone de Beauvoir, *The Second Sex*, trans. Constance Borde and Sheila Malovaney-Chevallier (New York: Vintage Books, 2011), 5.

8. Alessandra Tanesini, "The Practices of Justification," in *Epistemology: The Big Questions*, ed. Linda Martín Alcoff (Malden, MA: Blackwell, 1998), 157.

9. Peter Mundy and Lisa Newell, "Attention, Joint Attention, and Social Cognition," *Current Directions in Psychological Science* 16, no. 5 (2007): 269–74.

10. Lawrence Hatab provides a helpful analysis of the significance of research in joint attention for phenomenological inquiry into understanding. See, for example, Lawrence J. Hatab, *Proto-Phenomenology and the Nature of Language: Dwelling in Speech*, vol. 1 (Lanham, MD: Rowman & Littlefield, 2017), 45–46.

11. Linda Martín Alcoff, "Epistemologies of Ignorance: Three Types," in *Race and Epistemologies of Ignorance*, ed. Shannon Sullivan and Nancy Tuana (Albany: State University of New York Press, 2008), 44.

12. Especially influential in the development of this concern is the criticism of naturalized epistemology offered by Jaegwon Kim, who argues that Quine's naturalized epistemology entails an attempt to "discredit the very conception of normative epistemology" and the legitimacy of questions of justification. Jaegwon Kim, "What Is 'Naturalized Epistemology'?," *Philosophical Perspectives* 2 (1988): 385.

13. Hilary Kornblith, "Introduction: What Is Naturalistic Epistemology?," in *Naturalizing Epistemology*, ed. Hilary Kornblith (Cambridge, MA: MIT Press, 1994), 7.

14. Linda Martín Alcoff, *Real Knowing: New Versions of the Coherence Theory* (Ithaca, NY: Cornell University Press, 1996), 2.

15. "Suspicion of the category of reason per se and the tendency to reduce it to an operation of power actually pre-empt the very questions one needs to ask about how power is affecting our functioning as rational subjects; for it eradicates, or at least obscures, the distinction between what we have reason to think and what mere relations of power are doing to our thinking." Miranda Fricker, *Epistemic Injustice* (Oxford: Oxford University Press, 2010), 3.

16. Charles Mills, "Alternative Epistemologies," *Social Theory and Practice* 14, no. 3 (1988): 237–263.

17. Influential arguments for versions of internalism can be found in: Laurence Bonjour, "Externalist Theories of Empirical Knowledge," *Midwest Studies in Philosophy* 5 (1980): 53–73; Richard Feldman and Earl Conee, "Internalism Defended," *American Philosophical Quarterly* 38, no. 1 (2001): 1–18; Richard Fumerton, "The Internalism/Externalism Controversy," *Philosophical Perspectives* 2 (1988): 443–59; and Carl Ginet, *Knowledge, Perception, and Memory* (Dordrecht: Reidel, 1975).

18. See, for example, Lorraine Code, *Epistemic Responsibility* (Hanover, NH: Brown University Press, 1987).

19. Fricker, *Epistemic Injustice*, 150–51.

20. José Medina, *The Epistemology of Resistance: Gender and Racial Oppression, Epistemic Injustice, and Resistant Imaginations* (Oxford: Oxford University Press, 2013), 67.

21. Catherine Elgin, *Considered Judgment* (Princeton, NJ: Princeton University Press, 1996), 6–9.

22. Medina, *Epistemology of Resistance*, 12.

23. Elgin, *Considered Judgment*, 12.

24. As an imperfect procedural epistemology, epistemic justice theory can be understood as differentiating itself from the sort of pure internalism to which Edmund Gettier objected. Just as Gettier argued that it was possible for someone to have a correct belief and have excellent justification for it but still lack knowledge, epistemic justice theorists like Medina seem to argue that it is logically possible for someone to demonstrate what appears to be epistemic

virtue while ultimately being epistemically irresponsible, since our understanding of epistemic virtues and vices must be updated as analyses of social injustice are updated. For Gettier's argument against pure internalism, see Edmund L. Gettier, "Is Justified True Belief Knowledge?," *Analysis* 23, no. 6 (1963): 121–23.

Chapter 5

1. As Virginia Held has argued, the tendency to see emotion as irrational and thus to deny it any epistemic relevance has long been a chief mechanism of the subordination of women, since women have historically been associated with the emotions. This fact alone, for Held, is reason to consider the potential cognitive and ethical import of emotion more carefully. See Virginia Held, *The Ethics of Care: Personal, Political, and Global* (Oxford: Oxford University Press, 2007).

2. To be clear, feminist inquiry is not marginalized in all discursive spaces nor within all communities. Where feminist interests are seen as legitimate human interests of concern to all human beings, feminist inquiry functions smoothly as a form of reasoning. Nearly every culture today contains certain spaces within which feminist inquiry can operate smoothly, although the amount of tension between these spaces and the rest of the culture varies across cases.

3. Sara Ahmed, *Living a Feminist Life* (Durham, NC: Duke University Press, 2007), 38.

4. For an account of gaslighting as a form of epistemic and hermeneutic marginalization, see Kate Abramson, "Turning Up the Lights on Gaslighting," *Philosophical Perspectives* 28 (2014): 1–30.

5. Ahmed, *Living a Feminist Life*, 39.

6. Fricker describes hermeneutic injustice as "the injustice of having some significant area of one's social experience obscured from collective understanding owing to persistent and wide-ranging hermeneutical marginalization." Miranda Fricker, *Epistemic Injustice: Power and the Ethics of Knowing* (Oxford: Oxford University Press, 2007), 154.

7. Heidi Grasswick, "Feminist Epistemology," in *The Routledge Handbook of Social Epistemology*, ed. Ian James Kidd, José Medina, and Gail Polhaus Jr. (London: Routledge, 2020), 297.

8. Frederick F. Schmitt, "Socializing Epistemology: An Introduction through Two Sample Issues," in *Socializing Epistemology: The Social Dimensions of Knowledge*, ed. Frederick F. Schmitt (Lanham, MD: Rowman & Littlefield, 1994), 3.

9. See Simone de Beauvoir, "Woman's Situation and Character," in *The Second Sex*, trans. Constance Borde and Sheila Malovany-Chevallier (New York: Vintage Books, 2011), 638–66.

10. Hartsock's major contributions to standpoint theory during this period are collected in Nancy Hartsock, *The Feminist Standpoint Revisited and Other Essays* (Boulder, CO: Westview, 1998). Sandra Bartky's exploration of feminist consciousness as a phenomenology of oppression appears in Sandra Bartky, *Femininity and Domination: Studies in the Phenomenology of Oppression* (New York: Routledge, 1990).

11. Donna Haraway, "Situated Knowledges: The Science Question in Feminism and the Privilege of Partial Perspective," *Feminist Studies* 14 (1988): 584.

12. Haraway, "Situated Knowledges," 583.

13. Sandra Harding, "Strong Objectivity: A Response to the New Objectivity Question," *Synthese* 104 (1995): 337.

14. See also Helen Longino, *The Fate of Knowledge* (Princeton, NJ: Princeton University Press, 2002).

15. This example of feminist research in primatology is discussed at length by Elizabeth Anderson in "Feminist Epistemology: An Interpretation and Defense," *Hypatia* 10, no. 3 (1995): 50–84.

16. For an analysis of this research reconceptualizing divorce, see Elizabeth Anderson, "Uses of Value Judgments in Science: A General Argument, with Lessons from a Case Study of Feminist Research on Divorce," *Hypatia* 19, no. 1 (2004): 1–24.

17. For a variety of studies in this particular program of feminist economics, see Christine Baurhardt and Wendy Harcourt, eds., *Feminist Political Ecology and the Economics of Care: In Search of Economic Alternatives* (London: Routledge, 2020).

18. Harding, "Strong Objectivity," 346.

19. See especially Carol Gilligan, *In a Different Voice: Psychological Theory and Women's Development* (Cambridge, MA: Harvard University Press, 1982) and Nel Noddings, *Caring: A Feminine Approach to Ethics and Moral Education* (Berkeley: University of California Press, 1984).

20. See Andrea Nye, *Words of Power: A Feminist Reading of the History of Logic* (New York: Routledge, 1990) and Genevieve Lloyd, *The Man of Reason: "Male" and "Female" in Western Philosophy* (London: Metheun, 1984).

21. To be clear, feminist care ethics, in arguing for the general value of ethical practice grounded in a concern for social relations, *does* offer a normative ethics. While it draws from research in moral psychology on differences in moral development between girls and boys, its aim is not simply to describe this difference but to argue on behalf of ethical norms underappreciated because of androcentrism in moral theory.

22. Susan Haack, "Epistemological Reflections of an Old Feminist," *Reason Papers* 18 (1993): 37.

23. Haack, "Epistemological Reflections," 38.

24. See Susan Haack, "Staying for an Answer: The Untidy Process of

Groping for Truth," in *Scrutinizing Feminist Epistemology: An Examination of Gender in Science*, ed. Cassandra L. Pinnick, Noretta Koertge, and Robert F. Almeder (Piscataway, NJ: Rutgers University Press, 2003), 241 and *Manifesto of a Passionate Moderate: Unfashionable Essays* (Chicago: University of Chicago Press, 1998), 102–23. More recently, Michiko Kakutani has argued that feminist epistemology, with the value it puts on personal testimony, exacerbates the subjectivism and relativism that has pervaded political discourse in the "post-truth" era. See Michiko Kakutani, *Notes on Falsehood in the Age of Trump* (New York: Tim Duggan, 2018), 70–71.

25. See Medina's critique of the ideal of gender-blindness in José Medina, *The Epistemology of Resistance: Gender and Racial Oppression, Epistemic Injustice, and Resistant Imaginations* (Oxford: Oxford University Press, 2013), 36–37.

26. Ahmed, *Living a Feminist Life*, 1.

27. To be clear, discerning patterns in the way that women have been subordinated does not mean assuming that all kinds of women experience the same specific forms of subordination. Indeed, a comprehensive understanding of women's subordination requires that one understand how the form of subordination differs for different women depending on factors such as race, class, and geopolitical location.

28. Sandra Bartky, *Femininity and Domination: Studies in the Phenomenology of Oppression* (New York: Routledge, 1990), 14.

29. C. Wright Mills, *The Sociological Imagination* (Oxford: Oxford University Press, 2000), 3–4.

30. Virginia Held, *The Ethics of Care: Personal, Political, and Global* (Oxford: Oxford University Press, 2007), 61.

31. Lorraine Code, "Taking Subjectivity into Account," in *Rhetorical Spaces: Essays on Gendered Location* (New York: Routledge, 1995), 54.

32. Haraway, "Situated Knowledges," 579.

33. Sandra Harding, "Rethinking Standpoint Epistemology: What Is 'Strong Objectivity'?," in *The Feminist Standpoint Theory Reader: Intellectual and Political Controversies*, ed. Sandra Harding (New York: Routledge), 128.

34. Helen Longino, *Science as Situated Knowledge* (Princeton, NJ: Princeton University Press), 1989.

35. In an era where many conceive of feminism as concerned exclusively with the ills of patriarchy and of patriarchy as only one of several isolated forms of oppression, the claim that a feminist standpoint gives one greater access to the whole may appear to be an unfortunate relic of feminism prior to the turn toward difference brought about by the "third wave." It should be noted, however, that feminist standpoint theory professes to offer a more comprehensive understanding of the whole not because it holds that understanding those historical practices that organize social reality according to gender roles are sufficient for understanding the whole of that reality, but because it holds that thinking through

how the sexual division of labor works to shape social reality in a particular way provides valuable insight into the general processes by which social reality is organized—processes that are themselves historically diverse. As Kathi Weeks puts it, feminist standpoint theory is committed to what she calls "the project of totality" in that it involves "a methodological mandate to relate and connect, to situate and contextualize, to conceive the social systematically as a complex process of relationships," adding that it is for this reason that a genuine feminist standpoint grasps that "capitalism, patriarchy, and white supremacy are not isolated forces but rather systems that traverse the entire social horizon and intersect at multiple points." Kathi Weeks, "Labor, Standpoints, and Feminist Subjects," in *The Feminist Standpoint Theory Reader: Intellectual and Political Controversies*, ed. Sandra Harding (New York: Routledge, 2004), 184.

36. Feminist standpoint theorists are particularly influenced by the exploration of consciousness offered by György Lukács in *History and Class Consciousness: Studies in Marxist Dialectics*. On this point, see Frederic Jameson, "History and Class Consciousness as an Unfinished Project," in *The Feminist Standpoint Theory Reader: Intellectual and Political Controversies*, ed. Sandra Harding (New York: Routledge, 2004), 143–51; and Weeks, "Labor, Standpoints," 184–88.

37. Hartsock, *Feminist Standpoint Revisited*, 91.

38. While internalist forms of critical social epistemology have been the most dominant in recent decades, Charles Mills argues specifically on behalf of standpoint theory's externalism (what he calls "objectivism") on the grounds that only this approach is adequate for understanding the way epistemic vices are rooted in oppressive social structures. Mills worries, however, that classic standpoint theory cannot account for the existence of multiple axes of oppression (e.g., race, class, and gender). See Charles Mills, "Ideology," in *The Routledge Handbook of Epistemic Injustice*, ed. Ian James Kidd, José Medina, and Gail Polhaus Jr. (New York: Routledge, 2019), 100–111.

Chapter 6

1. Linda Martín Alcoff, *Real Knowing: New Versions of the Coherence Theory* (Ithaca, NY: Cornell University Press), 45.

2. Brice Wachterhauser, "Getting It Right: Relativism, Realism, and Truth," in *The Cambridge Companion to Gadamer*, ed. Robert Dostal (Cambridge: Cambridge University Press, 2002), 55.

3. Richard Rorty, *Philosophy and the Mirror of Nature* (Princeton, NJ: Princeton University Press, 1978), 357–65.

4. See, for example, Robin Schott, "Whose Home Is It Anyway? A Feminist Response to Gadamer's Hermeneutics," in *Gadamer and Hermeneutics: Science, Culture, Literature: Plato, Heidegger, Barthes, Ricoeur, Habermas, Derrida*, ed. Hugh

Silverman (New York: Routledge, 1991), 202–9; and Diane Elam, "Is Feminism the Saving Grace of Hermeneutics?," *Social Epistemology* 5, no. 4 (1991): 349–60.

5. Lorraine Code, "Introduction: Why Feminists Do Not Read Gadamer," in *Feminist Interpretations of Hans-Georg Gadamer*, ed. Lorraine Code (University Park: Pennsylvania State University Press, 2003), 7.

6. Sandra Harding, "Strong Objectivity: A Response to the New Objectivity Question," *Synthese* 104, no. 3 (1995): 342.

7. For Butler's theory of the need for ongoing critical self-reflection, see especially Judith Butler, "Contingent Foundations: Feminism and the Question of 'Postmodernism,'" in *Feminist Contentions: A Philosophical Exchange*, ed. Seyla Benhabib, Judith Butler, Drucilla Cornell, and Nancy Fraser (New York: Routledge, 1995).

8. Silja Freudenberger, "The Hermeneutic Conversation as Epistemological Model," in *Feminist Interpretations of Hans-Georg Gadamer*, ed. Lorraine Code (University Park: Pennsylvania State University Press, 2003), 280–81.

9. "In a tradition this process of fusion is continually going on, for there old and new are always combining into something of living value, without either being explicitly foregrounded from the other" (TM, 317).

10. Likewise, it is possible, on Gadamer's theory, that I encounter an object so entirely foreign that I cannot even generate a question about it and cannot even formulate what sort of claim it could possibly be making on my fore-conceptions. Gadamer briefly addresses this possibility when he argues that one cannot figure out if one agrees or disagrees with another if they lack entirely any common language (TM, 403).

11. See, for example, John Caputo, *Radical Hermeneutics: Repetition, Deconstruction, and the Hermeneutic Project* (Bloomington: Indiana University Press, 1987), 95; and Marie Fleming, "Gadamer's Conversation: Does the Other Have a Say?," in *Feminist Interpretations of Hans-Georg Gadamer*, ed. Lorraine Code (University Park: Pennsylvania State University Press, 2003), 128–31.

12. Emilio Betti, "Hermeneutics as the General Methodology of the *Geisteswissenschaften*," in *Contemporary Hermeneutics: Hermeneutics as Method, Philosophy, and Critique*, ed. and trans. Josef Bleicher (London: Routledge & Kegan Paul, 1980), 79.

13. Karl-Otto Apel, "Regulative Ideas or Truth-Happening? An Attempt to Answer the Question of the Conditions of the Possibility of Valid Understanding," trans. Ralf Sommermeier, in *The Philosophy of Hans-Georg Gadamer: Library of Living Philosophers*, ed. Lewis Edwin Hahn (Chicago: Open Court, 1996), 67.

14. Michael Forster, *German Philosophy of Language: From Schlegel to Hegel and Beyond* (Oxford: Oxford University Press, 2011), 312.

15. Kristin Gjesdal, *Gadamer and the Legacy of German Idealism* (Cambridge: Cambridge University Press, 2009), 216.

16. Gadamer understands this point both in terms of Hegel's concept of concrete universality and Kant's doctrine of reflective judgment. "That the universality of the rule is in need of application and that for the application of rules there exists in turn no rule, one could have been able to learn from Kant's *Critique of Judgment* and from its successors, especially from Hegel, if not from one's own insight." Hans-Georg Gadamer, "The Heritage of Hegel," in *Reason in the Age of Science*, trans. Frederick G. Lawrence (Cambridge, MA: MIT Press, 2001), 49.

17. Brice Wachterhauser, "Getting It Right: Relativism, Realism, and Truth," in *The Cambridge Companion to Gadamer*, ed. Robert Dostal (Cambridge: Cambridge University Press, 2002), 63.

18. David Liakos, " 'The Recovery of the Fundamental Hermeneutic Problem': Application and Normativity," in *Gadamer's Truth and Method: A Polyphonic Commentary*, ed. Cynthia R. Nielsen and Greg Lynch (Lanham, MD: Rowman & Littlefield, 2022).

19. Liakos, " 'Recovery,' " 178.

20. Cynthia Nielsen and David Utsler, "Gadamer, Fricker, and Honneth: Testimonial Injustice, Prejudice, and Social Esteem," in *Epistemic Injustice and the Philosophy of Recognition*, ed. Paul Giladi and Nicola McMillan, 63–87 (New York: Routledge, 2023).

21. Gadamer, "Heritage of Hegel," 49.

22. Miranda Fricker, *Epistemic Injustice: Power and the Ethics of Knowing* (Oxford: Oxford University Press, 2007), 150–51.

23. In Hegelian terms, standpoint theory regards forms of hermeneutic marginalization and the process by which they are resolved as a process of *determinate* rather than indeterminate negation. Like Hegel, too, standpoint theorists conceive of negativity as intrinsic to the reality they are investigating despite the fact that many "might wish to be spared the negative as something false, and demand to be led to the truth without further ado." G. W. F. Hegel, *Phenomenology of Spirit*, trans. A. V. Miller (Oxford: Oxford University Press, 1977), 22.

24. Fricker, *Epistemic Injustice*, 147. Fricker's worry about the ontological dimension of standpoint theory mirrors Gjesdal's worry about the ontological turn in Gadamerian hermeneutics.

25. Fricker's concerns relate to what Alessandra Tanesini calls standpoint theory's controversial "inversion thesis," that is, to the claim that the objective interests of the hermeneutically marginalized are epistemically privileged. As Tanesini explains, this is both the most controversial of those arguments standpoint theory puts forward and the one that most differentiates it from other forms of feminist epistemology. Alessandra Tanesini, "Standpoint Then and Now," in *The Routledge Handbook of Social Epistemology*, ed. Miranda Fricker et al. (New York: Routledge, 2020), 337.

26. Sandra Harding, "Strong Objectivity: A Response to the New Objectivity Question," *Synthese* 104 (1995): 346.

27. Donna Haraway, "Situated Knowledges: The Science Question in Feminism and the Privilege of Partial Perspective," *Feminist Studies* 14 (1988): 590.

28. See my discussion in the previous chapter of the problematic arguments presented by Andrea Nye and Genevieve Lloyd under the heading of "feminist epistemology."

29. As Nicholas Davey puts it, this event of truth "is not a bursting forth from a noumenal realm but a sudden shift of perspective that allows us to see that which we had not anticipated even though the elements of what we now know stood before us albeit in a fragmentary way." Nicholas Davey, *Unquiet Understanding: Gadamer's Philosophical Hermeneutics* (Albany: State University of New York Press, 2006), 120.

Bibliography

Abramson, Kate. "Turning Up the Lights on Gaslighting." *Philosophical Perspectives* 28 (2014): 1–30.
Ahmed, Sara. *Living a Feminist Life*. Durham, NC: Duke University Press, 2007.
Alcoff, Linda Martín. "Epistemologies of Ignorance: Three Types." In *Race and Epistemologies of Ignorance*, edited by Shannon Sullivan and Nancy Tuana, 39–58. Albany: State University of New York Press, 2008.
———. *Real Knowing: New Versions of the Coherence Theory*. Ithaca, NY: Cornell University Press, 1996.
Anderson, Elizabeth. "Feminist Epistemology: An Interpretation and Defense." *Hypatia* 10, no. 3 (1995): 50–84.
———. "Uses of Value Judgments in Science: A General Argument, with Lessons from a Case Study of Feminist Research on Divorce." *Hypatia* 19, no. 1 (2004): 1–24.
Apel, Karl-Otto. "Regulative Ideas or Truth-Happening? An Attempt to Answer the Question of the Conditions of the Possibility of Valid Understanding." In *The Philosophy of Hans-Georg Gadamer: Library of Living Philosophers*, edited by Lewis Edwin Hahn, 67–94. Chicago: Open Court, 1996.
Bacon, Francis. *The New Organon*. Edited by Lisa Jardine and Michael Silverthorne. Cambridge: Cambridge University Press, 2000.
Barthold, Lauren Swayne. *Overcoming Polarization in the Public Sphere: Civic Dialogue*. Cham, Switzerland: Palgrave Macmillan, 2020.
Bartky, Sandra. *Femininity and Domination: Studies in the Phenomenology of Oppression*. New York: Routledge, 1990.
Baurhardt, Christine and Wendy Harcourt, eds. *Feminist Political Ecology and the Economics of Care: In Search of Economic Alternatives*. London: Routledge, 2020.
Bernstein, Richard. *Beyond Objectivism and Relativism: Science, Hermeneutics, and Praxis*. Philadelphia: University of Pennsylvania Press, 1983.
Betti, Emilio. "Hermeneutics as the General Methodology of the *Geisteswissenschaften*." In *Contemporary Hermeneutics: Hermeneutics as Method, Philosophy,*

and Critique, edited by Josef Bleicher, 51–94. London: Routledge & Kegan Paul, 1980.

Bonjour, Laurence. "Externalist Theories of Empirical Knowledge." *Midwest Studies in Philosophy* 5 (1980): 53–73.

Butler, Judith. "Contingent Foundations: Feminism and the Question of 'Postmodernism.'" In *Feminist Contentions: A Philosophical Exchange*, edited by Seyla Benhabib, Judith Butler, Drucilla Cornell, and Nancy Fraser. New York: Routledge, 1995.

Caputo, John D. "Gadamer and the Postmodern Mind." In *The Gadamerian Mind*, edited by Theodore George and Gert-Jan van der Heiden, 435–38. London: Routledge, 2022.

———. *Hermeneutics: Facts and Interpretation in the Age of Information*. London: Penguin, 2018.

———. *Radical Hermeneutics: Repetition, Deconstruction, and the Hermeneutic Project*. Bloomington: Indiana University Press, 1987.

Coady, C. A. J. *Testimony: A Philosophy Study*. Oxford: Oxford University Press, 1992.

Code, Lorraine. *Epistemic Responsibility*. Hanover, NH: Brown University Press, 1987.

———. "Introduction: Why Feminists Do Not Read Gadamer." In *Feminist Interpretations of Hans-Georg Gadamer*, edited by Lorraine Code, 1–36. University Park: Pennsylvania State University Press, 2003.

———. "Taking Subjectivity into Account." In *Rhetorical Spaces: Essays on Gendered Location*, 23–57. New York: Routledge, 1995.

Culbertson, Carolyn. "Gadamer's Concept of Language." In *The Gadamerian Mind*, edited by Theodore George and Gert-Jan van der Heiden, 127–38. London: Routledge, 2022.

———. "Play in Conversation: The Cognitive Import of Gadamer's Theory of Play." In *Language and Phenomenology*, edited by Chad Engelland, 248–63. New York: Routledge, 2021.

———. *Words Underway: Continental Philosophy of Language*. London: Rowman & Littlefield International, 2019.

Davey, Nicholas. *Unquiet Understanding: Gadamer's Philosophical Hermeneutics*. Albany: State University of New York Press, 2006.

DaVia, Carlo. "The Role of Aristotle in Gadamer's Work." In *The Gadamerian Mind*, edited by Theodore George and Gert-Jan van der Heiden, 207–20. London: Routledge, 2022.

D'Alembert, Jean le Rond. *Preliminary Discourse to the Encyclopedia of Diderot*. Translated by Richard Schwab. Chicago: University of Chicago Press, 1995.

De Beauvoir, Simone. *The Second Sex*. Translated by Constance Borde and Sheila Malovany-Chevallier. New York: Vintage Books, 2011.

Dostal, Robert J. *Gadamer's Hermeneutics: Between Phenomenology and Dialectic*. Evanston, IL: Northwestern University Press, 2022.

Dreyfus, Hubert L. *Being-in-the-World: A Commentary on Being and Time, Division I*. Cambridge, MA: MIT Press, 1991.
Elam, Diane. "Is Feminism the Saving Grace of Hermeneutics?," *Social Epistemology* 5, no. 4 (1991): 349–60.
Elgin, Catherine Z. *Considered Judgment*. Princeton, NJ: Princeton University Press, 1996.
Elster, John. *Making Sense of Marx*. Cambridge: Cambridge University Press, 1985.
Fairfield, Paul. "Dialogue in the Classroom." In *Education, Dialogue, and Hermeneutics*, edited by Paul Fairfield, 77–89. New York: Bloomsbury, 2011.
Feldman, Richard and Earl Conee. "Internalism Defended." *American Philosophical Quarterly* 38, no. 1 (2001): 1–18.
Figal, Günter. "The Doing of the Thing Itself: Gadamer's Hermeneutic Ontology of Language." In *The Cambridge Companion to Gadamer*, edited by Robert J. Dostal, 102–25. Cambridge: Cambridge University Press, 2002.
———. *Objectivity: The Hermeneutical and Philosophy*. Translated by Theodore George. Albany: State University of New York Press, 2010.
Fleming, Marie. "Gadamer's Conversation: Does the Other Have a Say?" In *Feminist Interpretations of Hans-Georg Gadamer*, edited by Lorraine Code, 109–32. University Park: Pennsylvania State University Press, 2003.
Forster, Michael. *German Philosophy of Language: From Schlegel to Hegel and Beyond*. Oxford: Oxford University Press, 2011.
Fraser, Nancy. "False Antitheses." In *Feminist Contentions: A Philosophical Exchange*, edited by Seyla Benhabib, Judith Butler, Drucilla Cornell, and Nancy Fraser, 59–74. New York: Routledge, 1995.
Freire, Paolo. *Pedagogy of the Oppressed*. Translated by Myra Berman Ramos. New York: Continuum, 2000.
Freudenberger, Silja. "The Hermeneutic Conversation as Epistemological Model." In *Feminist Interpretations of Hans-Georg Gadamer*, edited by Lorraine Code, 259–84. University Park: Pennsylvania State University Press, 2003.
Fricker, Miranda. *Epistemic Injustice: Power and the Ethics of Knowing*. Oxford: Oxford University Press, 2007.
Fumerton, Richard. "The Internalism/Externalism Controversy." *Philosophical Perspectives* 2 (1988): 443–59.
Gadamer, Hans-Georg. "The Boundaries of Language." In *Language and Linguisticality in Gadamer's Hermeneutics*, edited by Lawrence Schmidt, 9–17. Lanham, MD: Lexington Books, 2000.
———. *The Enigma of Health: The Art of Healing in a Scientific Age*. Translated by Jason Gaiger and Nicholas Walker. Stanford, CA: Stanford University Press, 1996.
———. *Philosophical Hermeneutics*. Translated by David E. Linge. Berkeley: University of California Press, 1976.
———. *Reason in the Age of Science*. Translated by Frederick G. Lawrence. Cambridge, MA: MIT Press, 2001.

———. *The Relevance of the Beautiful and Other Essays*. Translated by Nicholas Walker. Cambridge: Cambridge University Press, 1986.
———. *Truth and Method*. Translated by Joel Weinsheimer and Donald G. Marshall. London: Bloomsbury, 2013.
———. *Wahrheit und Methode: Grundzüge einer philosophischen Hermeneutik*. Tübingen, Germany: Mohr Siebeck, 2010.
Gallagher, Shaun. *Hermeneutics and Education*. Albany: State University of New York Press, 1992.
George, Theodore. *The Responsibility to Understand*. Edinburgh: University of Edinburgh Press, 2020.
Gettier, Edmund L. "Is Justified True Belief Knowledge?" *Analysis* 23, no. 6 (1963): 121–23.
Gilligan, Carol. *In a Different Voice: Psychological Theory and Women's Development*. Cambridge, MA: Harvard University Press, 1982.
Ginet, Carl. *Knowledge, Perception, and Memory*. Dordrecht, Netherlands: Reidel, 1975.
Gjesdal, Kristin. *Gadamer and the Legacy of German Idealism*. Cambridge: Cambridge University Press, 2009.
Grasswick, Heidi. "Feminist Epistemology." In *The Routledge Handbook of Social Epistemology*, edited by Miranda Fricker, Peter J. Graham, David Henderson, and Nikolaj J. L. L. Pedersen, 295–303. London: Routledge, 2020.
Grondin, Jean. "Gadamer's Basic Understanding of Understanding." In *The Cambridge Companion to Gadamer*, edited by Robert J. Dostal, 13–35. Cambridge: Cambridge University Press, 2002.
———. "Vattimo's Latinization of Hermeneutics: Why Did Gadamer Resist Postmodernism?" *Phainomena* 55 (2006): 36–51.
Haack, Susan. "Epistemological Reflections of an Old Feminist." *Reason Papers* 18 (1993): 31–43.
———. *Manifesto of a Passionate Moderate: Unfashionable Essays*. Chicago: University of Chicago Press, 1998.
———. "Staying for an Answer: The Untidy Process of Groping for Truth." In *Scrutinizing Feminist Epistemology: An Examination of Gender in Science*, edited by Cassandra L. Pinnick, Noretta Koertge, and Robert F. Almeder, 234–43. Piscataway, NJ: Rutgers University Press, 2003.
Haraway, Donna. "Situated Knowledges: The Science Question in Feminism and the Privilege of Partial Perspective." *Feminist Studies* 14 (1988): 575–99.
Harding, Sandra. "Rethinking Standpoint Epistemology: What Is 'Strong Objectivity'?" In *The Feminist Standpoint Theory Reader: Intellectual and Political Controversies*, edited by Sandra Harding, 127–40. New York: Routledge, 2004.
———. *The Science Question in Feminism*. Ithaca, NY: Cornell University Press, 1986.

———. "Strong Objectivity: A Response to the New Objectivity Question." *Synthese* 104 (1995): 331–49.
Hartsock, Nancy. *The Feminist Standpoint Revisited and Other Essays*. Boulder, CO: Westview Press, 1998.
Hatab, Lawrence J. *Proto-Phenomenology and the Nature of Language: Dwelling in Speech*, vol. 1. Lanham, MD: Rowman & Littlefield, 2017.
Hegel, G. W. F. *Phenomenology of Spirit*. Translated by A. V. Miller. Oxford: Oxford University Press, 1977.
———. *The Science of Logic*. Translated by George di Giovanni. New York: Cambridge University Press, 2010.
Heidegger, Martin. *Being and Time*. Translated by John Macquarrie and Edward Robinson. New York: Harper & Row, 1962.
———. "Phenomenological Interpretations with Respect to Aristotle: Indication of the Hermeneutical Situation." Translated by Michael Baur. *Man and World* 25 (1992): 355–93.
Held, Virginia. *The Ethics of Care: Personal, Political, and Global*. Oxford: Oxford University Press, 2007.
Huizinga, Johan. *Homo Ludens: A Study of the Play-Element in Culture*. London: Routledge & Kegan Paul, 1949.
Jameson, Frederic. "History and Class Consciousness as an Unfinished Project." In *The Feminist Standpoint Theory Reader: Intellectual and Political Controversies*, edited by Sandra Harding, 143–51. New York: Routledge, 2004.
Kakutani, Michiko. *Notes on Falsehood in the Age of Trump*. New York: Tim Duggan, 2018.
Kant, Immanuel. "Answer to the Question: What Is Enlightenment?." In *Practical Philosophy*, edited by Mary J. Gregor, 11–22. Cambridge: Cambridge University Press, 1999.
———. *Critique of the Power of Judgment*. Translated by Paul Guyer and Eric Matthews. Cambridge: Cambridge University Press, 2001.
Kim, Jaegwon. "What Is 'Naturalized Epistemology'?" *Philosophical Perspectives* 2 (1988): 381–405.
Kitcher, Phillip. "Contrasting Conceptions of Socializing Epistemology." In *Socializing Epistemology: The Social Dimensions of Knowledge*, edited by Frederick F. Schmitt, 111–34. Lanham, MD: Rowman & Littlefield, 1994.
Kornblith, Hilary. "Introduction: What Is Naturalistic Epistemology?" In *Naturalizing Epistemology*, edited by Hilary Kornblith, 1–14. Cambridge, MA: MIT Press, 1994.
Kuhn, Thomas. *The Structure of Scientific Revolutions*. Chicago: University of Chicago Press, 1962.
Liakos, David. "Reading Oneself in the Text: Cavell and Gadamer's Romantic Conception of Reading." *Journal of Aesthetics and Phenomenology* 6, no. 1 (2019): 79–87.

———. " 'The Recovery of the Fundamental Hermeneutic Problem': Application and Normativity." In *Gadamer's Truth and Method: A Polyphonic Commentary*, edited by Cynthia R. Nielsen and Greg Lynch, 165–85. Lanham, MD: Rowman & Littlefield, 2022.

Lloyd, Genevieve. *The Man of Reason: "Male" and "Female" in Western Philosophy*. London: Metheun, 1984.

Longino, Helen. *The Fate of Knowledge*. Princeton, NJ: Princeton University Press, 2002.

———. *Science as Situated Knowledge*. Princeton, NJ: Princeton University Press, 1989.

Lukács, György. *History and Class Consciousness*. Translated by Rodney Livingstone. Cambridge, MA: MIT Press, 1971.

Mannies, Whitney. "Elements of Style: Openness and Dispositions." In *Inheriting Gadamer: New Directions in Philosophical Hermeneutics*, edited by Georgia Warnke, 81–101. Edinburgh: Edinburgh University Press, 2016.

McNeill, William. *The Fate of Phenomenology: Heidegger's Legacy*. Lanham, MD: Rowman & Littlefield, 2020.

Medina, José. *The Epistemology of Resistance: Gender and Racial Oppression, Epistemic Injustice, and Resistant Imaginations*. Oxford: Oxford University Press, 2013.

Mills, Charles. "Alternative Epistemologies." *Social Theory and Practice* 14, no. 3 (1988): 237–63.

———. "Ideology." In *The Routledge Handbook of Epistemic Injustice*, edited by Ian James Kidd, José Medina, and Gail Polhaus Jr., 100–111. New York: Routledge, 2019.

Mills, C. Wright. *The Sociological Imagination*. Oxford: Oxford University Press, 2000.

Morris, Michael. *Knowledge and Ideology: The Epistemology of Social and Political Critique*. Cambridge: Cambridge University Press, 2016.

Mundy, Peter and Lisa Newell. "Attention, Joint Attention, and Social Cognition." *Current Directions in Psychological Science* 16, no. 5 (2007): 269–74.

Nielsen, Cynthia R. and Greg Lynch, eds. *Gadamer's Truth and Method: A Polyphonic Commentary*. Lanham, MD: Rowman & Littlefield, 2022.

Nielsen, Cynthia R. and David Utsler. "Gadamer, Fricker, and Honneth: Testimonial Injustice, Prejudice, and Social Esteem." In *Epistemic Injustice and the Philosophy of Recognition*, edited by Paul Giladi and Nicola McMillan, 63–87. New York: Routledge, 2023.

Noddings, Nel. *Caring: A Feminine Approach to Ethics and Moral Education*. Berkeley: University of California Press, 1984.

Novalis. "Christianity or Europe: A Fragment." In *The Early Political Writings of the German Romantics*, edited by Frederick Beiser, 59–80. Cambridge: Cambridge University Press, 1996.

Nye, Andrea. *Words of Power: A Feminist Reading of the History of Logic*. New York: Routledge, 1990.
Palmer, Richard E. *Hermeneutics: Interpretation Theory in Schleiermacher, Dilthey, Heidegger, and Gadamer*. Evanston, IL: Northwestern University Press, 1969.
Poscher, Ralf. "Hermeneutics, Jurisprudence, and Law." In *The Routledge Companion to Hermeneutics*, edited by Jeff Malpas and Hans-Helmuth Gander, 451–65. London: Routledge, 2014.
Quine, W. V. O. "Epistemology Naturalized." In *Ontological Relativity and Other Essays*, 69–90. New York: Columbia University Press, 1969.
Risser, James. *Hermeneutics and the Voice of the Other: Re-reading Gadamer's Philosophical Hermeneutics*. Albany: State University of New York Press, 1997.
Rorty, Richard. "Being That Can Be Understood Is Language." In *Gadamer's Repercussions: Reconsidering Philosophical Hermeneutics*, edited by Bruce Krajewski, 21–29. Berkeley: University of California Press, 2004.
———. *Philosophy and the Mirror of Nature*. Princeton, NJ: Princeton University Press, 2009.
Schleiermacher, Friedrich. "General Hermeneutics." In *The Hermeneutics Reader: Texts of the German Tradition from the Enlightenment to the Present*, edited by Kurt Mueller-Vollmer, 73–86. New York: Continuum, 1985.
Schmidt, Dennis. *Lyrical and Ethical Subjects: Essays on the Periphery of the Word, Freedom, and History*. Albany: State University of New York Press, 2005.
Schmidt, Lawrence. "Back to Basics: The Forgotten Fore-conception of Completeness." *Duquesne Studies in Phenomenology* 1, no. 1 (2020).
Schmitt, Frederick F. "Socializing Epistemology: An Introduction through Two Sample Issues." In *Socializing Epistemology: The Social Dimensions of Knowledge*, edited by Frederick F. Schmitt, 1–28. Lanham, MD: Rowman & Littlefield, 1994.
Schott, Robin. "Whose Home Is It Anyway? A Feminist Response to Gadamer's Hermeneutics." In *Gadamer and Hermeneutics: Science, Culture, Literature: Plato, Heidegger, Barthes, Ricoeur, Habermas, Derrida*, edited by Hugh Silverman, 202–09. New York: Routledge, 1991.
Shotwell, Alexis. *Knowing Otherwise: Race, Gender, and Implicit Understanding*. University Park: Pennsylvania State University Press, 2011.
Simpson, Lorenzo C. *Hermeneutics as Critique: Science, Politics, Race, and Culture*. New York: Columbia University Press, 2021.
Tanesini, Alessandra. *The Mismeasure of the Self: A Study in Vice Epistemology*. Oxford: Oxford University Press, 2022.
———. "The Practices of Justification." In *Epistemology: The Big Questions*, edited by Linda Martín Alcoff, 152–64. Malden, MA: Blackwell, 1998.
Taylor, Charles. "Philosophy and Its History." In *Philosophy in History: Essays on the Historiography of Philosophy*, edited by Richard Rorty, J. B. Schneewind,

and Quentin Skinner, 17–30. Cambridge: Cambridge University Press, 1984.
Van der Heiden, Gert-Jan. *The Voice of Misery: A Continental Philosophy of Testimony*. Albany: State University of New York Press, 2019.
Vattimo, Gianni. *The End of Modernity: Nihilism and Hermeneutics in Postmodern Culture*. Baltimore: John Hopkins University Press, 1991.
———. "Nihilism as Emancipation." *Cosmos and History: The Journal of Natural and Social Philosophy* 5, no. 1 (2009): 20–23.
Vessey, David. "Gadamer and the Body across Dialogical Contexts." *Philosophy Today* 44 (2000): 70–77.
Vilhauer, Monica. *Gadamer's Ethics of Play: Hermeneutics and the Other*. Lanham, MD: Lexington Books, 2010.
Wachterhauser, Brice. "Getting It Right: Relativism, Realism, and Truth." In *The Cambridge Companion to Gadamer*, edited by Robert J. Dostal, 52–78. Cambridge: Cambridge University Press, 2002.
Walhof, Darren. *The Democratic Theory of Hans-Georg Gadamer*. Cham, Switzerland: Palgrave Macmillan, 2017.
Warnke, Georgia. *Gadamer: Hermeneutics, Tradition, and Reason*. Stanford, CA: Stanford University Press, 1987.
———. "Philosophical Hermeneutics and the Politics of Memory." In *Interpreting Gadamer: New Directions in Philosophical Hermeneutics*, edited by Georgia Warnke, 121–42. Edinburgh: Edinburgh University Press, 2016.
Weeks, Kathi. "Labor, Standpoints, and Feminist Subjects." In *The Feminist Standpoint Theory Reader: Intellectual and Political Controversies*, edited by Sandra Harding, 181–94. New York: Routledge, 2004.
Zuckert, Catherine H. "Hermeneutics in Practice: Gadamer on Ancient Philosophy." In *The Cambridge Companion to Gadamer*, edited by Robert J. Dostal, 201–24. Cambridge: Cambridge University Press, 2002.

Index

active ignorance, 112
Ahmed, Sara, 118–19, 131
Alcoff, Linda Martín, 51–53, 99, 101–02, 106–07, 110, 143–44, 154, 166n9, 170n6
algorithms, 18, 24
anti-epistemological reading of Gadamer, 6–10, 25, 34–36, 92, 98, 142–50
anti-foundationalism, 34–36, 85, 175n21
artwork: epistemic function of, 69–93, 160–61, 173n3, 173n4; non-representational, 72
Apel, Karl-Otto, 5, 35, 150, 154
application, 24, 26–27, 37–38, 116, 131, 149, 152–54, 162, 183n16
Aristotle, 20, 29, 69–72

Bacon, Francis, 58–60
Bartky, Sandra, 122, 132–33, 136, 138
Beauvoir, Simone de, 103–04, 121, 176n7
Betti, Emilio, 5, 24–26, 34–37, 145, 150, 153, 171n9
Bildung, 35, 38–39, 41, 69, 73, 84, 155–56
Butler, Judith, 147, 182n7

Caputo, John, 34–36, 86–89, 142, 165n3, 168n20, 169n24, 173n25, 175n17
Carnap, Rudolf, 101
circularity, 24–25
Chladenius, Johann Martin, 30
Coady, C. A. J., 120
Code, Lorraine, 4, 137, 146
coherence, 50–51, 107, 115, 150; maximizing comprehensive, 51–53, 156; procedural argument for, 53, 154–55, 166n9, 170n6
cognitivist model of knowledge, 102–03; social epistemological critique of, 104–06
communitarianism, 3
comprehensiveness, 90, 92, 122, 132, 138–40, 160, 180n27, 180n35. *See also* coherence
consciousness-raising, 121
constructivism, 4, 85–88; hermeneutic critique of, 89–91, 143
conversation: truth in, 77–86, 174n12; understanding in, 33–34, 91, 147, 156, 174n9, 174n11, 174n12
critical race theory, 172n22

D'Alembert, Jean le Rond, 58–59
datafication, 9, 18, 49, 106, 138

deconstruction, 21, 35, 87
Derrida, Jacques, 35
Descartes, René, 58–60

education, 38–39, 41–42, 48, 56, 69; banking concept of, 39–40, 169n25, 174n7; hermeneutic theory of, 40–41, 169n27
effective history (*Wirkungsgeschichte*), 22, 26, 39, 48–49, 154, 156–57
Elgin, Catherine, 113–14, 139, 159
Elster, Jon, 103
empiricism, 121, 137–38
Enlightenment epistemology, 30, 58–67, 94, 98, 100, 102, 143, 145, 162, 172n19; individualistic reduction in, 102; reactive responses to, 62, 122
epistemic justice, 55, 110, 112–15, 119–20, 156–59
epistemic virtues, 55–57, 110–15, 160, 171n10, 171n11; as critical thinking skills, 137; of feminist inquiry, 136–38; 155. *See also* virtue epistemology
epistemology as a field: Gadamer's critique of, 5, 9, 93, 143; narrow conceptions of, 8–9, 36, 94, 107, 143–44; as the priority of philosophy, 98–99, 144. *See also* social epistemological turn
existential phenomenology, 19–21, 167n4
externalism, 111, 140, 153–54, 156, 181n38

facticity, hermeneutics of, 19–21, 167n7
fallibility, 114, 139, 151
feminist consciousness, 121–22, 130–37, 139

feminist epistemology, 8, 101, 117–40, 166n11; genesis of, 120–22; essentialist forms of, 126–27, 129–30; internalism and externalism in, 140
feminist standpoint theory, 121–22, 138–40, 147; 180n35, 181n36, 181n38, 183n23; critiques of, 159–60, 183n24, 183n25
feminist theory: as a tool for responsible epistemic practice, 117–21, 125, 130–40; epistemic marginalization of, 118–20, 178n2
Figal, Günter, 88–93
fore-conceptions (*Vorbegriffe*): 20, 23, 25, 56, 66, 143; necessity of, 46–49, 145–46; problematization and revision of, 50–54, 81, 146–47, 153–54, 160–62
fore-structure of the understanding, 7, 19–20, 47–49, 167n6
Forster, Michael, 5, 151–52
freedom, 63–64, 66–67, 173n4
Freire, Paulo, 39–40, 169n25
Freudenberger, Silja, 148–49
Fricker, Miranda, 5, 110, 112, 158–59, 171n10, 171n11, 178n6, 183n25
fusion of horizons, 32, 148–49, 154, 161

Gallagher, Shaun, 40
gaslighting, 118–19, 178n4
George, Theodore, 86, 89
Gettier, Edmund, 177n24
Gjesdal, Kristin, 151–52, 183n24

Haack, Susan, 127–29
Haraway, Donna, 120, 123–25, 137, 159–60
Harding, Sandra, 9, 106, 120, 124–28, 138, 145–47, 159–60

Hartmann, Nicolai, 92–93
Hartsock, Nancy, 121–122, 139–40, 159
Hegel, G. W. F., 38, 81, 83, 152, 156, 172n19, 175n13, 175n16, 183n16, 183n23
Heidegger, Martin, 7, 19–21, 25, 47, 167n6, 167n7, 170n2
Held, Virginia, 134, 178n1
hermeneutic: circle, 25–26, 80–81, 131, 170n2, 170n5; fork, 142–145; theory of normativity, 151–55; postmodernism, 85–88, 169n24; realism, 89–93, 153; theory of truth, 6–7, 9, 76–94, 143, 155–57, 160–61; virtues, 55–58, 69, 80
hermeneutics: history of, 29–31; legal, 26–27, 168n17; theological, 26–27
Hirsch, E. D., 34, 145
historical consciousness, 2–4, 19, 21–27, 54, 57, 63–67, 92, 117, 152, 162, 173n24
historicism, 54, 64
Huizinga, Johan, 74
humanism, 87–88
humanities, 7, 18, 165n8, 169n1
Husserl, Edmund, 5, 19

immanence model of knowledge, 46, 58, 62, 66–67, 84, 97, 143
incommensurability, theory of, 85, 90; in feminist epistemology, 122, 129
individualistic reduction, 102–03
internalism, 88, 111–14, 116, 139–40, 153–60, 177n17, 177n24, 181n38

joint attention, 105–06
justification, 53–54, 59, 87–88, 109–15, 120, 155–60; in deliberative democracies, 87–88; comprehensiveness as a form of, 138–140. See also reason

Kant, Immanuel, 59–60, 81, 92, 102, 173n4, 183n16
Kim, Jaegwon, 177n12
Kitcher, Philip, 101–02
Kornblith, Hilary, 100–01, 109–10
Kuhn, Thomas, 85–86, 124

language, 16–17, 27–36, 78–79, 83, 163, 174n9; ideality of, 32; natural, 28
law, 26–27, 29, 168n17
lectures, 78, 174n7, 174n8
Liakos, David, 153–54
Lifeworld (*Lebenswelt*), 5, 17, 19–22, 36, 47–50, 105–07, 131, 138, 145, 148, 161–62
Lloyd, Genevieve, 126, 129
logos, 33–34, 80–82
Longino, Helen, 138

marginalization: epistemic, 118–20, 126; hermeneutic, 112, 135, 147, 158–61, 178n6, 183n23, 183n25
Medina, José, 112–14, 171n12, 177n24
meta-blindness, 55, 171n10. See also active ignorance
metaphysics, 98: dualistic, 93; postmodern critique of, 35, 168n20, 169n23, 169n24
Meno (Plato), 18, 82–83, 111
methodology, 5–7, 17–18, 42, 52, 57–60, 81, 84, 113–14, 124, 127–28, 150, 160, 175n13
Mills, Charles, 111, 181n38
Mills, C. Wright, 133–134

natural sciences, 6, 7, 100–01, 108, 120–21; beliefs about the neutrality of, 18, 124–30, 169n1

naturalized epistemology, 101, 108, 121, 141, 177n12
neo-Kantian idealism, 92–93
Nielsen, Cynthia, 155
nondifferentiation, 73–74, 83, 90–91
Novalis, 62–63, 172n21
normativity of knowledge, 18, 94, 104, 116, 126–29, 136–40, 150–155, 160, 162–63, 170n6
Nye, Andrea, 126, 129

objectivity, 26, 36, 49, 86, 123; hermeneutic theory of, 50, 88–91, 171n9; weak vs. strong, 138
objectivism, 9–10, 124–25
openness, 17, 56–57, 69, 80–81, 98, 153
ostension, 51–52

personal dimension of understanding, 8, 36–42, 118–19, 134–35, 153, 162. *See also* self-knowledge
perspectivism, 123–24, 129
procedural epistemology, perfect and imperfect, 113–14, 139, 159
performance, 37–39, 69–71, 73, 75–76
Plato 70, 81–82, 111
play, 74–76, 173n4
presentation, 72–73, 76–77, 79, 83, 91–92

questions, 16–17, 18, 22–23, 28, 40, 49, 53, 56, 82, 131–33, 137–38, 148
Quine, W. V. O., 101, 108, 121, 177n12

ratio cognoscendi, 103
reading, 25, 27–28, 31–32, 34, 47–48, 50–51, 53, 56, 78, 154–55
realism, 89–93, 137, 153

reason, 59–67, 86–88, 103–04, 108–12, 115–16, 118, 126–27; as embedded in social practices, 98, 101–02, 120, 153
recognition, 83: in aesthetic experience, 72, 90, 160; in conversation, 79–80
recollection, 82
referentiality, 71–72, 85, 88–91, 153
relativism, 108, 160, 162
Romanticism, 62–67, 30–31, 62–67
Rorty, Richard, 6, 34–36, 39, 41, 85–86, 88–90, 144–45, 175n17, 175n21

Schleiermacher, Friedrich, 30–31
Schmitt, Frederick, 101, 121, 166n10, 166n11
self-awareness, 3, 20, 26, 54–55, 61, 113–14, 147
self-knowledge, 37, 171n12
situated knowledge doctrine, x, 98, 122–29, 134–35, 137, 140, 145–46, 160
skepticism, 93, 115
social epistemological turn 99–100, 107, 115, 157; concerns about the, 108, 115
social epistemology: critical, 148, 158–60, 181; emergence of, 99–100; Gadamerian hermeneutics as, 145–49; normative dimension of, 110–16; replacement thesis of, 100, 109–10
sociological imagination, 133–34
symbols, 71

Tanesini, Alessandra, 102–06, 116, 153, 183n25
technological rationality, 9–10, 18–19, 24, 28, 42, 84, 92–93, 101, 142, 166n13

testimony, 107, 157, 171n11, 175n27
tradition, 1–4, 30, 46, 58–67, 102, 144, 146, 149, 151–54, 162
traditionalism, 46, 63–64, 66–67, 122, 173n25
transcendence model of knowledge, 17–19, 25, 36, 45–49, 58–60, 97–98, 141
transformation into structure, 75, 80, 85
trust, 33, 107, 174n12
truth, 31–36, 49, 159–60; correspondence theory of, 54, 86; hermeneutic theory of, 6–9, 76–94, 160–61; in interpretation, 84–94, 143

understanding: as distinct from knowledge, 7–8; of texts, 25–32, 34, 47–53, 148; ongoing task of, 51, 91–93, 125, 157–61; *see also* conversation
Utsler, David, 155

Vattimo, Gianni, 87–89
virtue epistemology, 55, 111–13; normative dimension of, 111–15, 136–37, 162

Wachterhauser, Brice, 144–45, 152
Warnke, Georgia, 22
Wolff, Christian, 30

www.ingramcontent.com/pod-product-compliance
Ingram Content Group UK Ltd.
Pitfield, Milton Keynes, MK11 3LW, UK
UKHW042009140426
5217IPUK00015B/1061